Working-Class Network Society

Working-Class Network Society

Communication Technology and the Information Have-Less in Urban China

Jack Linchuan Qiu

The MIT Press
Cambridge, Massachusetts
London, England

This book was set in Stone Sans and Stone Serif by SNP Best-set Typesetter Ltd., Hong Kong.

Library of Congress Cataloging-in-Publication Data

Qiu, Jack Linchuan, 1973–
Working-class network society : communication technology and the information have-less in urban China / Jack Linchuan Qiu.
    p. cm.—(Information revolution and global politics)
Includes bibliographical references and index.
ISBN 978-0-262-17006-2 (hardcover : alk. paper)
ISBN 978-0-262-54931-8 (paperback)
1. Information technology—China. 2. Telecommunication—China.
3. Diffusion of innovations—China. I. Title.
HC430.I55Q28   2009
303.48′330951—dc22
                                                    2008034818

For my parents, and Maggie

Contents

Foreword

This truly original book investigates the cultural, social, and institutional specificity of the network society in China while having broader theoretical implications. The network society is the social structure that characterizes the information age, as the industrial society characterized the industrial age. It is a social structure based on networks of communication, business, work, culture, sociability, science and technology, social movements, and politics. The networking form of organization is as old as the history of humankind but only recently became the predominant form of social organization because it harnesses the power of the revolution in microelectronics-based information and communication technologies that constituted a new technological paradigm in the 1970s and expanded in the twenty-first century into the global network of communication around the Internet (1.3 billion users in 2008) and wireless communication networks (3.4 billions subscribers in 2008).

Networks have no boundaries, so the network society is a global network society. Globalization is organized around a network of global networks. Globalization *is* the network society in its concrete manifestation. Networks are operated by the programs social actors inscript in their structures, always through conflict and always open to challenges from other social actors whose interests are ill represented in the network's program. In the current global network society, everything that has value according to the network's program is included in the network, wherever it is on the planet. Anything or anyone who has no value or becomes devalued is excluded from the network in a variable geometry of global dynamism and local despair. So the architecture of our world is composed of networks that include and exclude territories and people to form the uneven profile of globalization. Thus, all societies to some extent are network societies because their dominant sectors and functions everywhere are connected to the global network of networks from where they obtain access to wealth, information, and power. Furthermore, those who are not included in the networks are nonetheless defined in their existence by their exclusion and their drive to survive by creating alternative networks, be it the global criminal economy or networks of resistance to the dominant order.

The fact that the network society is global, bypassing in its dynamics the boundaries defined by the nation-state, is not tantamount to global social homogeneity. *The world is not flat.* The market is, but societies, cultures, and institutions that have been produced differentially by their historical and geographical specificity, by their identification in time and space, are not. Therefore, every society is at the same time a network society in its social structure and a specific network society in terms of its culture, institutions, and specific location in the international division of labor and in the world structure of power relationships. This is what a number of researchers from a variety of countries documented in the book I edited and coauthored in 2004, examining the network society in a cross-cultural perspective (Castells 2004). Jack Qiu takes this analysis one step further. He analyzes the specificity of the network society in China and proposes the concept of working-class network society. It may sound odd at first, as all innovative concepts do. But it becomes almost evident if we relate it to the usual vision that we have of China today. Most analysts agree that China is the manufacturing powerhouse of the planet in this early part of the century. What Western Europe was in the nineteenth century and the United States and Japan were in the twentieth century is China today: the industrial factory of the world. But this factory is networked to the entire global economy and is organized around the informational mode of development. It manufactures goods by incorporating information and knowledge into the labor process.

Thus, class divisions appear on the basis of differential access to and control of information processing tasks, ultimately embodied in differential access to information and communication technologies, at work and in life. The irony of history has located the largest exploited working class of the global information age in the last communist state inherited from the industrial era.

This book provides a systematic analytical framework to study both the differential dynamics of the global network society and the processes of new inequality and class formation in the context of informationalism. It relies on firsthand fieldwork research in China, documentary and statistical analysis, and a deep knowledge of the scholarly literature on global technological transformations. It opens a new path of inquiry that researchers and students around the world will follow. It also challenges us to think normatively and to shake up our detachment when contemplating the sea of injustice and human suffering that characterizes a process of economic growth and technological innovation that probably dwarfs the human drama of previous industrializations. Professor Qiu takes us away from the blind technological optimism of vendors of the future and into the harsh territory of the exploitative and exclusionary information age.

Manuel Castells
Santa Monica, California
March 2008

Acknowledgments

I first conceived this book in 2004, when I was doing postdoctoral research at the University of Southern California (USC) with generous support from the USC Zumberge Interdisciplinary Research Fund, USC Annenberg School for Communication, and USC Department of Geography. Since then, the School of Journalism and Communication at the Chinese University of Hong Kong (CUHK) and the Ford Foundation have provided essential institutional and financial resources. The project has benefited from research contracts from the Chinese Academy of Social Sciences, the Organization for Economic Co-operation and Development (OECD), the United Nations Children's Fund (UNICEF), the World Bank, and the U.K. Department for International Development.

I am most indebted to Manuel Castells, Carolyn Cartier, and Bu Wei, who have offered invaluable collegial support and continuous inspiration since the beginning of this research project. Robert Prior, Ernest Wilson, and William Drake gave important suggestions for the structure of the book. Yuezhi Zhao, Wen Tiejun, Arvind Singhal, Wang Shaoguang, Kuan Hsin Chi, Paul DiMaggio, and Arif Dirik shared critical comments and pointed to key references. Discussions with Huang Yu, Yang Guobin, Jonathan Donner, Li Dongming, Gordon Mathews, Deborah Fallows, and Joseph Turow proved to be stimulating and helpful.

I have been lucky to work with Guo Liang, Kate Hartford, Jing Wang, Paul Lee, Nicholas Jankowski, Steven Johns, Eric Thompson, Mark Levy, Taylor Boas, Mireia Fernández-Ardèvol, Araba Sey, Nina Hachigian, Harmeet Sawhney, Raul Pertierra, Patrick Law, Matthew Chew, Pun Ngai, Elisa Oreglia, Matt Zhou, and Lokman Tsui. All of them have helped me along this line of research through various collaborative projects. Li Yanhong, Kitty Chen, Hattie Tang, Chen Yun, Zhou Linghui, Liu Xia, Nick Zhang, Li Zhiping, Luo Yuan, Zhu Tian, Ding Wei, Cara Wallis, Lu Hui, and

Michael Qiu have accompanied me during fieldwork, providing me with research materials and facilitating the analysis process.

I am grateful to be a member of several intellectual communities that helped me sustain this book project. These include the Annenberg Research Network on International Communication, the Metamorphosis Project at USC, the Chinese Internet Research Group, the Mobile-Society Discussion Group, the China IT Discussion Group, as well as other networks of researchers in Hong Kong, the United States, Australia, the Philippines, and Singapore. The pillars of these communities are Sandra Ball-Rokeach, François Bar, Hernan Galperin, Peter Monge, Janet Fulk, Geoffrey Cowan, Larry Gross, Joseph Chan, Eric Ma, Anthony Fung, Chin-Chuan Lee, Peter Yu, Randy Kluver, Ken Grant, Monroe Price, James Katz, Erwin Alampay, Angel Lin, Leopoldina Fortunati, Larissa Hjorth, Gerard Goggin, Michael Keane, Ang Peng Hwa, Hao Xiaoming, and Eddie Kuo.

Sections of this book were presented in preliminary form at various conferences and symposia organized by the USC Annenberg School for Communication, University of Pennsylvania Annenberg School for Communication, the Canadian IDRC, Peking University, France Telecom R&D Beijing, the University of Philippines, University of California at Berkeley, Michigan State University, Texas A&M University, Rutgers University, Nanyang Technological University, Hong Kong Baptist University, the Chinese Academy of Social Sciences, and the International Communication Association and the International Association for Media and Communication Research.

Robert Prior, Margy Avery, Sandra Minkkinen, and Bev Miller at the MIT Press provided important editorial assistance. Melody Lutz at USC Annenberg helped with the coordination of the book project.

My sincere gratitude goes to all these colleagues and organizations. All the faults in the volume are, however, exclusively mine.

Abbreviations

ARPU	Average revenue per user
BBS	Bulletin board system
CASS	Chinese Academy of Social Sciences
CCP	Chinese Communist Party
CNNIC	China Internet Network Information Center
DECT	Digital enhanced cordless telephone
FDI	Foreign direct investment
GDP	Gross domestic product
ICP	Internet content provider
ICT	Information and communication technologies
ILO	International Labor Organization
IPO	Initial public offering
ISP	Internet service provider
MCD	Mobile communication division
MEI	Ministry of Electronic Industry
MII	Ministry of Information Industry
MMORPG	Massively multiplayer online role-playing games
MPT	Ministry of Post and Telecommunications
MoC	Ministry of Culture
MoE	Ministry of Education
MoH	Ministry of Health
MPS	Ministry of Public Security
NGO	Nongovernmental organization
NIE	Newly industrialized economies
OS	Operating system
P2P	Peer-to-peer
PAS	Personal access system
PHS	Personal handyphone system
PRC	People's Republic of China

SARFT   State Administration for Radio, Film, and Television
SARS   Severe acute respiratory syndrome
SEZ   Special Economic Zone
SMS   Short messaging services
SOE   State-owned enterprises
Sysop   System operator
Telco   Telecommunications operator
VoIP   Voice over Internet protocol
WLL   Wireless local loop
WSIS   World Summit on Information Society
WTO   World Trade Organization

1   Introduction

The small connecting cogwheel which revolves quietly is among the most essential parts of the machine.
—Leo Tolstoy

Do information and communication technologies (ICTs) help the poor, or do they promote the interests of the rich? Do they reduce inequality, or make it more acute? In an examination of the uneven development of ICTs and their social consequences, we often immediately think about the digital divide, the great social division between the information haves and the information have-nots. But this is a binary mode of thinking that simplifies things, people, and processes into two basic categories. We either have or do not have the gadget, the skill, or the access. There is either upward social mobility, or people would be "falling through the Net" (National Telecommunications and Information Administration 1995). Since the late 1990s, the concept of the digital divide has dominated many analytical accounts, policy debates, and planning documents (National Telecommunications and Information Administration 1999, 2000; Bolt and Crawford 2000; Norris 2001; Jung, Qiu, and Kim 2001; Murelli 2002). But is this all that is going on?

In summer 2002, I returned to China from the United States to conduct fieldwork. I had done some research on the digital divide and proposed a preliminary idea of informational stratification as a way to understand information inequality in China (Qiu 2002a). I traveled from China's coastal metropolitan areas to remote villages in the high mountains of the Southwest. I was in a high-tech exposition one day, amazed by the marvelous technologies offered to China's new rich; on another day, I set foot in a clay house with no windows, where people had no media access and could barely survive on potatoes.

Between these two extremes, the overwhelming part of my daily observation fell in the vast gray zone in the middle of the great divide, between the haves and have-nots. For the first time, I encountered short-messaging services (SMS) and Little Smart (*Xiaolingtong*), a low-end wireless phone (2007a, 2007b). For the first time, I realized how Internet cafés had penetrated the back alleys of both big cities and small towns, even in the less developed regions inland. For the first time, I witnessed the vulnerability of low-end users, the frustration of working-class service providers, and the myriad ways of ICT appropriation at the grassroots. So many things are quickly happening, but not without their own connections to each other. It took me a few years and more research to piece together the big picture that is the subject of this book (Cartier, Castells, and Qiu 2005; Qiu and Zhou 2005; Qiu 2006, 2007a, 2007b): the rise of working-class network society.

What Is Going On?

Questions about communication technology and inequality are particularly important issues in China because for millennia, elite dominance over ICTs has been a main characteristic in the nation's long history, with the ancient writing, printing, and dissemination systems reinforcing the rule of bureaucrats and the literati. Hence, in the social sciences, since Max Weber's milestone study on Confucianism and Taoism (Weber 1964), China has been the archetype for culturally sanctioned inequality. The Chinese Communist Party (CCP) attempted to end this legacy, but succeeded only partially and temporarily. When modern ICTs like the Internet and mobile phone appeared in the 1990s, they were predominantly for the elite and upper classes (Hu 2001, Qiu 2002a, Giese 2003). But since the turn of the new century, China has become home to the world's largest national population of mobile phone users (547.3 million in December 2007), and its Internet user population has overtaken that of the United States to become the largest in the world by March 2008 (Johnson 2008). By 2005, China also produced more than one-third of all personal computers and mobile phones in the global market (Zeng and Williamson 2007). With further technological diffusion beyond the initial core of highly educated and high-income urbanites, is the historic tendency of elite dominance being challenged? Or is it persisting as the country becomes an engine of growth for the global information technology (IT) industry (Organization for Economic Co-operation and Development 2006) and a pole of market growth for the world economy (Schiller 2005)?

At the global level, the theory of network society was systematically discussed in Manuel Castells's *Information Age* trilogy (1996, 1997, 1998). Using interdisciplinary research findings from around the world, Castells developed a comprehensive framework of network society to understand the informational mode of production, the global space of flows, and the political and cultural transformations of our age. The trilogy highlights inequality as embodied in the "new urban form" of the informational city, with its "distinctive feature of being globally connected and locally disconnected, physically and socially" (1996, 404). It also takes considerable effort to integrate China into the general framework of network society by examining, for example, overseas Chinese business networks, the Chinese developmental state, and the regional formation of the Pearl River Delta in South China as a "representative urban face of the twenty-first century" (1996, 409). Castells's seminal work provides a conceptual basis for our inquiry about ICTs and China, especially urban China, in the twenty-first century.

In the decade that has passed since the publication of the trilogy, the most pivotal change in urban and urbanizing areas of China has been the rise of working-class network society, which consists of three fundamental transformations. First, ICTs are becoming less expensive, more widespread, and more closely integrated with the life of working-class people. In this process, China has been shaping low-end ICTs in previously unexpected ways to meet the demands of domestic and international markets, thus producing a series of inexpensive working-class ICTs on a massive scale. These include informal businesses like the sales of second-hand phones, used computers, and pirated DVDs. They also include more quantifiable ones like Internet cafés, SMS, prepaid mobile service, and the Little Smart low-end wireless phone.

Table 1.1 summarizes the growth of working-class ICTs in China. Between 1999 and 2007, China's cybercafé user population rose from 0.98 to 71.19 million and Little Smart subscriptions from 0.6 to 84.5 million. Between 2000 and 2007, prepaid mobile phone subscription grew from 14.9 to 360.9 million, and SMS traffic volume from 1.4 to 592.1 billion messages per annum. These statistics are partial reflections of the sea change in China's ICT market from elite domination to more dispersed patterns of technology dissemination and grassroots communication involving working-class users and service providers of all kinds. This change also reflects intense competition in China's telecom sector and increasing saturation in high-end markets (Wilson 2004).

Second, the diffusion and appropriation of working-class ICTs have given rise to a new social category of the *information have-les:* low-end ICT

Table 1.1
Growth of working-class ICTs in China, 1999–2007 (year-end data)

	Internet café user population (millions)	Prepaid mobile phone subscription (millions)	SMS traffic volume (billion messages)	Little Smart subscriptions (millions)
1999	0.98	NA	NA	0.6
2000	4.64	14.9	1.4	1.3
2001	5.19	46.2	18.9	6.0
2002	11.47	88.6	90.0	13.0
2003	16.14	124.4	137.1	37.3
2004	23.03	187.8	217.8	65.2
2005	29.97	235.0	304.7	85.3
2006	44.25	290.6	429.7	91.1
2007	71.19	360.9	592.1	84.5

Sources: Compilation based on CNNIC (1999–2007), MII (1999–2007), *China Mobile Annual Reports* (2000–2007) and *China Unicom Annual Reports* (2000–2007).

users, service providers, and laborers who are manufacturing these electronics. I call them "have-less" because, compared to the upper classes, they have limited income and limited influence in policy processes, although they have begun to go online and use wireless phones.

As in the cases of the haves and have-nots, it is not easy to quantify the have-less, but it would be a serious mistake to ignore these people, treat them as exceptions, or equate them with either side of the digital divide. In China, the have-less population encompasses large proportions of the 147 million internal migrants, more than 30 million laid-off workers, another 100 million or so retirees, and a large number of the 189 million youth between the ages of fifteen and twenty-four, including about 30 million students as well as school dropouts, unemployed and underemployed youth.[1]

The emergence of the information have-less has become the definitive feature of informational stratification in Chinese cities, as shown in figure 1.1, which presents findings from an official random-sampling survey in Beijing.[2] Each stratum in the figure stands for the percentage of the total sample ($N = 1,722$) belonging to a similar technosocial position, defined by ICT access, ownership, knowledge, and skills, as well as associated ICT behaviors and attitudes. It reflects the general picture that the information have-less have become the largest demographic group in this stratified

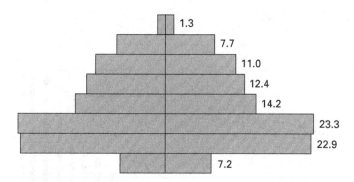

1.3

7.7

11.0

12.4

14.2

23.3

22.9

7.2

Figure 1.1
Informational stratification of Beijing residents: Percentage of respondents belong-ing to each stratum. *Source:* Informatization Office of Beijing Municipality (2005).

society: the two lower-middle strata represent 23.3 and 22.9 percent of the total sample, respectively, or about half of all respondents.

People in these have-less strata are typically migrant workers, laid-off workers, senior citizens, and microentrepreneurs with a family monthly income of about $160 to $220. Most of them have begun to use mobile phones or the Internet, but often in distinct ways of ICT connection. Many spend more than ten hours a week online, yet they do not know about search engines or possess personal e-mail accounts because they use the Internet mostly for entertainment. They have mobile phones yet seldom make a phone call because it is perceived as too expensive, so they text. The have-less people are marked by their own modes of networked con-nectivity, as this book discusses in detail.

Third, a range of political, economic, and cultural issues has emerged on the technosocial basis of working-class ICTs and the information have-less, producing distinct practices, new urban places, and critical events that pave the way for a fledgling working-class network society. Central to this process is the making of a new working class, *network labor*, that is indis-pensable to China's economic boom and its rise as a global IT power. Although not all members of the have-less population belong to this new informational working class, as this group becomes more organized in ICT-based social networks, the process of class formation has begun.

Most important, the ICT-based class-making process is embedded in ongoing urban transformations, as shown in figure 1.2. In less than thirty years, the majority of the Chinese population has moved from agriculture to the industrial and services sectors, and private sector employment has become the predominant mode of work in Chinese cities. These are crucial

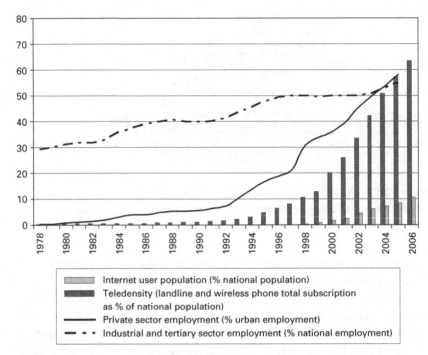

Figure 1.2
Urban transformations and ICT growth in China, 1978–2006. *Sources:* Compilation based on *Almanac of China's Population* (2006), MII (1999–2006), CNNIC (1998–2007).

changes that were well under way before the wide spread of ICTs, which was measured in figure 1.2 by combined teledensity (fixed line, Little Smart, and mobile phone) and Internet penetration per hundred people. With rising mobility, workers and working families have lost much of the welfare that they previously enjoyed, including job security. They have to maneuver to find affordable housing, health care, education, and other necessities of urban life, which are all being increasingly privatized and commercialized. The rise of working-class ICTs and the information have-less in this sense results from microlevel social innovations responding to the challenges posed by large-scale transformations of industrialization, privatization, and globalization in the context of contemporary urban China.

Construed as such, the emergence of working-class network society is about the fundamental enlargement of network society through processes of social differentiation and networked connectivity that crystallize the issues and questions facing China's new working class. This is a pivotal process through which hundreds of millions of have-less people from diverse backgrounds begin to share common experiences related to digital media—experiences of uplifting, risk taking, community building, and suffering from persistent structural inequality. In so doing, networked communication technologies have become essential to human existence among the information have-less at the lower strata of the Chinese informational city, a fertile technosocial foundation for the rise of working-class network society.

Bring Class Back In

This book provides a panoramic view of working-class ICTs and the information have-less and develops a systematic examination of the emergent working-class network society in urban China. At stake are not only technological and economic issues of network formation, national development, and market competition but also sociopolitical and cultural issues of inclusion and exclusion, institutional reform, and grassroots innovation, along a peculiar trajectory of Chinese informationalism that holds tremendous relevance to developing regions of the world.[3]

This is a worthwhile undertaking because networked communication technologies like the Internet and mobile phone are too often seen as elite privileges, designed for the upper class. The global cyberspace in this sense represents a flat, classless social imagination. Although many scholars devote themselves to studying the uneven development of ICTs, attention is usually paid to social divisions along the lines of age, gender, race, and ethnicity, but seldom to class.

Research about the digital divide, an umbrella term that covers a range of studies about ICTs and inequality, emphasizes a particular social reality: that of a two-tier society (Servon 2002, Van Dijk 2005, Koh 2005). In Western postindustrial societies, this conception correctly captures the polarization of wealth distribution, the decline of manufacturing and the traditional middle class, and the general transformation of the informational city toward a "dual city" characterized by social and spatial schism between the rich and the poor (Castells 1989, 1999). However, this book contends that the binary model is inadequate to reflect the technosocial dynamics in a rapidly industrializing society like China, where the problem is not only about access but also about class formation, collective identity, and political power under the structural parameters of a large, developing country. The metaphor of an overarching divide does not do justice to the significance and complexity of the Chinese experience, which is emblematic of the new technosocial reality emerging in much of the global South.

Consider small-scale telecom operators (microtelcos) in Latin America (Galperin and Mariscal 2005, Galperin and Bar 2007), community multimedia centers and ICT-equipped fishermen in South Asia (Slater and Tacchi 2004, Jensen 2007), microentrepreneurs using wireless phones in Africa (Donner 2004, 2006), and prepaid mobile phone service in the Philippines (Pertierra et al. 2002, Toral 2003). There is an entire array of low-end ICT uses and applications around the globe, such as inexpensive wireless communication, that has appeared from Asia to Africa to Latin America (Castells, Fernandez-Ardevol, Qiu, and Sey, 2006; Qiu and Thompson 2007). Many of these new users do not personally own any ICT equipment since they depend on Internet cafés or telephone collectives for access. Others may be able to purchase only used phones, thus creating a huge market for refurbished digital equipment, for instance, in Indonesia (Barendregt 2005).

We see a full range of working-class ICTs in China's urban and urbanizing areas that have emerged in recent years to serve the information have-less. The crucial transformation is taking place among ordinary city dwellers and in small towns that have actively engaged in using and appropriating low-end ICTs as tools of individual struggling and familial connectivity, of place making and community building. Are these people already information haves, or are they still have-nots? When the question is posed in this way, it is difficult to talk about the important phenomena and processes with coherence, let alone analyze them systematically with respect to their unique patterns and multifaceted manifestations.

Moreover, is it a single divide or multiple strata in the distribution of ICT resources that serve as a new seedbed for class formation? Is it a single dimension of social differentiation, moving vertically upward or downward? Could there be other ways of movement: horizontal, inclined in different angles, interacting with institutional and cultural factors, or even going astray? Conceptualizing working-class network society opens up these alternative ways of seeing and thinking and, in so doing, developing a more refined and realistic analytical tool. It builds on the recognition of the digital divide but goes beyond. Its goal is not to substitute the binary model with another simplification but to delve into the evolving structures of informational stratification and class formation, into the vast middle ground between the haves and have-nots that is populated by the information have-less.

In discussing the relevance of Castells's urban theory in Third World contexts, Peter Evans maintains that "the network society is more plastic in its potential than it first appears" (2002, 12). In an interview with the *Chinese Journal of Communication*, Castells states, "How applicable my theory (which is a general theory) is to China can only be established by Chinese researchers, by applying it, and modifying it, to the Chinese reality" (2008, 3). This is how and why, in analyzing low-end ICTs in China, we shall bring class back in for a broader understanding of the Chinese experience as well as network society in general.

The most crucial development here is the transformation toward a new working class—an informational working class centered on network labor. This is a dynamic formation of workers, and their relationships with others, under new conditions of industrialization, globalization, and networked connectivity. The dichotomous contradiction between "self-programmable" and "generic" labor is a known pattern of flexible capitalism in postindustrial network societies (Castells 1998). However, under the historical and institutional conditions of contemporary China, industrialization and informatization (*xinxihua*, i.e., the spread of ICTs throughout the economy and society) are juxtaposed, which entails more complex and multilayered labor formation.

The result is yet another brand of informationalism, *Chinese informationalism* one might call it, whose central components are the network enterprise, including multinational and domestic IT corporations; the network state, including not only the Chinese government but also the Chinese Communist Party (CCP); and network labor, or the new working class. In other words, a critical result from China's new developmental paradigm is the rise of network labor in relation to network enterprise on the one hand and network state on the other.

Network labor combines self-programmable labor with programmable labor (those who perform simplified skilled tasks in the new information industry) and generic labor, creating the basis for China's working-class network society.[4] This basis draws directly from the social repertoire of the information have-less, a broad category of low-income consumers and providers such as rural-to-urban migrants, laid-off workers, retirees, and youth who have gained access to ICTs since the turn of the century. Defined as such, the creation of working-class ICTs as a growing category of low-end ICT products and services is in itself a necessary though insufficient process for the making of network labor.

To complete class formation in this new development of network society, two additional criteria need to be stressed. First, the goals of working-class ICTs, working-class connectivity, and working-class networks are essentially about meeting the basic information needs of have-less people, shaped fundamentally by China's contemporary urban reforms in the commercialization of housing, education, and health care. The wide spread of ICTs is therefore indicative of growing information needs at the grassroots level to deal with this social upheaval. Although consumerism and individualism are popular frames of interpretation, the development of working-class ICTs has to be understood, first and foremost, as resulting from the changing urban conditions that give rise to concrete everyday existential demands of workers, working families, and working-class communities for such indispensable needs as employment, child care, and health care.

Second, at both the discursive and practical levels, the making of a new working class is necessarily a process of collective empowerment. Otherwise, it will revert back to the trap of elite domination and patron-client networks that have characterized the past. Empowerment in this case is the process through which the information have-less gain control over the situation around them (Rogers and Singhal 2003) and become members of the newly empowered network labor. This is not only an individual process. Although it often starts as individual suffering and individual struggle, the endeavor has to go beyond the private and enter a public realm. It has to connect scattered clouds of networked individualism and give them solidarity in order to bring about social change at higher structural levels.

Given the above recognitions, this book raises and explores the following questions about working-class network society:

• What constitutes working-class ICTs? How widespread are they in China's urban and urbanizing areas? Who belongs to the information have-less? What are the specific goals and distinct social and behavioral patterns of have-less ICT users and service providers? What obstacles do they face in using networked connectivity to meet their informational needs?
• How does the spread of working-class ICTs among the information have-less contribute to the making of China's new working class and the formation of working-class network society? Why does working-class network society emerge, and under what sociohistorical conditions? What are its origins in China's economy, politics, and media system? What is the trajectory of Chinese informationalism, seen from a renewed perspective of class analysis, in the broader contexts of industrialization, urbanization, and globalization?

- What are the economic, political, and cultural manifestations of working-class network society? How do they reflect, reinforce, and reorganize the fundamental power structures of China? How do they reveal critical issues about network labor, above and beyond what is known about network enterprise and network state? How do they relate to age-old debates on equality and stratification, technology and control, working-class community and informal economy, and the role of traditional social networks?
- What are the consequences of working-class connectivity? Does it encourage horizontal communication and bottom-up networking in opposition to the elite domination of the past? Does it empower the information have-less or disempower them? How does this entail new policy, new understanding of the Net and the self, and new perspectives in analyzing ICT and development? What does the Chinese experience tell us about key issues of network society in the twenty-first century—local and regional, national and global?

This book answers these questions on the basis of empirical evidence collected since 2002 in more than twenty Chinese cities in Guangdong, Hong Kong, and Macau of South China; Shanghai, Zhejiang, and Jiangsu of East China; Sichuan of West China; Hubei of Central China; and Beijing, Tianjin, and Hebei of North China (see the methodological appendix at the end of the book). The project connects scattered pieces of information gathered through interviews, focus groups, surveys, participant observation, and sociospatial mapping, and links them with a number of key issues and debates about communication technology, working-class people, and have-less urban conditions, which have so far received little research attention.

Original research findings, official statistics, and archive data are synthesized to construct a broad picture of working-class network society, from its genesis and internal structure to its ongoing transformation and impact on the have-less population, as well as the power dynamics of urban society at large. To gain a deeper understanding, more targeted analysis is carried out to focus on specific working-class ICTs (wired or wireless) and particular have-less social groups (such as migrants, youth, females, and seniors). A series of case studies is then carried out under specific organizational settings (factories, stores, and online gaming companies), in particular urban places (migrant enclaves, university dormitories, and labor markets), and during critical events that provide a window for us to be informed about and understand the suffering, struggling, and social innovation at the grassroots of the Chinese network society.

Confronting a Technosocial Emergence

The reality that confronts us cannot be clearer: hundreds of millions of have-less people have gained access through low-end ICTs. The Internet and mobile phones are no longer luxuries. With the newly available working-class connectivity, local, translocal, and regional networks have sprung up to become the substance of new urban places, which seek to resist, supplement, and even thrive on the basis of the global space of flows in such realms as the financial market, international trade, and digital content. In this reality, the technological and the social are two parts of the same puzzle that merge into each other as working-class innovations emerge from networking and problem solving among the have-less. To China and the rest of the world, this is a definitive transformation, the beginning of an era.

However, we must exercise caution because the process has just begun. In any examination of this technosocial change, it is important to refrain from oversimplification and hasty conclusions. For example, the existence of the information have-less as a broad social stratification category should not be equated with the rise of a new working class. That is, the information have-less may be seen as a "class in itself", defined by similar techno-social positioning in the marketplace of ICTs, but it is not yet a "class for itself", which requires more organizational, cultural, and political processes that produce collective identity, class consciousness, solidarity, and empowerment. Creating such a social class in the full sense is particularly complicated in China given the rule of Chinese authorities that has combined the world's largest Communist party with one of the world's most successful developmental states since the end of the Cold War.

Similarly, it is far too early to predict that the ascendance of working-class network society will cause a social revolution comparable to Mao's attempt to systematically erase elite domination. This is particularly so because the stage of technology diffusion we are in now seems at first glance to be apolitical and asocial, because it is often interpreted only in frameworks of the market economy, commercial culture, and technology. So far, the technosocial emergence has only created openings for social change, whose realization is not predetermined. Instead, it is contingent on many other factors in the real world at both the grassroots and structural levels, whose outcome may also be the unmaking of class, depending on how the ICTs are put to use, by whom, and for what goal.

This technosocial emergence is full of potential, with opportunities for both progressive change and regressive control. There is indeed a chance that the emergence of network labor as a process of class formation may never be fully complete. Even if a new working class finally rises, it may or may not coexist harmoniously with upper-class network society. It is therefore important to exercise prudence in research. A more suitable way to do so is to adopt a neo-Weberian approach and conceptualize this class formation process as a stratified distribution of life chances, whose consequence and broader social impact can be found only in concrete institutional and cultural settings.

Despite the uncertainties, we can be relatively confident in disentangling three crucial processes of emergence that can serve as basic coordinates for our discussion. First is the fundamental process of informational stratification in network society. Second is the central problematic of class emergence on the technosocial basis of working-class ICTs and the information have-less. Third is the key development of network formation and its empowerment or disempowerment effect on network labor.

Informational stratification has increasingly occurred in the enlarged network society, meaning that different social strata, including the information have-less, are capable of interacting with digital media and integrating them into their modes of communication and ways of life. This is a key transformation as the Internet and mobile communication are being transformed from elite privilege for the upper classes into basic instruments necessary to human existence itself. Migrants, laid-off workers, retirees, and students from low-income families are, in this sense, not merely vulnerable groups (*ruoshi qunti*), as they have been called in China's mass media and policy circles. The official term downplays the agency of the have-less and sees them as passive and weak, itself a problematic assumption. On the contrary, this book emphasizes the potential role of the information have-less as agents of social change—not only individually at the microlevel but also collectively through the networking of their families and communities—albeit under structural constraints.

Meanwhile, in the context of a vast industrializing society like China today, class and class differentiation need to be viewed as a primary aspect of social research (C. K. Lee 2002a, 2002b; Sun 2006), in this case, from a perspective of media and communication. The central problem is the making of a new working class on the technosocial basis of the information have-less. The specific constitution of the have-less people is contingent on economic structure, institutional setting, and the demographic makeup of a given society. But "less" does not necessarily imply inferiority; it could also mean less information overload or less commitment to the status quo.

Recent social transformations in China have disproportionately inflicted the have-less. Rural-to-urban migrants and laid-off workers have been uprooted from agricultural and industrial production systems. The lack of social welfare has left many retirees with little or no pension, and college students from working families have been forced to deal with skyrocketing tuition and plummeting prospects for employment. It is in this merciless process of structural transformation that the have-less people are gaining access to ICTs on an unprecedented scale—in order to cope with the tremendous uncertainties of the world they are thrown into—precisely because their right to communicate and their needs for information, entertainment, social support, and social services in general have been systematically underserved by the media—public and private, old and new.

The rise of the new working class is therefore above all a social and historical process. It consists of countless daily struggles at the grassroots that give rise to a new category of not only end users but also ICT manufacturers and providers, all of whom we call the information have-less. And this is not to mention the massive army of laborers behind the burgeoning electronics industry; members of the have-less working in Internet cafés, second-hand equipment markets, and stores selling prepaid phone cards and pirated DVDs. New forms of entrepreneurship are taking shape along with new ways of exploitation and alienation. Innovative modes of technology appropriation emerge, sometimes of questionable legality and almost always dependent on the discourse of the rich and the powerful. It is hence not unimaginable that the consequence of this technosocial emergence may work against the interests of the have-less and against the making of the new working class. This is a crucial paradox that this book revisits.

Finally, the emergence of the new working class is about the formation, evolution, and impact of networks. These are social networks that materialize through working-class ICTs, whose popularity results from their low cost. Their quality may not be guaranteed, which is quite different from high-end services that emphasize signal reliability and channel "redundancy" (Graham 1999). Despite the limitations, working-class ICTs are tools of networking, facilitating information exchange, grassroots coordination, and mutual support, particularly important in places where unions are weak and families are far away.

These working-class social networks existed before. But with the help of digital media, they have expanded locally and translocally; their networking process has accelerated, with an increasing transnational reach. The nature of these networks depends on who is using the technology and under what conditions. A factory, a school, a residential community, or a prison cell: through the intermingling of people and place, the information have-less and working-class ICTs reconfigure each other in complex ways, giving rise to infinite variations and producing a kaleidoscope of communication patterns. While these network dynamics may serve as a fertile seedbed for the fostering of network labor, it remains an open question whether the informational tools for the lower class to deal with issues of existence (e.g., housing, employment, and senior care) can also facilitate independent solidarity and political mobilization, or whether they will become networks of class reconciliation, even ways of disempowerment. Whatever the outcome, working-class ICT networks have been, and will continue to be, central to the unfolding answer.

At stake is the making of China's new working class, economically, politically, and culturally, which, in important ways, parallels the "making of the English working class" (Thompson 1966). The differences are that the Chinese process is of a larger scale and is changing faster as it relies on ICT-based network connectivity. Due to the persisting power of the CCP in China and that of neoliberal doctrine worldwide, this new Chinese working class in the making probably will not assume the same organizational and cultural characteristics of the old industrial proletariat. It would be also erroneous to postulate the simple return of Maoist class politics. Rather, this is a new period of class formation with distinct elements, dynamics, and points of engagement, many of which, as will be discussed in this book, are built on the basis of working-class networks that have expanded into a most critical technosocial issue today.

Structure of the Book

This book is divided into three main parts. Part I, "Networks Materialized," discusses diverse forms of working-class ICTs—their patterns of diffusion, transformation, and the broader implications. Part II, "The People of Have-Less," examines different groups of the information have-less—their informational needs, the way they use and appropriate communication technologies, and the dilemmas they face. Part III, "Working Class in the Making," investigates how the have-less people and their technologies come together to produce concrete urban places and critical events that mark the beginning of a new class formation process in the enlarged network society.

We start with a discussion on China's cybercafé, or "Net bar (*wangba*)," business in chapter 2. Despite repetitive crackdowns, a defiant upsurge of cybercafé continues to occur throughout the country, giving rise to a unique collective space for Internet access. How does this shared mode of access (as opposed to individually based modes of access at home or at work) evolve? What are the different types of cybercafés and their characteristics? What are the forces shaping this particular informational commons of the have-less people, revealing what issues and challenges in the coevolution of market dynamics and state regulation, with what potentials in grassroots network formation?

Chapter 3 is about the historical trajectory of wireless phone or *shouji* ("hand-phone" in Chinese) from an elite device to a common component of everyday life. This change has happened as a massive IT industrial complex emerges to include China's domestic mobile handset manufacturing sector and a number of low-end wireless services such as SMS, Little Smart, prepaid services, and pagers (which have almost disappeared), all of which hold important lessons about working-class connectivity. Like chapter 2, chapter 3 seeks to piece together the basic policy environment and labor conditions for each working-class ICT as well as the processes of bottom-up networking.

Chapters 4 and 5 concentrates on the have-less people: how their informational needs are shaped, neglected, or satisfied in processes of structural transformation and the subsequent problems and dilemmas. Mobility is the central organizing concept of chapter 4, which provides an overview on the basic conditions of have-less migrants under conditions of industrialization and urbanization in a global context. It discusses how migrants use and appropriate ICTs, for what purpose, and with what empowerment effect, drawing on six survey groups that combine qualitative and quantitative design with action research. Have-less migrants are heterogeneous on the basis of their gender, ethnicity, and regional identity. These groups are extending their traditional translocal networks while also forming new cultural communities of bloggers, Internet poets, and art troupes. They are being transformed into network labor under the new organizational settings of cost innovation, a definitive feature of the up-and-rising Chinese informationalism.

In chapter 5 we look at two lower-mobility social groups: youngsters and senior citizens, particularly those in have-less families, who have also begun to turn to Internet and wireless service. These groups of people, young or old, have to cope with the fundamental changes triggered by the one-child policy and neoliberal reforms of education and health care, which have had a profound impact on the family unit. They face formidable issues that create motivations for adopting and appropriating working-class ICTs to meet their increasing needs for information, communication, and networking. These bottom-up informational needs have led to innovation at the level of local state behavior and the marketing strategy of some firms, especially in the wireless business, making it imperative to rethink the notion of welfare in a new era of networked connectivity.

Part III deals with concrete urban places, specific institutions and networks, and the central problematic of class formation. Chapter 6 provides an overview on the making of working-class communities where the information have-less and working-class ICTs are most concentrated, for example, factory dormitories and the migrant enclaves known as urban villages. While new technologies facilitate the new process of place making within and beyond the global space of flows, they also expose old conflicts between migrants and long-term residents, between labor and management, between bottom-up forces of change and top-down means of control. The process of class formation is molded in the seesaw battle between power domination and power contestation, when active members of the new working class struggle to play a decisive role in the making of their own places of living and the shaping of the Chinese informational city.

Chapter 7 addresses the serious consequences of the technosocial emergence if we fail to understand and act on the vital issues facing the information have-less. Already the new means of communication have been used to assist the informal economy, due to long-standing problems of unemployment, organized crime, and official corruption. This chapter develops a critical appraisal of three new media events: the Lanjisu cybercafé fire in 2002; the killing of a migrant, Sun Zhigang, in 2003; and the Ma Jiajue dormitory murder case in 2004. Why did these tragedies happen? What did they reveal about deep-seated social problems in working-class network society? How did they trigger reactions in public opinion, the escalation of urban control policy, and cross-class ties? In a comparative light, this chapter contends that death is not only the ultimate expression of systemic suppression and the despair they inflict, but also a powerful way of struggle for equality and dignity in the "city underneath." It highlights concrete working-class efforts to create history and collective memory outside "timeless time" as network society is enlarged to include more marginal social groups.

Finally, the book closes with a summary on the main lessons set out here. It reflects on the complex role of working-class ICTs and the resilience and vulnerability of translocal networks among the have-less in a larger historical and transnational context. From stratification to equality to network labor, from sustainability to community building to social innovation, the ramifications of working-class network society are numerous and profound for the future of Chinese informationalism and a new class analysis of the twenty-first century.

Diverse as they are, the information have-less—their working-class ICTs, their families and communities, their daily struggles and participation in the class-making and history-making process—are the silent cogwheels of the enlarged network society. For too long they have been overlooked. It is time to scrutinize their trajectories of transformation; their social, economic, political, and cultural dynamics; and their consequences, intended or unintended. From this working hypothesis, we embark on the intellectual journey of this book.

I   Networks Materialized

2 Internet Cafés

When commercial Internet began in China in 1995, the Internet café was the center of action. "How far is China away from the Information Superhighway?" asked the most famous Internet advertisement of the time. "Go north, 1500 meters" (*China Youth Daily* 1997). A thick arrow was drawn pointing at one of the earliest cybercafés in the Zhongguancun area of Beijing, China's main IT hub. It was in this area, also in an Internet café, that in 1996 I got my first e-mail account. Set up by graduates from the Computer Science Department of Peking University, this place was conveniently located in the old *hutong* alleys outside the East Gate of the campus. There were about twenty terminals, of which nineteen used the UNIX system showing monotonous green texts. Only one had Netscape 1.1, and it cost a prohibitive hourly rate of twenty yuan ($2.40) to surf the Web.

To me and most of my fellow users, e-mail was the only activity. One of the shop owners taught me the commands and explained how they charged by the volume of international data flow. It was international because half of the customers were foreign exchange students, and everyone else, myself included, was applying for schools overseas. It was good business, as the delivery of international mail took at least one week and more than 4 yuan, whereas an e-mail took only a few minutes and less than half a yuan. The place was not fancy, but it was quiet and clean, with the smell of instant coffee floating in the air.

Since then, Internet café in China has gone through a remarkable metamorphosis. Enter an average cybercafé in 2008, and you are immediately surrounded by the dazzling colors and sounds of online gaming, streaming video, poster ads, and young people talking loudly to each other or to their microphones. Almost all computers are equipped with earphones and a microphone. People flock in not to pursue further studies, but to be entertained. It would be uncommon to see anyone checking e-mail and even harder to find anyone retrieving foreign-language content. The coffee smell has been replaced by cigarette smoke. From time to time, you see people eat instant noodles or snooze in front of the monitor. Very few of them are trying to get out of the country. They barely want to get out of their seats.

The machines are also different. In the mid-1990s, computer terminals in Internet cafés were identical to personal computers (PCs) at home or at work in terms of hardware and software. A decade later, they evolved into a special-purpose appliance optimized for collective entertainment. From standardized headsets to heavy-duty waterproof keyboards, from the officially authorized operating system (OS) to the latest online gaming programs, these computers are well equipped, although they rarely have a USB harbor, a CD-ROM, or Word. They have become a particular species with their own technical design and service requirement that a full commercial plaza has emerged in Guangzhou specializing in cybercafé computers.

Even the Chinese phrase for Internet café has changed. Ten years ago, it was called *wangluo kafeiwu*, meaning literally "network coffee house," a place of enlightenment, culture, and taste for the brainy and foreign minded. Ten years later, it is known simply as *wangba* or "Net bar." The short term succinctly signifies the loss of its elite appeal and descent into a working-class ICT. Cybercafés have become a kind of inexpensive bar, where the information have-less kill time, relax and socialize, and get intoxicated in cyberspace and the physical place. A 2004 survey found that 91.4 percent of China's Net bars charged no more than 2 yuan (25 cents) for hourly access (China Youth Network 2004).

Nevertheless, a few things remain unchanged. Most customers—students as well as tourists and migrant workers—are young, and many of the café owners, like their customers, are male with relatively high levels of education by local standards. Their employees, particularly attendants in larger cafés, include more females, who tend to be young, less educated, and poorly paid; they work long hours, in almost complete silence.

For working-class network society, the Internet café offers a collective mode of access. It is an informational commons of exceptional value because a large number of potential Internet users in the country are either unable to afford their own PC (or unwilling to pay for it) and get their own Internet access (Murray 2003). This is not only a matter of income. It also requires domestic space and a relatively stable residence. Users also have to deal with Internet service providers (ISPs) and take care of maintaining and upgrading their computer. In contrast, the Net bar rents shared scarce ICT resources. It offers a cost-effective solution for members of the information have-less to meet their informational needs, while building and extending working-class networks from the bottom up.

This is, however, a skewed market, where individual decisions in investment and sales, as well as the life prospects of the customers and staff, are constrained by larger structural forces. ISPs frown at the idea of sharing, just as phone companies turned away from party line service in early-twentieth-century North America (Martin 1991). Schools and upper-class communities dislike Net bars because thugs and criminals may hide there. There are indeed thieves and drug dealers, and a number of young people have vanished due to gang activities or fire. These events, publicized and dramatized by the mass media, cause nationwide public panic and a call for strict regulation by government in yet another process of arrogant elites silencing the information have-less.

It is against this backdrop that the market of Net bars coevolves with state regulation at national and local levels, while the technical design and business model of cybercafés are being upgraded and differentiated. The role of government intervention thus assumes vital importance beyond the model of Chinese developmental state due to the class dynamics concerning collective access. But how strong is the state when it comes to the technosocial emergence of grassroots networking? How tenacious is the grassroots networking that supports the working-class ICT service of cybercafé and wider social formations of network labor? Based on field observation, interview, and archive research, I examine these questions by providing an analytical overview of Internet cafés, their historical trajectory, internal differentiation, and implications for working-class network society.

The Defiant Upsurge

When an Internet café hits the headlines, it is almost always associated with at least one of the following terms: *qingli* (clean-up), *daji* (crackdown), *guanbi* (close-down), and *zhengdun* (rectify, or following official regulations). This has become a press routine, both in and outside the country, as revealed by these typical press accounts: between April and October 2001, 17,488 Net bars were closed nationwide (XinhuaNet 2001); in December 2002, another 3,300 were cracked down on (Associated Press 2002); between March and November 2004, 18,000 had their business suspended and 1,600 lost their licenses permanently (CCID Net 2004). This is, of course, not just objective news but stories magnified out of proportion, designed to create a chilling effect. Be they nationwide or local campaigns, the operations are almost always high profile in order to deter the allegedly unscrupulous from illegal cybercafé operations, also known in Chinese as black Net bars (*heiwangba*).

The Chinese government has established an institutional framework to mobilize resources and implement measures of control at various levels, involving both public and private stakeholders. Restrictive regulations were stipulated in 1998, 2001, and 2002. A number of government agencies, including the Ministry of Information Industry (MII), the police, and the Ministry of Culture (MoC), have joined forces in the rectification campaigns, giving rise to a new "national regulatory regime" (Qiu and Zhou 2005).

But what is the consequence? Does the combination of stringent regulation, frequent rectification, and society-wide media campaigns stop people from visiting or opening up their own Internet cafés? A meta-analysis of data from the China Network Information Center (CNNIC), the official monitor of the country's Internet industry, reveals surprisingly that despite the crackdowns, the growth of the Internet café in China has been exponential and robust.

From January 1999 to January 2008, the Internet café user population increased from about 60,000 to 71.2 million. Meanwhile, café users as a percentage of the total Internet user population leaped from 3 percent to 33.9 percent. Until 2007, there was only a single dip in the growth curve, from July 2000 to July 2001, most likely due to a severe clampdown at the time, and one slowdown of market expansion in the first half of 2003 when severe acute respiratory syndrome (SARS) forced people to stay home. Except for these two brief periods, the upsurge of Internet cafés is indisputable (figure 2.1).

The growth of the Internet café as a working-class ICT is more remarkable when compared with other modes of access (figure 2.2). The only comparable trend is in the case of home access, whose proportion of total Internet user population climbed from 44 percent in January 1999 to 67.3 percent in January 2008. This achievement, however, results from the unceasing efforts of both ISPs and the government to promote access at home. Meanwhile, contrary to the experience of Internet cafés, there has been very little policy hindrance to the spread of home access. The percentage of home-based users has therefore gone up, although more gradually but rather smoothly until 2007.

During the same period, from 1999 to 2007, the percentage of people accessing the Net from their office went through a significant downswing, dropping from 50.0 percent to 24.3 percent. CNNIC released data on school access between January 2001 and July 2007. In this period, the ratio

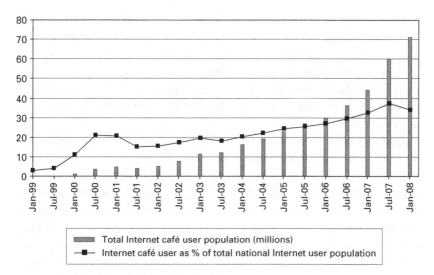

Figure 2.1
Growth of Internet café user population in China, 1999–2008. *Source:* Compilation based on CNNIC (1999–2008).

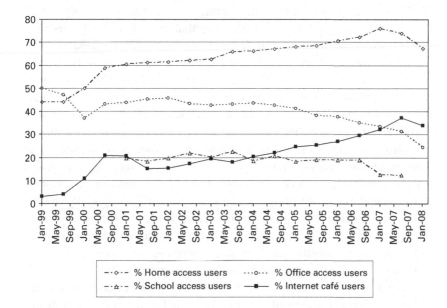

Figure 2.2
Percentage of total Internet user population using four modes of access: Home, office, school, and Internet café. 1999–2008. *Source:* Compilation based on CNNIC (1999–2008).

of users going online from school was quite stable, from 19.7 percent at the beginning of 2001 and remaining at this level for several years, until it dipped to about 12 percent in 2007. Now, with more than one-third of China's Internet users going online from a shared informational service, the cybercafé has become the second most important, and the most rapidly growing, mode of Internet access in the country, serving have-less netizens on massive scale.

Another piece of evidence, which must be viewed with some caution, is the total number of Internet cafés in China. It is difficult to count these small businesses because many of them are illegal or semilegal, and available reports rarely explain how they came up with their estimates. A widely circulated official Xinhua article claims that the government had registered 110,000 Internet cafés in February 2003 (Xinhua News Agency 2003a). This figure was, however, reported at the end of a major rectification campaign that started just after a large cybercafé fire in Beijing in June 2002, when the total number was reported to be about 200,000 (L. Shen 2003).

More recently, it was reported that there were at least 1.8 million cybercafé outlets in China in October 2004, citing an MoC official (*China Daily* 2004), and more than 2 million of them in September 2005 (McLaughlin 2005). According to another official press release, this one in July 2006, China had 112,264 cybercafés, with more than 6 million computers and 786,000 employees (*Guangming Daily* 2006). The wide discrepancies in these estimates is not uncommon, as in other types of macrostatistics in the country, generated by unexplained methodology in the framework of a complicated bureaucratic system. However, the observation remains that the Internet café business is huge despite the restrictive regulatory regime.

This growth pattern flies in the face of suppressive policies and refutes the derogatory upper-class discourse that looks down on cybercafés as a doomed ghetto business. In so doing, it vehemently challenges the problematic commonsense that the joint efforts of the state and the upper classes would exert control over matters regarding ICTs—especially in this sphere of working-class technology that is now being claimed by the information have-less. As the high-end market gets saturated, the importance of Net bars as a collective mode of access becomes even more prominent as they continue to drive the expansion of Internet into the lower social strata of urban China, from low-income communities in major metropolitan areas to second- and third-tier cities and small towns in the hinterland. The question is how and why, over the course of a decade, this particular Internet access service has shown such an upsurge.

Selecting a Path

How did the Internet café evolve from an upper-class service, provided by and for the elite, to a working-class ICT? How did it become a crucial technosocial basis for the expansion of working-class networks among the information have-less? The process encompasses several transformations. First, the customer base of Internet cafés shifted from elites in the 1990s to the information have-less of the twenty-first century. Second, the main function changed from offering a two-way communication flow of information to the delivery of increasingly one-way entertainment. Third, the Internet café used to be a symbol of the new economy. But Net bars face a major public image crisis caused by the crackdown, stigmatization, and an increasing number of black Net-bars. Gone is the image of the Internet café as a place of enlightenment. Net bars are now widely perceived as a social problem in urban China.

These currents of devolution were not predestined. This path was not a matter of bad luck or a linear process of increasing regulation or a continuously expanding market. It in fact started as a set of messy forces interacting with events embedded in the social reality of the Chinese informational city, including street-corner societies in contemporary China, which are often misunderstood by the urban mainstream.[1]

Despite the apparent lack of order, we see a systemic trend of Internet cafés being locked in and forced into a downward spiral without other choices, especially since the key transitional period of 1999 to 2002. Alternative ways of technology shaping are suppressed, leaving Net bars under the dual pressures of political control and commercial survival. Some cybercafés have vanished. Others were left with no choice but to become what they are today.

We can construct four basic types of collective Internet access venues in China: (1) promotional cafés, (2) elite cafés, (3) mass-service Net bars, and (4) illegal or semilegal black Net bars, including unlicensed or partially licensed ones, many of which fail to have valid licenses due to uncontrollable reasons such as policy change and official discrimination against Net bars. We can find a notable example of each of these four types in the Haidian District of Beijing, in or near Zhongguancun, all within a short bike ride from the cybercafé where I got my first e-mail address. Unfortunately, none of these examples still exists. Financial reasons contributed to the decline of the first two. Urban reconstruction forced the third to relocate. The last was torched.

Promotional and Elite Cafés

The first prototypical venue of collective access was the Science Education House (*kejiaoguan*) of Info Highway Ltd (*yinghaiwei*), China's leading Internet firm in the mid-1990s (*China Youth Daily* 1997). The famous cybercafé advertisement mentioned at the beginning of this chapter was set up by Info Highway to guide people to the Science Education House, which I visited in 1996. The place had a modern look with glass walls and a white ceramic floor—but only two computers. Going online was free because the objective was to spread knowledge about the Internet and attract potential subscribers to the company's Internet access service. When Info Highway foundered in 1998 and finally closed down in 2004, this cybercafé also disappeared.[2]

There are, however, a number of promotional cafés throughout China. In 1996, China Telecom opened Information Time-Space (*xinxishikon*) in Guangzhou, designed to encourage people to use ChinaNet.[3] In 2002, free promotional Internet services could be spotted in restaurants and saunas in South China as well as computer malls in southwestern China. In Shanghai, East China, a bookstore next to Fudan University offered free Internet access to customers, who queued up for free Web-surfing sessions.[4] But promotional cybercafés have become increasingly rare because the owners determined that such free services no longer attract their target audience: the upper strata of the consumer market. Given the emergence of the information have-less, the Internet itself has lost most of its promotional appeal as something special for China's new rich.

There are also elite cafés, whose operations differ from promotional cafés, although the client basis is similar. A famous elite café was Sparkice (*shihuakai*), located in the southern part of Zhongguancun; it opened in November 1996 not far from Beijing's Friendship Hotel. Charging a high hourly rate of 20 yuan ($2.40) in 1999, it served mostly foreign tourists and a small number of the young and affluent of the local population. With the Internet boom of the late 1990s, Sparkice expanded to a chain of fourteen cybercafés nationwide. The company, however, withdrew from the business during a crackdown campaign on Net bars in summer 2002 "in order to be more focused on B2B [business-to-business] service" (*Business Weekly* 2002).

Nevertheless, many elite cybercafés continue to exist in major metropolitan areas, serving mostly high-end game players. One such café that I visited in January 2004 was on the Huaihai Road in Shanghai's main commercial district. It charged 10 yuan ($1.20) per hour, in contrast to 3 to 5 yuan for ordinary Net bars in the city. Here the computers were better maintained and had faster connections. Customers could also enjoy more space, more privacy, and a nonsmoking area. The access fee included unlimited free drinks. It is important to note, though, that such elite cafés rarely exist outside megacities like Shanghai, Beijing, and Shenzhen. The market share of elite cafés is declining because the strong growth is in smaller cities and towns, not big cities (Guo 2004).

Feiyu and Mass-Service Net Bars

Mass-service Net bars are large cybercafés or a large number of small shops that offer affordable access service to diverse groups of the have-less. The best example of large-scale Internet cafés is Feiyu, whose superstore along the South Wall of Peking University once had about fifteen hundred computers.[5] This is probably the largest single-site Internet café that ever existed in China, and it may be also a world record. Founded in February 1998 with twenty-five computers, Feiyu went through two and a half years of extraordinary expansion, taking over nine nearby businesses to form a massive 6,000-square-meter space both above and below the ground (Xiao 2001). This was the renowned Feiyu Net bar street in the center of Zhongguancun.

Feiyu's owner, Wang Yuesheng, was an entrepreneur from the Shanxi countryside, where he had made a fortune selling construction materials and gasoline. Because of his personal background—he was from the lower strata—Wang believed that his Internet access service should be socially inclusive, serving not only the elite. This is why he adopted the name *Feiyu,* using two simple Chinese characters so that the less educated would recognize this brand (Dong 2003).

The gigantic Net bar was divided into several sections in order to target diverse user groups with different goals for Internet access, including the less wealthy. Computers in each section had different configurations; some were older and slower models, and others were newer and had flat-screen monitors. A flexible pricing scheme was applied that varied with the time of day.[6]

Table 2.1 shows that Feiyu catered to a wider spectrum of users compared to most Net bars today. The Internet was free between 7:00 and 9:00 A.M., and low-income students from nearby universities would line up on weekends for free Internet access (Rong 2000). According to Guo Liang at the Chinese Academy of Social Sciences, young female migrants working in nearby barber shops also started to go online at the time because of the free access.[7] Moreover, Feiyu provided special training and discounts for laid-off workers and those above age sixty (Zhu and Zhao 2000).

Table 2.1
Rates at Feiyu Net-Friend cybercafé (8.27 yuan = $1.00)

Service items	Time	Hourly rate
Internet access	7:00 A.M.–9:00 A.M.	Free of charge
	9:00 A.M.–noon	3–5 yuan
	Noon–2:00 A.M.	4–10 yuan
	2:00 A.M.–7:00 A.M.	3–5 yuan
Printing	1 yuan per page (A4 size)	
Photocoping	0.2 yuan per page (A4 size)	0.4 yuan per page (A3 size)
Scanning	4 yuan per page (A4 size)	
No other service charges		
Drinking water provided for free		
20 percent discount for VIP card and student ID card holders		
Internet access charge calculated by the minute		

Note: A4 and A3 are the commonly used printing paper sizes in China, A4 is 8.3 by 11.7 inches; A3 is 11.7 by 16.5 inches.

Feiyu also offered printing, scanning, and photocopying service, which is extremely rare in Net bars today, where word processors are scarce or even nonexistent. The provision of free drinking water and by-the-minute cost calculation is also rare today in China. In 2000, Feiyu asked its customers to pay after they finished going online, whereas standard operation today is to pay up front (H. Xin 2000a). Such seemingly small matters showed that Feiyu was not just another commercial IT company. More than anything else, it treated its have-less customers with respect.

Then in December 2000, more than two hundred police descended on Feiyu. In about two hours, they checked 860 computers and found "pornographic" content on 56 (6.5 percent) of them (H. Xin 2000b). The penalty included 10,000 yuan ($1,208). The mass media soon began to associate this prominent Net bar with the corruption of morals among youth. Peking University, which owned the land, reconsidered whether the Feiyu Net bar street should be allowed to continue to exist. In April 2001, four months after the police raid, Peking University cut Feiyu's electrical service in order to force it to relocate (*New Weekly* 2001). The new location provided by Peking University was at a nearby but less accessible site in a high-rise building. It had more than 2,000 square meters for about 1,200 computers, as opposed to the previous setup of 6,000 square meters for 1,500 computers (Xiao 2001).

Feiyu has never recovered from the eviction. To prepare for similar "abrupt interruptions," Wang had to "diffuse risk" and "diversify" his business into dozens of small Net bars in ordinary residential communities in Beijing, each having 50 to 100 computers (Xiao 2001). Feiyu was thus transformed into a series of small-scale operations—and not by choice. Following the move, its daily revenue per computer plummeted from 74 yuan ($8.94) to 20 yuan ($2.42), a decline of 73 percent.[8] Feiyu suffered yet another police raid in February 2002. This time the penalty was more severe, including suspension of the business for three months (Wang and Zhang 2003).

Feiyu had been reshaped from a large entity dominating an entire street in Zhongguancun into a typical mass-service Net bar, consisting of a series of much smaller and lower-profile operations. Scaled down and scared off, it now had to let go its aspirations to serve diverse user groups including the less privileged. It had to focus on survival, like most other Net bars since this time.

Black Net Bars

Black Net bars (*heiwangba*) are Internet cafés that engage in "illegal" activities: they operate without a license or, more commonly, without one or a couple of the several officially required licenses. Even a fully licensed cybercafé can be labeled "black" if it admit minors under age sixteen. But since it is so easy to lose licenses and minors constitute such a major chunk of the cybercafé market, there is a frequent slippage in China's urban discourse between black Net bar and cybercafé in general, to the extent that the two are often regarded as synonyms.

By far the most notorious black Net bar is Lanjisu, located next to the University of Science and Technology, Beijing (USTB). It began operations in late May 2002, about three months after the February 2002 police raid on Feiyu. But just two weeks later, on June 16, Lanjisu was set on fire at 2:30 A.M.. Earlier, the Net bar attendant had refused to admit two minors, aged thirteen and fourteen (Shanghai Oriental TV 2004). As revenge, the teenagers poured gasoline at the gate of the cybercafé and set it alight. Because the door was locked and the windows were bolted with metal bars, the fire killed twenty-five and injured thirteen. Among the dead, twenty-one were USTB students, nine of them from the same class majoring in computer science (Bai 2002).

In several ways, Lanjisu was quite similar to one of the smaller-scale mass-service Net bars that Wang Yuesheng would deem appropriate then. It had close to one hundred computers on the second floor of an old building standing in an average residential community. It charged 3 yuan per hour for Internet access and 12 yuan for service between midnight and 8:00 A.M. (Bai 2002). Chapter 7 will discuss how the incident revealed deep-seated social problems facing the information have-less. Here, we focus on one question: Should the crackdown on Internet cafés be blamed for this tragedy?

For too long we have been told that the Lanjisu fire triggered severe crackdowns on Internet cafés in China. The implicit messages are that black Net bars are by nature evil; they were operated by greedy evildoers who despise the law and the well-being of youth; therefore, these operators brought the misfortune onto themselves. This, however, is misleading because it contradicts the basic chronology of the events. If one juxtaposes the Lanjisu tragedy with the ups and downs of Feiyu (located nearby), given the tightening of control before the fire, the direction of causality should be clear.

In the Feiyu case, the serious crackdown in Beijing started at least as early as December 2000 and continued into 2001 and the first half of 2002. Regulations targeting Internet cafés appeared in December 1998, whose six generic articles were expanded to twenty-five articles and twenty-eight subitems in April 2001, indicating an obvious heightening of regulation (Qiu and Zhou 2005). The owners of Lanjisu, for instance, had operated two Net bars, both located in Beijing's Haidian District, starting in early 1998, roughly the same time that Feiyu was established. By April 2001, they had received six citations from the authorities (J. Li 2003, Li and Ma 2003), indicating the level of regulation that had affected the shop prior to the fatal fire.

Of course, the arsonists and the Lanjisu operators have their share of responsibility for the fire. But the evidence points to the excessive crackdowns, which must be viewed as a major factor contributing to the high tension that led to the catastrophe. This argument applies nationally, not just in Beijing.

According to official CNNIC data (figure 2.1) the largest percentage decrease in cybercafé user population occurred between July 2000 and July 2001. In the first half of 2001, about 5 million cybercafé users were lost nationwide. Between April and October 2001, 17,488 Internet cafés were shut down across the country (*Wenhuibao* 2001). As upper-class members of urban society finally celebrated China's entry into the

World Trade Organization (WTO) in November 2001, the Internet café business was barely surviving after the most serious crisis ever recorded in its history. All of this happened prior to rather than after the fire in June 2002.

Nineteen days before the Lanjisu fire, my colleague Bu Wei and I happened to be in Xichang, Sichuan Province, a small city in southwest China. At 6:00 A.M., we found out it was a common practice for local cybercafés to operate overnight behind locked doors. The fact that this Net bar was more than a thousand miles away from Beijing revealed that something systematic was wrong at the time.

Increasing control over Internet cafés at the turn of the millennium was not an isolated development. Nor was it was a matter that concerns the information have-less only. As figures 2.1 and 2.2 demonstrate, 1999 and 2000 witnessed the fastest growth of Internet café user population ever recorded in China. This was the time when the country's mass media organizations, all under the auspices of the CCP, started to move online, squeezing private dot-coms during this critical period of global IT slowdown. The year 2000 was a key moment for the escalation of control over Internet content: four new state regulations were promulgated in a single year, tightening up measures with regard to Internet content providers (ICPs), chatrooms, and online forums such as electronic bulletin board systems (Qiu 2004, Cheung 2003).

Between 1998 and 2001, the Internet café, the most important venue for collective Internet access, also played a significant role in assisting nationalistic hackers who were launching cyberattacks against perceived enemies of China. After the riots in Indonesia against ethnic Chinese following the fall of Suharto's regime in 1998, a Net bar in the Communist Youth City (Gongqingcheng) of Jiangxi Province offered free access for "patriotic and capable hackers" to attack the Indonesians. Such collective hacking from Net bars became more common shortly after the NATO bombing of the Chinese embassy in Belgrade in 1999 and during the U.S.-China plane standoff in 2001, when an American spy plane and a Chinese fighter jet collided over the South China Sea.[9]

It was also in this turbulent period, beginning in summer 1999, that the government began its crusade against Falun Gong in the first nationwide mass criticism (*dapipan*) campaign since Tiananmen. It swept across society, reinforcing the dominance of the authorities. Yet at the same time, it was a common practice for cybercafés to use www.anonymizer.com as default home page for its Internet browsers, allowing anonymous browsing beyond the official "Great Firewall", China's infamous Internet filtering and censorship system (Barmé and Ye 1997). This was the case in one café I visited in January 2000, an operation owned by China Telecom Beijing. Although the practice had been around for a while, used by people searching for a range of unauthorized content from prodemocracy movements to gambling and pornography, the campaign against Falun Gong became the most powerful imperative to clamp down on the dissemination of "harmful" information through Net bars.

The authorities finally decided to intervene for political and economic reasons. In so doing, they initiated a domino effect that ultimately forced Net bar operators to cut back on the uses associated with this shared mode of ICT service. It was too risky to retain all the social and political functions of a cybercafé, from alternative speech to collective hacking. The same is true for organized efforts to include laid-off workers and retirees as well as other have-less groups, as happened at Feiyu.

Entertainment is, after all, the lowest denominator with significant market potential. Cast in narrowly defined commercial terms, as long as the market expands and café owners can make some money, the boundary between mass-service Net bars and black Net bars does not matter much. Hence, benign as some of the original intentions might have been, the suppressive policies created rather than solved the Net bar problem. Short-sighted decisions made for immediate troubleshooting turned out to accelerate the descent from elite to working-class ICT, which eventually hurt the long-term well-being of Internet cafés through its particular mode of disempowering devolution.

Upgrades

A key to the process of state intervention, and of artificially heightened competition caused by the involvement of state-sponsored corporations, is a discourse of linear progression, best captured by the term *upgrade*, by which we understand a technical expression that now assumes social, political, and cultural meaning under the technocratic system of contemporary China. Just as average PC users often need to upgrade hardware and software without knowing the exact content of the upgrades, at the policy level Net bar users and managers are seldom involved in deciding how to upgrade their collective places of access. Although cybercafés are often run by have-less entrepreneurs for have-less consumers in have-less communities, their fate nonetheless depends on elite decision makers, who care more about upgrades than the actual informational needs of the information have-less.

The discourse, policy, and practices of top-down upgrading have done serious harm to the booming cybercafé sector. "Open a Net bar, and kill yourself (*yaozisha, kaiwangba*)" is now the motto instead of its late-1990s version, "Open a Net bar, and be well-off (*yaoxiangfa, kaiwangba*)." But the puzzling question remains: Why, under such formidable circumstances, does the Internet café market continue to expand? Does this mean the upgrades somehow help cybercafés or that they were not powerful enough to stop Net bar growth? Does this suggest the upgrades may even produce opportunities for the information have-less to build new alliances and appropriate the logic of upgrading in unexpected ways?

Regulation and Resistance: National and Local
From 1998 to 2002, China issued three official directives regarding the operation of Internet cafés, with the measures of control becoming increasingly strict, for example, by requiring higher network security standards, closer cooperation with enforcement agencies, and more severe penalties for noncompliance (Qiu and Zhou 2005). During this period, the leadership role in the national regulatory regime shifted from the Ministry of Public Security (MPS) in 1998 to the Ministry of Information Industry (MII) in 2001 and finally to the Ministry of Culture (MoC) in 2002, indicating significant alterations in the policy goals being pursued. As of 2008, MoC is still the main regulator of Internet cafés. Its Regulation on the Administration of Business Sites of Internet Access Services, effective since November 15, 2002, remains the key ordinance regarding the Net bar business.

Why does China need to impose a regulatory regime, now that it already has a considerable set of general-purpose Internet regulations controlling everything from infrastructure and content to providers and users? This intriguing question was posed by legal researcher Murray (2003). The ineffectiveness of existing Internet laws and the lack of central coordination among enforcement mechanisms are two possible answers. Another is the logic of power maximization when there are few checks and balances against regulation. But these do not explain everything, especially why since 2002 there has been less effort to upgrade Net bar regulation at the national level even more.

That not much has changed since 2002 does not suggest that the situation is satisfactory. MoC's main undertaking has been the chain store model of Net bar management, which has so far failed to achieve its stated goals. An understanding of the regulatory updates requires going beyond the directives because regulations are not only developed and imposed through formal institutions, they also have to grow and respond to issues in the larger society.

In this larger social environment, mass media, especially China's new commercial media emerging since the 1990s, have to be factored in (Y. Zhao 1998, 2002; Lee 2000, 2003). As I learned in several interviews, it was from the deluge of media messages in the mid- and late 1990s that many Net bar operators were convinced to believe in the promising future of this business. Commercial mass media then started to stigmatize the same people whom they lured into the trade in the first place. The real problem here is not consistency but the journalistic practice of sensationalism. Thus, it was no coincidence that the rosy digital future depicted a few years ago looks drastically different from the stark reality of Net bars, yet both were constructed and dramatized by media.

At the same time, no sensational effect can last for long. The manipulated tidal wave of public opinion has to subside eventually, and commercial media have to move on to other targets. This is probably why there has been no major crisis in the media pressing for new government intervention since 2003. In this sense, the regulatory environment for the Internet café business has in fact relaxed, which in part explains the steady growth of the café user population since July 2003.

The regulatory relaxation also results from the inability of MoC, the main national regulator, to dominate policy implementation below the national level. Most provincial branches of MoC are active in their control efforts, which are, however, not comparable to provincial MPS authorities, which previously took the lead in the overall regulatory regime. With limited resources for MoC subbranches, its activities are fairly uneven at and below the city level, where the priorities of City Informatization Offices often prevail because the latter are directly authorized by city governments to coordinate ICT-related tasks of all kinds.[10]

The local policy environments for Internet café regulation therefore reflect the complex dynamics of urban politics. Conflict, compromise, coalition, and battle between stakeholders have occurred. It is common to observe discontinuity in the local interpretation and implementation of nationwide regulations. One city may take a more lenient approach to Net bars, while the next city may take a completely opposite approach, as found in the cases of Shenzhen versus Dongguan or Foshan versus Nanhai in Guangdong Province in 2002 (Qiu and Zhou 2005). Local conditions may also vary within a city or fluctuate over time, depending on the relative strength of the have-less communities in relation to suppressive authorities and the urban elite.

The crucial importance of local dynamics is highlighted in China's first citywide Net bar strike in Lishui, a small city in the mountainous region of southern Zhejiang Province, which had a population of about 259,600 in 2003.[11] On November 15, 2004, *Chuzhou Wanbao*, Lishui's local newspaper, ran a full-page front page muckraking report on "problematic" cybercafés in the city, accusing them of poor management and moral corruption, especially among youth. Following the usual pattern, this soon triggered a local crackdown.

Up to this point, the Internet café regulator in Lishui had been the City Bureau of Public Security, not the City Bureau of Culture, which again shows the degree of local variation. Under pressure created by the report, public security officials claimed to have insufficient manpower to oversee Net bars. The city government then passed a resolution, without consulting Net bar operators, to delegate the regulatory authority from the city level to the street-level police units of *paichusuo*, who were empowered to enforce a strict penalty system with heavy fines and random checks at any time and, by any member of their staff (W. Yang 2004).

Angry Net bar operators decided to take collective action in unprecedented resistance. Starting on November 22, 2004, all sixty-one Net bars in Lishui went on strike. Signs posted on their closed doors said, "Completely disheartened . . . Net bars stop business!!! (*Wanban wunai . . . wangba tingye!!!*)." Strike organizers collected Internet routers from the shops to guarantee unified action. All of a sudden, thousands of Net bar customers were sent to the streets (W. Yang 2004).

The strike lasted only two days, but it produced important results. For the first time, it forced the local regulator, in this case the public security authority and the city government, to sit down and negotiate with Net bar operators. Lishui officials made some compromises by specifying which police officers could rectify Net bars and agreeing on the correct procedure in this situation. Although the Net bar business did not achieve its full demands (for example, the penalty remained heavy), the strike demonstrated the potential power of have-less operators to play a considerable role in shaping local urban politics. However brief the action was and however small the city, it showed a rare but important example that imposed decisions to upgrade the regulatory system could be stalled at the grassroots.

Technical Design: Compulsory Measures and Beyond
The upgrading of Internet cafés also involves a technical dimension that reflects top-down as well as bottom-up dynamics. In 2000, Feiyu's

superstore in Beijing offered a range of services, from printing and photo-copying to scanning, catering to customers at different income levels, from a variety of backgrounds, and with different needs. Such arrangements have now almost entirely disappeared.

Most Net bar computers today are configured for entertainment. They are optimized for online gaming, chatting, and video watching, with the help of regularly updated hardware and software, from webcams and LCD displays to the latest programs. Because they do not have a CD-ROM, a USB harbor, or an external disc reader for fear of computer virus infection, they are unsuitable for international travelers, bloggers, or hackers. They are powerful in delivering games and full-length movies but crippled in fostering more creative user-driven content. The technology has spawned a new generation of users who visit Net bars to kill time, be amused, and play. Many of them stopped checking e-mail partly because they cannot store their messages on the computers and Web mail is slow, and partly because they already have SMS and can transfer files through QQ, the popular Chinese online chatting service provided by Tencent Ltd.

The technical upgrades have create a huge market, considering that China has at least 112,264 Net bars equipped with about 6.1 million computers that needed to be updated every couple of years (*Guangming Daily* 2006). This produces significant business opportunities because in order to attract customers in this competitive market, all Net bars have to use up-to-date software and regularly upgraded equipment.

The decisions for making upgrades, however, are also made for rather than by the Net bar operators. The size of the market and the heavily regulated nature of the industry mean that authorities and corporations both want a large piece of the pie. For example, Filter King (*Guolvwang*), an Internet café content-filtering system, has been widely adopted because it is what the police require. Produced by Zetronic, a software company in Zhuhai, Filter King was among the first to be endorsed by the MPS at the national level. It soon became the most common system required by provincial and city police authorities. Between 2002 and 2005, it matured from Version 1.0 to Version 2.8 with increasing functions in monitoring, tracking, and filtering information, while the number of its Net bar subscriptions nationwide grew to more than 50,000.[12]

Filter King works with a central server located in a local police bureau, controlled and maintained by the local Internet police task force. At the user end, all computers in registered Net bars in the area have to install Filter King software and connect to the central server. Data exchange occurs between the server and individual computers to ensure surveillance over all online communication. To ensure this data exchange, subscribing Net bars have to run the same version of Filter King as the one used by the local police. This means that every time the police upgrade their system, all connecting Net bars have to follow suit, a costly process of mandatory upgrading.

The MoC also attempted to create its own surveillance market, although with less success. Its main filter system, Clean Net Pioneer (*Jingwangxianfeng*), encountered more difficulty in diffusion and was relatively easy to bypass (Su 2005). Its installation fee is calculated on a per-computer basis, which is much more expensive than Filter King. Most Net bar operators were reluctant to install it because they believed it was buggy and incompatible with the existing system used by the police. Programs designed to disable Clean Net Pioneer can be found online for free download, which is unlikely to happen to systems like Filter King given the formidable power of the police. Since March 2005, MoC has promoted its "Sunny Plan (*yangguang jihua*)" for the Net bar industry, which encompasses not just filtering technologies but everything from computer hardware to service provision to the improvement of the public image of Net bars. But the program was too ambitious and propagandist to produce real impact.

Local companies with government backgrounds can be another major factor. This is the case of Pubwin, the most widely used Net bar OS in the country, developed by Hintsoft (*Haoyi*), a software company founded in November 1998 under the auspices of the Shanghai Municipal Informatization Office.[13] After being deployed in Shanghai and nearby cities for a few years, the Pubwin system was upgraded to Version 4.0 and finally received endorsement from the MPS. In 2005, Hintsoft was further upgraded to Pubwin EP, designed for large-scale Net bars. By this point, it accounted for more than 50 percent of the national market share (*YeskyNet* 2005).

Important to note in these cases is the involvement of multinationals. Hintsoft received venture capital from the International Data Group (IDG) in July 2005. Corporate sponsors of MoC's Sunny Plan included global players such as Intel and Philips (*Blogchina* 2005). According to John Du, director of Intel China Research Center in Beijing, his company places particular emphasis on China's Internet cafés by helping them "do upgrades, monitor their PCs, and do maintenance," because they constitute a main part of "the next usage model" (Einhorn 2006). Since 2005, Intel has been a prominent player in China's cybercafé hardware market.

The technical upgrading of Net bars has its own dynamics. Although regulation and state sponsorship still matter, there is relatively more of a market component, less dominance by the MoC (or even MPS), more

chances for local products to spread, and more involvement of transnational players. In this area of operation, Net bars are recognized as an
important and legitimate business rather than something problematic by
nature that can survive only at the mercy of officials. But this is at the
same time a highly manipulated market of entertainment machines,
serving a small spectrum of the informational needs, narrowly defined for,
rather than by, the information have-less.

Business Models: Old and New
The Internet café business started in the 1990s with a simple idea. For
almost everyone then, computers and Internet access were expensive and
required technical expertise. Therefore, café owners could make a profit by
purchasing access bandwidth at the wholesale rate and selling it through
retail to end users. There were investments on equipment and site renova-
tion as well as operational costs for rent, labor, and maintenance. But this
simple business model proved to be effective in yielding a decent profit,
given the significant difference between wholesale and retail prices at a
time when there was strong public curiosity in everything related to the
Internet.

This original model had to respond to changes in policy, technology,
and market dynamics, and in so doing, it became more complicated. At
the turn of the century, with the emergence of mass-service Net bars,
advertising in the form of posters or computer wallpapers became ubiquitous, promoting not only online games but also computer software and
hardware. Stores previously selling only coffee started to offer a variety of
drinks, cigarettes, and snacks ranging from instant noodles to tea-flavored
eggs. The service expanded to include prepaid cards for long-distance
phone calls, dial-up Internet access, and online gaming. The new poster
ads and add-on retail business brought in extra revenue.

But more important, the modified model had much higher costs under
the new regulatory system of licensing, taxation, and mandatory technology upgrades. Until the late 1990s, no license was required to open an
Internet café. But to register a Net bar today requires at least four licenses:
from the local bureau of cultural affairs, the public security bureau, the
bureau of industry and commerce, and the telecom authority. Net bars
are required to display all these licenses prominently, a discriminatory
treatment seldom found in other IT-related businesses. The number of
required approvals can run up to more than a dozen, for example, in
Sichuan.[14] Some city authorities have even suspended cybercafé registration altogether. A black market for Net bar licenses thus came into being.

In Shanghai, for instance, licenses needed for one Net bar could be sold for 240,000 yuan ($29,000) in early 2004.[15]

Registration is only the beginning of the additional costs. Because Internet cafés are officially categorized as the entertainment trade (*yule hangye*) or special trade (*tezhong hangye*), it is subject to a heavy taxation of 20 to 40 percent of the profit.[16] This stands in stark contrast to other IT sectors that enjoy much lower or zero tax rate, not to mention government subsidies that Net bar owners cannot even dream of.

The upgrading of surveillance devices required by regulators is another expense. In 2002, a Pubwin system cost about 500 to 600 *yuan* (about $$61 to $73) to install and 100 to 200 yuan (about $12 to $24) for annual updating, which included all computers in a Net bar. Clean Net Pioneer has charged 45 yuan ($5.50) per terminal since 2003, which is expensive because the cost can run easily into thousands of yuan.

Moreover, harsh fines, suspension of business, and confiscation of machines need to be considered increasingly as a part of a Net bar operating budget. Through licensing, taxation, mandatory updates, and fines, the business operation of Net bars has become tied to the income of some local governments. This explains why local state authorities are active in clampdown, yet they do not want to eliminate the cybercafé business. These are predators positioned high up in the food chain in an odd ecology of revenue sharing. At the end of the day, it is in their interests to see growth in this working-class ICT. This symbiotic relationship—an imposed patron-client relationship—then forced cybercafés into a downward spiral, a pathetic lock-in that should be blamed for spawning black Net bars.

Meanwhile, the truly profound transformation took place. The original business model of the Internet café targeted high-end customers in major metropolitan areas. But now upper-class professionals in Beijing and Shanghai have Internet access at work or at home, and their informational and entertainment needs are taken care of by mass media and mainstream cultural institutions. Why would they want to visit cybercafés? It is only natural for Net bars to serve primarily the information have-less in the back alleys, at the city peripheries, and in small towns. In such small cities as Guangshui, Hubei Province, and Yima, Henan Province, cybercafés play a central role in Internet dissemination (Guo 2004). They have also appeared in the countryside, where some cybercafés "charged as little as one yuan ($0.12) for several hours of use" (Harwit 2004).

The flight from the elite market has produced results. To save on rent, cybercafés in most downtown areas moved from prominent street-level stores to either above-street-level quarters or basements. New Net bars in general avoid city centers. They popped up in suburbs and low-profile communities, including places like labor markets where high-mobility populations are concentrated. Some Net bars went underground, putting up signs of computer schools, or no sign at all, admitting known customers only.[17] Some others are set up in private households like the clay-cave homes of Yaodong in northwestern Shaanxi Province (Guo 2004). All of these are bottom-up business responses by have-less service providers to the decline of profitability under the pressure of state regulation and public scrutiny, drawing on local and regional network resources.

The materialization of the Net bar business model is a highly localized process contingent on local situations. While most Net bars followed an entertainment-oriented model, in Shenzhen, China's largest special economic zone (SEZ), there is more complexity and diversity in local business models owing to the combination of two factors. First, this is a city of young migrants, with workers from different backgrounds. Second, transborder activities, particularly with Hong Kong, account for a large part of the local economy. As a result, the local government has limited the scope of its regulation, which in effect has shielded local Net bars from the national pattern of homogenization.

WiseNews, the world's largest Chinese-language news search engine, is headquartered in Hong Kong, but most of its data processing employees work in Shenzhen. According to Ringo Lam, the CEO of WiseNews, one attraction of Shenzhen has to do with the cybercafés, because when there is a network failure or power outage at his Shenzhen facility, employees can still meet deadlines by using Net bars conveniently nearby.[18] Obviously, computers in these cybercafés are more than one-way entertainment machines. They are equipped with the necessary hardware and software to support transborder work activities, in this case, the preprocessing and processing of large quantities of news articles, including cleaning up the text, tagging, and working on the same database from multiple locations. It is not a coincidence that these Internet cafés exist in Shenzhen.

At the national level, a main issue of contention during recent years is the chain store model (Qiu and Zhou 2005). According to the MoC in April 2003, the goal is to upgrade Net bars into "large-scale chain-stores with themes and brands (*guimohua, liansuohua, zhutihua, pinpaihua*)." To achieve this goal, ten companies, mostly affiliates of MoC, were licensed to create national chain stores, and each province was allowed to set up three provincial chain stores. To force new Net bars to join chain stores, a national freeze on the licensing of individual cybercafés has been recommended since 2003. The chain store model was advocated as a panacea serving everyone's interests because it could supposedly improve the public image of Net bars. It was expected to facilitate the implementation of café regulation by bringing individual shops under a standardized organizational structure. It might also help Net bars through collective purchase and maintenance at larger economies of scale, as advocated in MoC's Sunny Plan (*Blogchina* 2005).

The reality of the chain store model, however, is quite different given the reality of local urban politics. Most Net bar operators I interviewed saw this new business model as nothing but another attempt at exploitation. They have to pay a sizable fee for chain store membership, yet they seldom receive the promised services. The equipment and software sold by chain store operators to individual stores are often seen as shoddy and overpriced. A main "service" of the chain-store company was, in fact, to alert its members to incoming official inspections so that they could be prepared, an act countering the moralistic goal of regulation that justified the chain store model at the first place.[19]

A few years after MoC's advocacy, the chain store model still looked marginal in the national Net bar industry. As of 2006, only five of the ten national enfranchises had been set up, and chain stores accounted for only 5.7 percent of all cybercafés (D. Zhu 2006; *Guangming Daily* 2006). The failure is unsurprising because MoC picked its affiliates with no experience in Net bar operation, parachuting them into the industry, assuming they would be commercially viable because of this official blessing. In this process, they excluded existing chain stores like Feiyu in Beijing and the EastdayBar (*Dongfangwangdian*) in Shanghai, which were better positioned with much better brand recognition to develop coalitions nationwide than any of the ten handpicked licensees.

The failure of the national chain store model demonstrates the capacity of have-less ICT providers in resisting the logic of top-down upgrading. Although so far there have been few incidents of direct confrontation comparable to the Lishui Net bar strike, the rallying of small café operators has given rise to a series of online forums such as World Net Alliance (*Tianxia wangmeng*), by far the largest one, with more than 500,000 members by June 2007.[20] There are also smaller forums like www .netbarguide.com that function as platforms of information exchange as well as social support, through which individual Net bar providers, scattered as they are, come to recognize their shared issues and collective effort in resistance and empowerment.

A key model for the business operation of Net bars is based on China's burgeoning online gaming industry, whose total sales revenue reached

3.77 billion yuan ($460 million) in 2005, with an average annual growth rate of around 50 percent (IDG and WCGCP 2006). The leading online game company, Shanda, had approximately 600 million user accounts by the end of 2007,[21] and its CEO, Chen Tianqiao, was once China's richest man (H. Fan 2004). The tremendous growth of the gaming industry has been so impressive that it was regarded as a fresh business model for China's Internet industry in general, paralleling earlier models centered on online advertisement, e-commerce, and then SMS. Even the Chinese government has decided to foster the industry by investing $2 billion in online games (Taylor 2006). The main justifications include the country's aspiration for its own creative industry, the need for Chinese gamers to gain independence from Korean and Japanese games, and the centrality of online gaming in the life of Chinese youth.

Cybercafés are crucial for online gaming in three ways. First, they provide a major channel of service and content delivery, especially to the vast low-end market that could not have existed without the collective mode of Internet access. Second, Net bars collect fees from gamers by selling prepaid gaming cards produced and distributed by Shanda and other game companies. This is particularly important because most members of the information have-less do not have credit cards or even bank accounts. Third, because Net bars are the main place where have-less gamers gather, they also offer a venue for targeted advertising and promotion of new game products.

These games play an indispensable role for Net bars by attracting customers to the cafés, retaining them, and letting them consume all the products and services provided there. There is therefore a tight symbiosis between Internet cafés and online gaming because neither could have reached the current scale without the other. In this sense, one may regard gaming as the most strategic industry partner of Net bars. One may even expect the more favorable official policy toward gaming to spill over to cybercafés and legitimatize them, or at least mitigate the systematic discrimination against them.

But is this true? A closer examination reveals a surprisingly high degree of tension between Net bar operators and the gaming industry. In the Second Internet and Entertainment Content Expo of China at the end of October 2004, Net bar owners challenged and embarrassed Chen Tianqiao, Shanda's CEO, by accusing his company of doing nothing for cybercafés. In response, Shanda launched its Winter Sysop Care Program (*Dongji wangguan guanhuai jihua*) within a month and claimed it to be "the first-ever service program for Net bar system operators provided by the [gaming] industry" (W. Lu 2004).

A few opinion leaders in the online forums of cybercafé operators, however, showed no sign of compromise. Three days after Shanda launched its Winter Program on November 28, the Manifesto on Boycotting Shanda Games appeared online. It soon spurred a deluge of accusation among Net bar operators against Shanda and the entire online gaming industry. One widely circulated poem at the time ended with this call for action:[22]

Arise, Net bar, challenge the hegemony of the gaming industry over the right to profit!
Arise, Net bar, break the monopoly of the gaming industry over huge wealth.
Arise, Net bar, undermine the means by which the gaming industry controls gamers!
Arise, Net bar, breach the battlefront of the gaming industry built on content.
Arise, Net bar, we constitute an immense sales platform.
Arise, Net bar, we have the terminals to be consolidated.
Arise, Net bar, together let's say NO at the top of our voice to the gaming industry!
Arise, Net bar, let's overthrow the unreasonable profit structure from tip to toe!
Ah, Net bar,
Sound your bugle call for battle!
Winter has arrived. Can spring be far behind?

The author of this poem, using the name Li Hongli, is undoubtedly among China's more literary Net bar operators. Drawing from the PRC national anthem and Shelley's "Ode to the West Wind," the lines mix militant language, typical in the Maoist age, with the terminology of the New Economy. Strong emotions are cast against the gaming industry, whose actual "hegemony" is far from comparable to other monopolies like MoC, MPS, MII, the national chain stores, predatory local state agencies, or even the mass media.

Such a burst of anger might have resulted from Chen Tianqiao's rise to China's richest man a few months earlier in 2004. It was also based on the emergent Net bar forums and online social networks of Net bar operators throughout the country. The gaming industry was singled out because it was a soft target that could not retaliate like the authorities. Unlike the official and quasi-official stakeholders, gaming companies, including Shanda, face intensive domestic and international market competition. It was within such market structures that the call to boycott could make sense. Another reason is that polemics against online games may spread more widely and stay online longer compared to discursive challenges to the authorities and their commercial affiliates, which probably would be censored in the first place or erased soon.

The dispute with the online gaming industry nonetheless demonstrates the political awareness of working-class providers, which has increased over the years, as shown by the expansion of their online forums and networks and critical incidents like the Lishui Net bar strike. However, collective actions remain rare. When they do happen, online or offline, their scope of influence tends to be so limited that it is still too early for them to challenge and alter elite domination at the structural level. Also important is to note that with such limited collective actions, we hear mostly about Net bar owners and operators, but rarely from their employees, who are mostly less educated migrant workers and laid-off workers, especially female labor, and ordinary café users, mostly youth.

The Commons of the Have-Less

Cybercafés offer a collective mode of access. They provide working-class connectivity that is inexpensive and shared to members of the information have-less. In so doing, they constitute an informational commons at the local level, generating hope and aspiration, conflict and despair, through the experiences of grassroots entrepreneurialism and everyday urban politics.

But is "commons" a misnomer, given the nearly universal drift toward privatization and commercialization? In contemporary China, with the decline of Maoist socialism, shared collective spaces of all kinds are being eroded, if not eradicated, in most social, economic, political, and cultural domains. Why, then, should collectivity matter at all? Why is it important, especially to the formation of network labor?

This is where the previous analysis can inform us. First, there were in fact multiple alternatives for Internet cafés to evolve, including but not limited to promotional cafés, Feiyu's free morning hours and training sessions for seniors and laid-off workers, and Net bars supporting hackers during the "patriotic cyberwars," although most of these have evaporated with the crackdowns and relentless upgrading. Second, in the absence of public sponsorship, spaces of the commons have little choice other than relying on private ownership and commercial deployment. This is particularly true when it comes to a fast-changing ICT business trying to survive in the context of contemporary urban China. However, just as privately owned bars served a public function for the emerging bourgeois of nineteenth-century Europe, so can privately operated Net bars sustain a space of shared experience for the new working class of the twenty-first century.

An important trend in recent years has been the growth of cybercafé-based virtual guilds (*gonghui*). Some of these guilds consist of gamers spontaneously organized on the basis of horizontal grassroots friendship networks, for example, among classmates and coworkers. Others include more vertically organized commercial units of the so-called Chinese gold farmers: those who collect "in-game currency in Massively Multiplayer Online Role-Playing Games (MMORPG) for the purpose of selling it to other players for real world currency."[23] These guilds represent a more flexible and yet networked mode of labor organization, an emerging form of network labor based on user-generated content, which would be hard to imagine without the widespread of Net bars (H. He 2005, Chew and Fung 2007).

Besides collective gaming (and collective work in the case of the gold farmers), a more traditional way of labor reorganization proceeds among the average staff members of Internet café below the level of Net bar owners. These are the people who sweep the floor and work at the counter. These are migrant workers from the countryside, who account for the bulk of the workforce for Net bars in the more developed regions of coastal China, as well as unemployed or underemployed youth, who fill in the lowest strata of jobs in the cybercafé business, especially in the inland provinces.

Chen is a young attendant in the remote city of Xichang in West China. At age twenty-two, he was already a laid-off worker from a bankrupt iron and steel factory, where he had worked for three years. In 2002, when I interviewed him, he was one of the two attendants at a small Net bar. Working a twelve-hour shift, seven days a week, Chen did not have health insurance or legal labor contract. With food and housing provided by the owner (a local China Telecom employee), his monthly salary was 300 yuan ($37). Yet he was happy because he could surf the Internet for free.

A similar position in the cybercafé market may provide a shared basis of class formation among these low-end have-less service providers. But it is important to note that economic domination also leads to discursive and political disempowerment. Ji is another attendant at a large-scale chain store, who migrated with his family from northeast China to Guangzhou in the South. At one of the most revealing moments, Ji confessed: "Now, even my folks feel it's sort of a shame for me to work at a Net bar. You know, talking about Net bar today is like talking about nightclubs in the 80s."[24]

There was a lot of truth in this revelation, considering especially that the interview was done in the wake of the Beijing café fire in summer 2002.

But had I seen Ji again, I probably would ask: Why should there be a problem? Put aside the European bourgeois more than a century ago, industrial workers, including those in China, before or after the founding of the PRC, had hangouts: working-class pubs, evening schools, and teahouses. Why shouldn't the urban underclass today be entitled to have a workers' bar in a new technological environment based on the Internet?

But as happened to corner bars and pool-table halls in Western societies, urban control over places of collective activity is often an entangled issue because class is seldom taken as the fundamental dimension of the problem. Instead, the question is usually about moralistic protection—of youth in all these cases—that overshadows the welfare of the commons on the policy agenda.

Of course, young people should not wander around by themselves in the streets late in the evening or play games in the wee hours in cybercafés or at home. But why do so many parents fail to keep their children home? Why can't universities open their computer labs for longer hours and use more appropriate regulations so that students do not need to visit black Net bars at night? Black Net bars are not by nature more magnetic than other places. They are popular among have-less youth because of the failure of existing institutions like school and family to establish full connections with the new technological environment of the Internet, including its entertainment and social networking functions. Too often the new media are supposed to serve only "productive" ends, narrowly defined by powerful stakeholders. Too quickly all other modes of uses are dismissed as "mindless" or "harmful."

In order to make the Internet café a better sphere of the commons, families and schools need to rethink their relationship with Net bars as an increasingly integral component of their local community rather than just a commercial service that comes and goes. In so doing, traditional institutions, including the state, need to redefine the scope of appropriate technology goals. They need to address problems in themselves and be more receptive to the informational and entertainment demands of the younger generation and migrant populations. Their responsiveness to the needs of the information have-less is in fact a major reason that Net bars can attract so many from traditional institutions, mainstream media, and even new media in traditional institutional frameworks like PCs at home. But this responsiveness is not without its limits under the constraints of skewed regulation as well as the biases of the market mechanism itself.

This explains why, to write an essay, design a Web page, or produce a Flash animation, one usually still has to use a personal computer in more exclusive settings. This also explains why so many cybercafés are filled with smoke and noise and pose security problems, including violations of the fire code, theft, robbery, and gang activities. Net bars have become, and not by their own choice, excessively entertainment oriented and "mass" oriented to the extent that they are now excluding not only the elite but also a significant proportion of the have-less population, especially females. In this sense, Net bars have to lift themselves from the downward spiral in order to transform themselves into a genuine information commons—a new sphere for fostering working-class network society.

The rethinking has to take into account the fast-changing, multimodal, and multimedia information environment. That Net bar customers no longer use much e-mail, for example, can be interpreted as a sign of the popularity of online games. But at the same time, this may also result from the diffusion of SMS, the common use of chat services, and the increasing capacity for chat applications to support asynchronous message exchange and file transfer. Much of such chatting exists because of Net bars.

Another usual charge against the devolution of cybercafés is that even those with just basic literacy can go in, click on some icons, and be entertained. The hard question is, What is literacy under the new technosocial condition? Wouldn't it be desirable for access to require minimum efforts at the Net bars so that Internet technology can be perceived as easy to try and not too complicated, factors known to facilitate the diffusion of innovations (Rogers 1962)?

Besides the wider spread of the Internet among have-less populations, there is also a potential uplifting effect on Net bar owners and operators, whose numbers are growing in tandem with the Net bar user population. A decade ago, China's new IT business elite launched the first generation of Internet cafés in order to spread enlightenment and help foster the information superhighway. In contrast, members of the information have-less today work in the Net bar industry in spite of tight regulations and low wages. They do so because there are few other job opportunities but strong market demand for collective Internet access. Many of them work as Net bar attendants because they can go online for free.

The job of a Net bar operator is demanding. Operators must know not only the basics about computers and the Internet, including both hardware and software, but also be able to keep learning because the systems are constantly upgraded by the authorities and corporations. Moreover, they need to be able to meet the technical challenges posed by customers who may want to contest the power of Net bar systems by disabling or modifying control devices such as Pubwin or Filter King. Even more so, Net bar operators have to learn to manage their business in a suppressive policy environment. They have to find out how to survive while being forced to take a leap in the dark. They have to deal with commercial competition and public stigmatization at the same time. It is this experience of struggle and a collective will to survive that provide the cornerstone of the new class dynamics. This trend is evidenced by emerging networks of café operators that were behind their online forums and the Lishui Net bar strike.

But coalition building remains a weak link, and the tragedy of the commons still hounds the cybercafé business. Market competition leads to a serious lack of mutual trust. Net bar operators are divided along myriad lines of demarcation with regard to their relationships with the regulators, chain stores, online gaming companies, equipment providers, telecom operators, and so on, many of them characterized by vertical patron-client ties. There has also been increasing confrontation, including violent incidents, between have-less users and have-less providers in recent years. Consequently, it is extremely rare to find the organizational solidarity to sustain something like the Lishui strike. Although collective identification among Net bar operators is advancing, they seldom seek to expand their horizontal networks to include other players or even the cybercafé workers they hire.

3 Going Wireless

Working-class ICTs not only take the wired form of Internet café but also a number of wireless modes, each having its own process of emergence, transformation, and, in certain cases, decline. Some of them, like SMS and prepaid services, have been emerging worldwide in industrialized nations as well as the global South (Castells et al. 2006). Others are more specifically Chinese, such as the country's domestic handset manufacturing industry and the Little Smart wireless system. Together they offer new modes of working-class connectivity to China's urban underclass, most of whom never owned telephones previously. To these have-less people, a mobile handset, or *shouji*, is often their first phone. In many cases, it is also their first personal ICT device of any kind.

How has the mobile phone become a working-class ICT? What wireless services are offered to China's information have-less? How and why do these working-class wireless technologies materialize, through what institutional processes, on the basis of what grassroots networks? What are the associated challenges, latent or manifest, and the general lessons to be drawn?

This chapter first examines the reform context of China's telecommunications sector, which sets the stage for the emergence of *shouji*. A central part of this process is the rise of a domestic handset manufacturing industry. We then look at a few specific parts of the burgeoning wireless market: the Little Smart, SMS, and prepaid mobile services. These services have helped wireless technology reach large numbers of have-less users while creating significant job opportunities for the urban underclass. These services do face commercial competition and persisting government control in selected social domains, which shapes the mode of use, technology design, and patterns of service and content provision. Finally, we consider the waxing and waning of pager service and its implications for working-class ICTs in general.

Telephone entered China in the late nineteenth century through European settlements along the coast, especially Hong Kong and Shanghai. A national telephone system was established by the end of the Qing dynasty (Baark 1997), which was expanded during the Republican era until the 1949 Communist takeover (He 1997). By then, penetration was 0.5 phones per 1,000 people, and nearly 30 percent of the lines were in Shanghai (Harwit 2004). As at the beginning years of the Internet, the telephone was mostly a technology for foreigners and a tiny fraction of the urban elite.

From the 1950s to 1970s, the gap in telephone access significantly narrowed between rural and urban areas as a result of Maoist policies that prioritized development in the countryside (Harwit 2004). But with market reform under Deng Xiaoping, the pendulum swung back to the cities, and urbanites again enjoyed faster telephone growth than rural residents (He 1997). At the end of the 1980s, the telephone remained a luxury and a symbol of power. It was usually an exclusive means of communication paid for by the government, installed only in important public offices and the residences of high-rank cadres.

By this time, the slow growth of fixed-line telephony had been widely regarded as a major bottleneck for the expansion of the Chinese economy. This was reflected in the country's Eighth Five-Year Plan (1991–1995), which attached special importance to telecommunications, along with energy and transportation. Major reform of the telecom sector was proposed and implemented to foster a more competitive market, serving not only the authorities but also others who could afford telephones (Mueller and Tan 1997).

The first analog mobile phone service appeared in China in 1987, when the old telephone system was under serious stress. National teledensity was 0.75 phones per 100 people. There was a huge untapped market, and Beijing was trying to boost telecom growth. However, mobile communication did not take off until the mid-1990s (figure 3.1). Several factors thwarted faster diffusion in these years: not only price and service quality but also the economic and political unrest of the late 1980s, culminating in Tiananmen, and the subsequent unpredictability of the early 1990s. Investment priority within the industry was given to landlines, microwave service, and the emerging ICT of the time, the pager.

After China entered a new phase of "neoliberalism with Chinese characteristics" in 1992 (Harvey, 2005), investment, especially foreign direct investment (FDI), significantly increased. China Unicom was established in 1994, breaking China Telecom's monopoly (Mueller and Tan 1997). That year also marked three other milestones in the wireless market: total

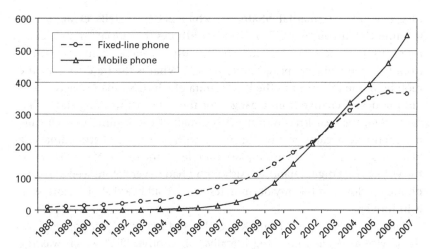

Figure 3.1
Year-end total subscriber population: fixed-line and mobile phones, 1988–2007 (millions). *Source:* MII (1998–2007).

mobile subscription reached 1 million; the Mobile Communication Division (MCD) was set up inside China Telecom; and the country's first digital service, using GSM, was launched by Unicom (Harwit 1998; Le, Qiao, and Sun 2006). Throughout the 1990s, the mobile market maintained an average annual growth rate of 141.8 percent. The diffusion curve tipped in 1998–1999, when MCD was separated from China Telecom and became China Mobile, the biggest player in the mobile market.

At the turn of the century, wireless communication finally began to spread to the lower social strata, a development that brought a sea change to the entire mobile phone industry. By October 2003, the number of mobile subscribers surpassed that of landline. By the end of 2007, China had the world's largest national mobile subscriber population: 547.3 million plus 84.5 million low-end Little Smart subscriptions. In comparison, the United States had 241.8 million mobile phone subscriptions in 2006 (FCC 2008). The much larger Chinese market would be difficult to imagine without the information have-less, who provide not only a crucial consumer basis but also the essential labor for this new and extraordinary mobile phone industry.

The Fateful *Shouji*

The term *shouji* was popularized by a blockbuster movie a few years ago about how the mobile phone influences upper-class Chinese families,

especially in extramarital affairs (Y. Zhao 2004; Castells et al. 2005).
Commercial discourse in urban China continues to associate mobile communication devices almost exclusively with the urban elite. Departing
from this conventional perspective, we ask, What is the trajectory for the
mobile phone to spread to the lower strata of China's urban society? How
did the device change from a gadget for the elite to a working-class ICT?

In 1996, the year I received my first e-mail at the Beijing Internet café,
my friend Kent came to my dormitory with something extraordinary: a
black Motorola 3200, the exemplary mobile phone of the 1990s. This was
the world's first digital handset. Although I had never before seen a mobile
phone up close nor had my dormmates, we had all heard about it and seen
it in movies.

Gangster movies from Hong Kong played a major role in popularizing
the device as *dageda*, meaning literally "Big-Brother-Big," which was the
default nickname for a mobile phone in the 1990s. Socially, *dageda* was
very different from *shouji*, although the underlying technology was roughly
the same. One has to be a Big Brother (*dage*, i.e., a powerful man) to enjoy
dageda connectivity. The assumption is gendered, excluding gang outsiders, and very much about power hierarchy. In the movies, *dageda* is
usually used by the Big Brother of some group to negotiate drug deals or
send out fateful commands such as assassination orders or the release of a
hostage. Sometimes it is also an assault weapon because it is thick and
heavy.

So Kent had his *dageda*, and everyone, including people across the corri-
dor, took turns touching and admiring the device. We felt lucky to be able
to see this phone up close, and indeed we were, because this was not an
ordinary dorm but one in a privileged university, and my friend Kent
worked for a resourceful government office. Like most other mobile users
at the time, Kent did not need to pay anything out of his pocket for the
phone. His *danwei*, or work unit, paid for everything: the phone, the accessories, the monthly bill (at least 10,000 yuan or about $1,208), and another
several thousand yuan for activating the phone number. Although the
Motorola 3200 was an import and we called it by a Hong Kong nickname,
the social structure underneath it was a continuation from the tradition of
Maoist socialism, when telecom was less a business than a public service
"serving the people"—specifically, the people in key work units, the elite.

Were it forty or just ten years earlier, the underlying organizational
structure built on high fees, official use, and market monopoly would have
remained intact longer. After all, why would stakeholders choose to
abandon their privileges, especially the more imposing ones, like the

dageda and the prestige it carried? But this was a different time, and the pace of change had to be considerably faster because China's telecom industry had begun to reform.

The establishment of China Unicom in 1994 as the second national telco dealt the first blow to China Telecom, the traditional monopoly. Unicom's first major move was about the mobile phone. In 1995, one year after its funding, Unicom started to provide GSM (global systems for mobile communications) digital service. In a little more than three years, its GSM subscription reached 1 million. In contrast, although China Telecom had a lot more resources, it was hesitant about building its digital mobile networks (Le, Qiao, and Sun 2006).

Unicom had the latecomer's advantage. It did not have much in the way of a landline or analog mobile system, so it could concentrate on everything digital. In 2002, Unicom launched China's first CDMA service (CDMA stands for code division multiple access, an advanced digital mobile communication standard at the time), putting additional pressure on the incumbent. Although Unicom has gradually lost its strategic position as a formidable market contender, it did play a historic role in pushing up competition and driving down prices in the market. Even today, Unicom usually offers less expensive services and is particularly active in small towns and working-class neighborhoods as compared to China Mobile.[1]

The biggest challenge to China Telecom, however, came from within. The MCD was set up within China Telecom in 1994, and by 1999 it had grown into an independent corporation, China Mobile. As the divorce concluded in 2000, China Telecom was relieved of its mobile telephony license, and China Mobile became the leading company in the wireless market. The most critical change brought by China Mobile is arguably in the investment structure of the industry.

Since the funding of the PRC, insufficient state investment had been a key obstacle to the growth of telephone in China (He 1997). To solve this problem, China Mobile was set up as an experiment to connect the national telephone sector with the global flows of capital, thus introducing the logic of the stock market. In 1997, China Mobile became the first Chinese telco ever listed on the New York Stock Exchange and the Stock Exchange of Hong Kong.[2] One by one, the three other national telecom operators followed suit: China Telecom and China Unicom in 2002 and China Netcom, which received half of China Telecom's assets, in 2004.

For the information have-less, this entry into the global capital market was both a blessing and a curse. It had the positive effects of diluting and bringing down the old elitist model of operation centered on the top levels of China's urban society. In order to be listed on the stock exchanges, even before the initial public offering (IPO), companies needed to show that they were running a business with not only high profitability but also growth points (*zengzhangdian*): new areas for capital accumulation. In China, the mobile market has been a prominent growth point since the late 1990s.

The extraordinary commercial expansion of the mobile market was due only in a small part to official mobile subscription as in the case of Kent's *dageda*. The decisive factor was that the mobile phone can now be adopted by a large number of ordinary people, especially members of the have-less. To this end, telecom companies had to offer less expensive handsets while providing better services to attract and retain customers. Market competition in this way destabilized the traditional elite model and made the technology more affordable and accessible. Hence, it was after the initiation of such a market-oriented process that we had the term *shouji*, meaning literally "handset" or "handphone," which indicates a technosocial relationship much more inclusive than *dageda*. Finally, wireless service is not just for the Big Brother; it is for everyone.

In 2008, one can buy a used domestic-brand *shouji* for as little as $1 in Shenzhen. Yet is *shouji* a real equalizer or source of empowerment for the have-less? The answer is complicated. Access to mobile phones, although beyond the traditional boundaries of elite-based landline systems, is still limited to those who can pay. Money takes the centrality previously attached to political power. The commercial model propels technology diffusion into the lower social strata but will not by itself lead to universal, quality service for have-less users. Nor will it automatically create a social structure that is fundamentally different and conducive to working-class formation.

Exclusion is obvious in the operation of the capital market at the macro-levels. Because all four of China's national telcos are now listed on stock markets, the notion of average revenue per user (ARPU), the key indicator for profitability, has thoroughly penetrated this industry. It is this corporate obsession with higher ARPU, rather than bottom-up consumer demands, that has led to the aggressive promotion of value-added services in recent years such as ring tone downloads, games, and the provision of a variety of content, such as news, jokes, greetings, and sex-related topics. The hard sale is sometimes imposed by mandatory upgrades of service packages and sometimes through SMS spam from the telcos and their partners. They also appear in advertisements, online, on billboards, in newspapers and magazines, in public transportation—indeed, throughout the landscape of the Chinese informational city.

In this process, have-less subscribers seldom have control other than bearing the annoying bombardments and, from time to time, paying a fee knowingly or unknowingly for services they may not need. They had little choice in the duopoly structure of the mobile phone market, with China Mobile being the dominant provider. As a female migrant in Guangzhou told me, she once tried to sign off mobile phone content service she had never requested, but her service provider did not allow her to do so. She was very upset to find out that her only solution was to shift to a new phone number to avoid the unreasonable fee, which means she lost contact with some of her friends.[3] In other cases, the *jiqunwang* (concentrated collective network) system has been implemented to use mobile phones to enforce social control, for example, in the development toward the "wireless leash" (Qiu 2007b) among factories in south China, as will be discussed in detail in chapter 6.

It is premature to take market expansion as equivalent to sociopolitical empowerment. Under the traditional structure of telecom provision, members of the have-less may still be subject to abuse and discriminatory treatment even after their absorption into the marketplace as consumers.

Besides reform in telecom service provision, an equally important change took place in the electronics manufacturing sector: the emergence of China's domestic mobile handset industry. This new industry, almost nonexistent in the 1990s, has made startling progress on a massive scale. In 2005, China produced 303.67 million mobile phones, or 40 percent of the world's total output. Of this number, 228 million were sold overseas, creating a total export value of $20.6 billion (Xie 2006). In 2006, the total output increased by 58.2 percent to 480.14 million sets, resulting in an export revenue of $31.2 billion (Ministry of Information Industry 2007).

Although we do not have specific labor statistics, a huge number of working-class jobs have been generated to support this rapidly expanding industry. Through these jobs in the manufacturing, transportation, wholesale, retail, services, and used phone markets, some of the sales revenue has trickled down to blue-collar workers, working families, and, through their grassroots networks, other have-less populations.

Particularly crucial to the market of low-end mobile handsets is the rise of China's domestic brands, which played an instrumental role in lowering handset price and spreading the technology to smaller cities and towns. By 1999, the handset market was dominated by foreign brands such as Motorola, Nokia, and Eriksson, the three of which took up fully 95 percent of total sales (J. Zhang 2004). However, with policy support from the State Council and MII,[4] domestic manufacturers began to produce their own models by late 1990s, and their market share surged to reach the record of 55.8 percent in 2003 (*People's Telecommunications Daily* 2003). Beginning in 2004, foreign brands fought back. As a result, the total share for domestic brands declined to 40.6 percent by the end of 2005, which was nevertheless still impressive considering the monopoly of foreign brands in the 1990s (Lin 2006).

China's leading brands—Bird, TCL, and Xiaxin—are known as the "Three Musketeers" (J. Wang 2005a). The most exemplary among them is Bird (*bodao*), located in Ningbo, south of Shanghai. Founded in 1992, Bird was initially a township enterprise making pagers and was later incorporated to produce mobile phones in 1999. It has since become the most famous domestic producer, selling more handsets than any other domestic brand for five consecutive years (H. Zhao 2006).

Bird exemplifies domestic firms in that its products cost only a fraction of the price of foreign-brand phones. In its take-off period from 1999 to 2003, the company bypassed the major metropolitan centers and went directly to small cities and towns using the sales expertise that it had accumulated while selling pagers. In so doing, it not only avoided clashing with foreign brands at their strongholds of Beijing, Shanghai, and Guangzhou but also developed a strategic network of sales, marketing, and post-sales services throughout the country, beyond the scope of influence of the multinationals (J. Wang 2005a). As of 2006, Bird's nationwide network included thirty-six customer service centers at the provincial level, close to four hundred at the city and prefecture levels, and more than two thousand at the county and township levels.[5]

By pushing the frontier of competition into the low-end market, domestic handset makers like Bird forced foreign brands to respond in ways that are favorable to the information have-less. Hence, the Motorola C117 phone in 2005 cost merely 399 yuan ($48), making the handset more affordable (IT168.com 2005). Nokia spread its sales and service centers to more than three hundred cities nationwide, making itself more accessible to have-less customers (J. Zhong 2004). All these were efforts to reclaim lost market shares by better serving the have-less.

Accompanying the competition between domestic and foreign brands were three unanticipated developments. First, the industrial formation far outpaced market expansion, resulting in a serious surplus production capacity. By the end of 2004, domestic manufacturers had accumulated a stock of about 40 million handsets (*YeskyNet* 2004). The total number of licensed mobile phone producers also rose to more than sixty in 2005 (Jin 2005).

Surplus production capacity soon led to the second development: huge exports from China—on the scale of 228 million handsets in 2005 (Xie 2006). In 2006, the total export revenue of mobile phones was $31.2 billion, with a 51 percent increase from 2005 (Ministry of Information Industry 2006). Most of these exports bear foreign brands like Nokia and Motorola, although domestic brands like Bird have also made some inroads in fast-growing international markets such as India and Vietnam (Pday Research 2006).

Meanwhile, a series of Chinese companies emerged specializing in the manufacture and export of handset parts and accessories. BYD in Shenzhen, for example, once produced about half the world's wireless phone batteries (Fishman 2005). Its key to success is to subject migrant labor and key equipment to a novel management system of process flexibility, which essentially uses constantly retrained workers to "deliver a high variety [of batteries] at low cost" and, in so doing, outcompete expensive manufacturing in other countries, particularly Japan (Zeng and Williamson 2007). This is an exemplary model for programmable labor and network labor underlying Chinese informationalism, which is discussed in detail in chapter 6.

The third unexpected development is the surfacing of "black," or illegal, *shouji*, which is starting to display characteristics of the black Net bar. Black *shouji* are handsets coming from illegal channels: smuggling, unlicensed manufacturers, and the underground recycling of used (and sometimes stolen) phones. They have emerged because China's first-generation mobile users in the big cities are updating their handsets while market demand for inexpensive phones remains strong. Moreover, there is an army of have-less workers, many of whom are underemployed, who can provide the cheap labor for refurbishing and trading these illegal handsets, as in other parts of the world (Mooallen 2008). The result was, not surprisingly, a rectification campaign launched by MII, MPS, and five other ministries between November 2005 and March 2006 to clean up the market of second-hand mobile phones, confiscate black *shouji*, and round up illegal handsets dealers (*China Electronics Daily* 2005; China News Agency 2006).

The spread of *shouji* undermines the traditional monopoly in service provision and equipment production while giving rise to a new industry more responsive to market needs. It contributes to the laying off of employees of the traditional public phone system, from male line erectors to female operators, in the name of technology upgrading, competition, and the logic of the stock market. But it also creates a large number of working-class job opportunities for those involved in manufacturing handsets as well as in sales, services, and second-hand markets. The results of both transformations converge to increase the number of the information have-less while restructuring the labor relationship in the general framework of network enterprise. This provides a fundamental basis for the emergence of network labor as a hallmark of China's contemporary network society.

The development of *shouji* runs parallel to the trajectory of the Internet café with the initially elite-oriented technology evolving into a working-class ICT, triggering market expansion and new network formation at the grassroots level. But unlike Net bars, which spread from big cities to smaller ones, wireless working-class ICTs sometimes started in smaller cities before being adopted in megacities. This is the general trend for China's domestic-brand handsets like Bird. It is also the case for Little Smart, the low-end wireless service.

Little Smart

Little Smart, or *Xiaolingtong*, was the name of the main character in a popular science-fiction series by Ye Yonglie, China's most famous science-fiction writer (Y. Lin 2005). It was later adopted as the brand name for this working-class ICT service that uses wireless local loop (WLL) technology to connect handsets with traditional landline networks. With its own set of base stations, switchers, and handsets, the technology is much cheaper than GSM or CDMA. Although a reception signal is not always guaranteed, Little Smart allows subscribers to enjoy mobile service at the price of landline, or more precisely, limited mobility service, because the system typically works only within one city. The limitation on spatial movement may not appeal to elite travelers, but it fits the lifestyle patterns of a large segment of the have-less population, like retirees and small storekeepers, who rarely venture beyond city limits (Qiu 2007a; Tan, Chen, and Liu 2005).

Internationally, there are two main types of WLL: the European digital enhanced cordless telephone (DECT) and its variant, corDECT, which is deployed in India (Castells, Fernandez-Ardevol, Qiu, and Sey 2006). The other is the Japanese personal handyphone system (PHS), brought to China by UTStarcom, a company founded by former Chinese students in the United States who then modified PHS into the personal access system (PAS) that underlies Little Smart. Although these various kinds of WLL technology have been applied elsewhere, the Chinese Little Smart stands out as a singular case revealing the internal structure, market dynamics, and challenges of wireless working-class ICT.

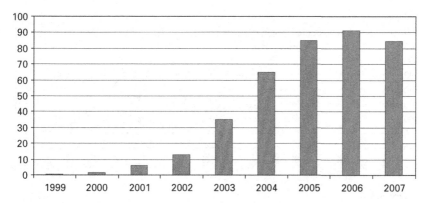

Figure 3.2
Year-end total subscriptions for Little Smart wireless service in China, 1999–2007 (millions). *Source:* MII (1999–2007).

Since the late 1990s, Little Smart has spread from small cities in China's coastal regions to inland provincial capitals and finally to Beijing and Shanghai, using the Maoist guerrilla strategy of "countryside surrounding cities (*nongcun baowei chengshi*)," as noted by industry commentators (XinhuaNet 2003). As figure 3.2 shows, the number of Little Smart subscribers grew from 600,000 in 1999 to 91.1 million in 2006, before it dipped to 84.5 million in 2007. This market is the world's fourth largest wireless user population following regular mobile user populations (GSM and CDMA users) in China, the United States, and Japan, and it is more than the entire population of Germany, which is about 83 million.

In regulatory terms, official statistics put Little Smart under a special category of wireless city phone (*wuxian shihua*). Thus, Little Smart users were not counted as part of China's total 547 million mobile subscriptions by the end of 2007. This separation of statistics facilitates comparison between Little Smart and regular mobile phones. As figure 3.3 shows, Little Smart expanded much faster than regular mobile service on the national level from 2000 to 2005. Since 2005, the trend has reversed, with an unprecedented decrease of 6.7 percent recorded for Little Smart in 2007.

How could Little Smart emerge so quickly and amass such a huge market? What is behind its phenomenal success and precipitous deceleration? There was certainly an inevitability for Little Smart to do well in a market like China, including the obvious factor of low cost. For suppliers, it is relatively inexpensive to deploy Little Smart on top of the existing fixed-line system (Tan, Chen, and Liu 2005; Wu 2007). It only takes about three

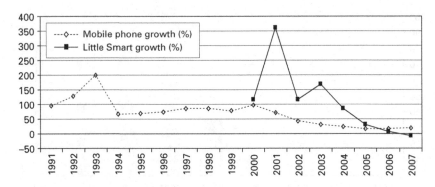

Figure 3.3
Annual growth of regular mobile phone and Little Smart subscriptions, 1991–2007.
Source: MII (1991–2007).

to four months to set up Little Smart services in a large city of 10 to 12 million potential users (Frost and Sullivan 2003). For subscribers, the price of a Little Smart handset usually ranges from less than $30 to $100, while a mobile phone often costs between $100 and $850. The monthly bill is also about one-third to one-half the amount for regular mobile service because of Little Smart's one-way charging scheme and its incapacity to roam. These, however, correspond to the expectations of have-less users because they do not want to pay for airtime while receiving calls (as is the case for regular mobile service), and many of them do not need roaming at all.[6]

Why didn't Little Smart, or WLL technology in general, materialize elsewhere on similar scale, not even in India?[7] A careful examination of archives and my interviews reveals several other facilitating factors in the processes that were coincidentally overlapping with each other at the moment of its emergence. Without any of these factors, the spread of Little Smart would have been much slower and the service might well have evolved into something much less appealing to the information have-less. Therefore, this is an "accidental accomplishment" of a working-class ICT (Qiu 2007a), which also explains the rapid slowdown of Little Smart diffusion since 2005 because the conducive conditions have largely disappeared.

The first of the accidental factors was the political legacy of China Telecom as the only telephone provider in the country until 1994. As indicated by the Eighth Five-Year Plan, the government at the time had an urgent need to increase teledensity in order to break the bottleneck imposed by the underdevelopment of telecom on economic growth and reach universal service, a goal that Beijing had been trying to attain since the Maoist age (Harwit 2004). It was under such circumstances that China Telecom decided in the mid-1990s to experiment with the hybrid solution of WLL, using limited mobility technology built on fixed-line networks (Y. Lin 2005).

At this time, the initial justification was that this could be an economical way to increase teledensity in China's mountainous regions. Thus, when the first Little Smart trial site opened in Yuhang of East China in 1997 and when the first commercial launch started in Zhaoqing of South China in 1998, no one paid much attention. No one anticipated the service to become such a major success on a national scale because Little Smart was perceived as a supplement to the landline system, an "enhanced cordless phone" that would be deployed only in small towns in the mountainous areas (Y. Lin 2005).

Right after the Little Smart experiment in Yuhang and Zhaoqing began, large-scale change began to occur in the telecom sector, starting with the listing of China Mobile on the stock market in 1998 and its ultimate separation from China Telecom in 2000. Old phone business went through a quick—and, for China Telecom, painful—process of transformation from an integral part of the public sector to a new domain of competition and accumulation. The logic of ARPU weighed in, while China Telecom, now left with just its landlines, was going through its struggle of reform and restrategizing before the initial public offering with the help of Chinese authorities.[8] In this context, prioritizing Little Smart as a main growth point of China Telecom was unsurprising given the remarkable performance of the wireless market at that time.

From a larger historical perspective, it was coincidental that China's telecom industry was going through these structural changes right after the adoption of Little Smart. Had these changes taken place earlier or later, the story of Little Smart would have been less astounding.

China Telecom should have stayed away from the wireless sector after being stripped of its mobile operation license and its MCD. But it nonetheless invested heavily in Little Smart to tap the low-end wireless market. The mobile license holders, China Mobile and China Unicom, cried foul. As a result, between 1999 and 2002, MII issued a series of commands against expanding Little Smart, ordering, for instance, the canceling of all new Little Smart projects in October 1999, the suspension of all Little Smart operations in May 2000, and the exclusion of Little Smart from big cities in February 2001 (Qiu, 2007a).

Yet, curiously enough, despite these official orders from Beijing, Little Smart continued to spread in leaps and bounds. It was precisely during this period, 1999 to 2002, that some of the highest growth rates were recorded. It was also during this period that the number of cities with Little Smart jumped: from about eighty in 1999 to more than two hundred in 2000, and then to nearly four hundred in 2002 (Y. Lin 2005).

This dissemination process was punctuated with local clashes between Little Smart and its opponents, sometimes leading to major breakdowns, for instance, in the northwest city of Lanzhou in August 2000 (Y. Lin 2005). But the technology sailed forward despite temporary turbulence and was finally deployed in Beijing and Shanghai in 2003 and 2004, respectively. Notably, throughout the process, regardless of the large number of local violations of its policies, MII never penalized China Telecom in a substantial way.

Decisive to this process of "countryside surrounding cities" was the important role of the local state. Local officials had worked with the local branches of China Telecom for decades, and there was inertia for the old trust relationship to continue, especially in small cities and towns, which China Mobile had barely set its eyes on. With the decentralization of decision making in the post-Mao era, local states, particularly those in less developed regions, assumed almost total responsibility for fostering the telecom sector by themselves, with little dependence on Beijing.

Moreover, there was political incentive for local states to achieve a high teledensity rate because it was one indicator of local economic development and therefore one assessment criterion for the performance of mayors and township leaders. This political drive to get better assessment results happened to overlap with the commercial interests of local China Telecom branches. It was this peculiar relationship of mutual support at the local level that effectively resisted top-down MII orders against Little Smart.

Equally important, the emergence of Little Smart was heavily owed to transnational processes, especially the role of UTStarcom due to its connection with telecom investors (Softbank) and PHS equipment manufacturers in Japan. This connection existed, however, by chance, because one of UTStarcom's cofounders, Hung Lu, had befriended Masayoshi Son, the owner of Softbank, when both were students at the University of California, Berkeley many years earlier. Softbank provided the first major venture capital for UTStarcom ($30 million in 1995), and the Japanese connection helped the company play a unique role by importing PHS base stations and handsets from Japan (Qiu 2007a).

UTStarcom, however, did not intentionally choose to focus on the low-end wireless market. Its corporate strategy from the beginning has leaned toward optical communications and Internet access solutions, with the wireless business occupying only a secondary position.[9] UTStarcom initially simply bought equipment from Japan and sold it to China Telecom. Although the role of UTStarcom in refining the PAS standard is not to be denied, as a technology company it did not concentrate its R&D resources on Little Smart at this early stage. Its corporate focus did not shift to the have-less market until late 2001, when UTStarcom began producing its own Little Smart handsets and equipment and remodeling the Little Smart base station so that it could better fit the spatial characteristics of Chinese cities.

In this case, the coincidence is not only the personal ties between Hung Lu and Masayoshi Son but also the status of the wireless market in Japan. Although it was essentially the same technology, PHS had limited success in Japan because of different user demographics, different regulatory structures, and different marketing strategies by the mobile (not landline) operators (H. Liu 2004). As a result, Japanese manufacturers were happy to sell their surplus products at negotiable prices, and local China Telecom branches were equally eager to purchase and deploy them. The complementarities between the Japan and China markets had little to do with the technology itself, but it significantly reduced the risk for UTStarcom and thereby enabled the company to play a critical bridging role in technology transfer.

With all the facilitating factors discussed above, one should note that there were many arguments against the deployment of Little Smart. From the beginning, China Mobile and Unicom have called Little Smart "outdated (*guoshi*)," referring to the status of PHS in Japan (however, not corDECT in India). They also criticized Little Smart's lack of roaming capacity and charged that its radio frequency would interfere with the forthcoming 3G mobile telephony (Jiang 2003, Bao 2004).

The most important accusation is about the poor reception signal of Little Smart systems. Users in some cities thus gave nicknames to the service such as "weiwei call" because one keeps saying, "*Wei! Wei!* (Hello! Hello!)" while using Little Smart (Kuo 2004). In February 2006, I carried a Little Smart handset in Shanghai for a couple of days. The reception signal was indeed quite unreliable. Even in downtown Shanghai, there was a lot more background noise using this Little Smart phone (a product by UTStarcom) as compared to ordinary mobile service.

Yet comparatively speaking, large metropolitan centers in general have worse reception signals than small cities do, with the technical deployment of Little Smart being quite uneven at the local level.[10] This again has to do with the localized nature of the diffusion process, in which local agencies decide largely independently how the service is to be set up. In places where the incentives are strong, Little Smart can reach the same level of service quality as regular mobile systems. For example, in Zhoushan, Zhejiang Province, local landline operators gave users sizable rewards (about 1,000 yuan or $120) for identifying blind spots where the Little Smart signal was inadequate. Using such mechanisms, signal quality can be improved quickly, leading to stronger customer satisfaction. One retiree whom I interviewed in Ningbo, Zhejiang Province, chose to use Little Smart as his only phone line, his "lifeline," indicating the reliability of the service in this medium-sized city.[11]

Little Smart does not have to offer low-quality service as long as the local telcos are committed to improving it. Telcos in Shanghai have much less incentive because the city adopted Little Smart rather late in the process, when its affluent residents already had regular mobile phones. For these companies, meeting the informational needs of the have-less, who are more sensitive to price, is but one of its many goals. In contrast, price sensitivity is much higher in the mainstream market of smaller cities like Ningbo, Zhoushan, and Xi'an, where Little Smart systems also happened to be deployed several years earlier than in the key metropolis. Small-town telcos therefore are more likely to capitalize on this working-class ICT.

But commercial incentives often exist only in the short run. Given the vicissitudes of market dynamics involving such fast-changing factors as technology and capital flows, there is no guarantee that the incentives will last. They may also become detrimental to the spread of low-end ICTs. After all, despite the size of the market, Little Smart's ARPU is low because subscribers choose the service precisely to lower their phone bill. With this realization in mind, it is odd to try to increase user expenses for Little Smart because to do so would drive away working-class consumers. Yet the logic of ARPU is dominant, and it meshes with the discourse of technology upgrading, as in the case of Internet café.

Consequently we see a number of efforts to make more expensive Little Smart handsets—some with color display, some with a dual-mode switching function between PAS and GSM, and some costing about 3,000 yuan, or $360 (*China Telecom World* 2004). Since 2003, SMS and VoIP (voice over Internet protocol) services have been added to Little Smart systems, which have been well received, as well as Internet access functions (such as general packet radio service or GPRS) and ring-tone downloading; neither, however, took off. A controversial proposal appeared in 2004 when some China Telecom and China Netcom employees proposed to add roaming capacity by a mandatory upgrading of all Little Smart systems, including handsets, on May 17, 2005, World Telecom Day. This proposal triggered immediate opposition among telecom analysts and has been indefinitely postponed (Shen 2005).

These upgrading efforts have intensified since 2005, but they do not lead to the continued prosperity of this working-class ICT. On the contrary, Little Smart entered a period of deceleration and market contraction, evidenced in the subscription figures of 2006 and 2007. UTStarcom's financial performance is another telling indicator. In 2003, the company had total sales revenues of $1.97 billion and a net profit of $216 million, mostly from Little Smart. In 2005, its revenue was $2.87 billion, but with a net loss of $533 million. In 2006, revenue declined to $2.46 billion, and it still lost $117 million.

As of 2008, Little Smart remains a prominent Chinese wireless working-class ICT despite unfavorable arguments from mobile operators and the self-destructive tendencies within the industry itself. Its value should be recognized not only for low-end consumers but at the level of China's entire wireless communication market. Little Smart has challenged mobile operators to lower prices by launching, for example, a variety of package (*taocan*) services that are getting increasingly close to the cost level of Little Smart. In May 2006, China Mobile Beijing also began to experiment with one-way charging packages, an obvious response to competition from Little Smart (Mao 2006).

Little Smart is a typical wireless working-class ICT that is being shaped under the conditions of Chinese informationalism. It is probably the most successful wireless development in the first five years of the twenty-first century, provided by fixed-line operators under the pressure of the stock market. The socialist legacy, the decentralized, local-state-centered policy implementation structure, and the presence of a Chinese American company with strong Japanese ties were all indispensable to the success of Little Smart, which is, in this sense, a product of a historical moment, not of a social structure with long-term stability.

Short Message Service (SMS)

China has more mobile subscribers than any other country and the world's largest national SMS (short message service) market. Sending one SMS usually costs 0.1 yuan, or a little more than one U.S. cent. As figure 3.4

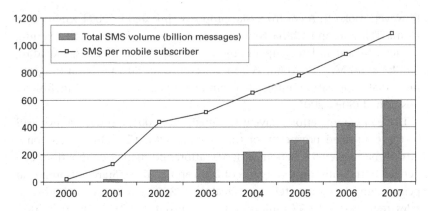

Figure 3.4
Growth of SMS traffic volume in China, 2000–2007. *Source:* MII (2000–2007).

shows, since China Mobile launched SMS in May 2000, the annual traffic volume has shot up from 1.4 billion in 2000 to 592.1 billion in 2007.

This is a remarkable expansion even considering the sheer size of the Chinese market. The growth of SMS significantly outpaces that of mobile phone subscribers. On average, a Chinese mobile subscriber sent 131 messages in 2001 and 1,082 messages in 2007. The more than eightfold increase in per capita volume indicates that there is something more profound than the diffusion of yet another ICT service. Behind the phenomenal growth of SMS is a real change in user behavior, the industrial structure of the telecom sector, and the concept of the telephone itself. Going wireless is not just about removing wires; it is also about adding computer-like capacities to the phone: the entry, storage, and retrieval of data; the receiving, sorting, sending, and forwarding of information; and, most crucial, the creation of meaning and the expansion of grassroots networks through *shouji*.

On the level of user behavior, SMS serves the functions of e-mail (asynchronous communication) since, in China, Internet use still lags far behind mobile use in terms of user population (figure 1.2). Voice call via mobile phone is often perceived as overpriced, especially among the information have-less, because it usually costs around 0.5 to 0.7 yuan per minute for both the sender and the receiver of a phone call. SMS, costing 0.1 yuan per message for the sender only, therefore provides an inexpensive alternative for working-class networking.

As in other countries, the appeal of SMS is most prominent among young users, given the challenge of entering and retrieving information on a small interface. An English SMS is often limited to seventy letters. Alternatively, it may consist of seventy Chinese characters, which can contain more information than an English message of the same length due to the two-dimensionality of the Chinese ideographic characters, now usually entered through phonetic pinyin input and the word association function.[12]

For less wealthy groups, especially youth, there is another explanation for heavy SMS use. Many of them buy relatively expensive mobile phones as a status symbol.[13] They use their savings to purchase trendy handsets but cannot afford voice call. Yet their handsets will become outdated in a short time. Therefore, it makes sense to use SMS for not only personal communication but also public performance with a trendy gadget whose color and ring tones enhance the consumer experience.[14] This type of conspicuous consumption and communication is particularly obvious among young migrant workers and students from low-income working families.

But how widespread is the diffusion of SMS in the stratified structure of Chinese society? Admittedly, we do not have empirical data to answer this question fully on the national scale. But it is clear that the technology has connected young users from across the class structure, including members of the working class—for example, among migrant factory workers (Law 2006). Radio and TV stations have been instrumental in promoting SMS across social strata and various social groups as in the reality TV contest, *Super Girl* (*chaoji nusheng*), the Chinese version of *American Idol*. In its first season, *Super Girl* drew in more than 8 million SMS votes in a single evening of its finale night (Yardley 2005).

Senior citizens have also begun to text, including my mother living in Wuhan, Hubei Province, who has her full share of technophobic issues, especially due to her poor pinyin (so it is difficult for her to input Chinese characters) and failing eyesight. The reason she uses it is that she has a brother with a hearing disability who lives in southern Jiangxi Province, several hundred miles away, and my uncle, also a pensioner, bought a special handset for the hearing impaired in March 2006. The device is for texting only; it is always set to vibration mode. It thus allows unprecedented translocal connectivity between my uncle and my mother, who has managed to learn texting through her Little Smart phone. In this case, SMS turns out to be a solution that satisfies previously unmet informational needs.

The spread of SMS use has brought structural change to the ICT industry by enabling a new business model. Before SMS, there were few value-added telecom services, and online content distributors could barely break even with the small revenue generated by Internet advertising or membership fees. The key missing link in China, as in most other developing countries, is the absence of credit cards. But mobile phone plus SMS could be functionally equivalent to credit cards by being a conduit of cash flow. Firms can now send content (e.g., news) and services (e.g., m-tickets that allow ticketing service to be delivered through SMSs) to customers while putting the charge on their phone bill, which users now can pay with their prepaid cash credits or through their monthly statements.

This business model benefits mobile operators, especially China Mobile, because they get the largest chunk of the revenue. But since mobile operators seldom provide attractive SMS content, they need to share part of the revenue with content producers, especially the country's major Web portals and broadcasting stations. The consequence is the emergence of a new industrial complex that integrates mobile operators with content and service providers, from Web sites to mass media, from IT companies to a wide range of traditional services such as fast food and financing, all using SMS as the technological platform (Qiu 2007b). Together they produce a large quantity of content: news updates, jokes, m-coupons (similar to m-tickets but distributed for free), greeting messages, soft porn, promotion of ring tones (*cailing*), multimedia messaging service (MMS, or *caixin*), and different types of advertisements that are sometimes basically spam.

While SMS delivery is automated, the creation and sales of content and the provision of subscriber services entail intensive labor. Key Internet portals thus all have their SMS task forces, known as SMS writers (*duanxin xieshou*), who produce, on a regular basis, large numbers of crisp, sexy texts to be sold or spammed to mobile subscribers. In general, SMS writers are paid poorly, although at times of high market demand like the Lunar New Year, they can make a weekly salary of up to 10,000 yuan (about $1,242) (Lan 2005). It is such new professions of informational labor, with huge disparities in their skill and income levels, that support the explosive growth of SMS, providing a material basis for the formation of China's new working class.

As in the case of Little Smart, telcos embrace SMS because, after being listed on stock markets, they have to strive for higher ARPU. To this end, SMS is not just another data service but a strategic one that serves as a launch pad for other value-added services. By taking full advantage of SMS, content providers like Netease may do extremely well on Nasdaq. For example, in 2003 when the stock price of Netease went through dramatic growth, William Ding, the owner of Netease, became China's richest man

(Xinhua News Agency 2003b). SMS may also help smaller firms attract venture capital or strike better deals when merging with multinational corporations, many of which have entered China's wireless market with plans to acquire promising local start-ups.

A crucial aspect of this industrial complex is its close ties with the authorities. In principle, the telcos are state owned, and, in general, China has shown no attempt to loosen its grip on other content and service providers, including private dot-coms. But the government had not paid much attention to SMS until the 2003 SARS epidemic, when SMS first demonstrated its capacity for alternative information exchange beyond official control (McDonald 2003). Yet once Beijing decided to intervene, it used state-owned mass media, exerted its influence over telcos, and effectively undermined the "rumors" about the pandemic spread of some "strange disease"—although only for a few weeks, until the authorities were forced to confront SARS, now in full swing (Castells, Fernandez-Ardevol, Qiu, and Sey 2006). Despite the change of attitude toward SARS, the Chinese government held its critical stance against those who used SMS to "spread rumors," arresting about a dozen people during the epidemic (Reporters without Borders 2004).

These mobile users could be tracked down, detained, and charged because it is relatively easy to sort and search billions of text messages. SMS have to go through state-owned pipelines, through a gigantic "remote searchable database" (Lyon 2003). Technically, mobile handsets are also more difficult than computers to be reconfigured in order to avoid censorship, filtering, and the "panoptic sort" (Gandy 1993). On the other hand, it is easy for the authorities to produce new regulations against the "abuse" of SMS, given the country's legal and regulatory structures.

The specific instance of "abuse" is often a moving target with notable arbitrariness and selectivity. It could be about "rumors" at one time, and "indecent content" at another (Lanfranco 2005). Yet when a female primary school teacher in a small city in Yunnan Province was sexually harassed by her boss using SMS, the local mobile operator refused to provide legal evidence of the abusive messages (Qiu 2007a). In this peculiar manner, SMS has been transformed into a "wireless leash" for elite-dominated social control over and through the processes of texting.

Does top-down control pose an obstacle to the commercial operation of SMS? The answer is both yes and no. At the beginning, when the MII announced its attempt to rectify sex-related SMS in 2003, just the announcement itself sent the stocks of content providers like Netease into a major slump (Lanfranco 2005). But entrepreneurialism proves to be as malleable as the technology itself, responsive to the structural conditions imposed by the authorities, thus adding to the growth of the SMS industrial complex at the conjuncture between the state and the market.

A case in point is Venus Info Tech Inc., headquartered in the Zhongguancun area of Beijing.[15] Like UTStarcom, it was founded by former overseas Chinese students, and it has carved out a new market: SMS surveillance. Venus was among the first in China to receive authorization from the MPS to develop a real-time surveillance system for SMS. Its main invention is the Cybervision SMS filtering system, the first of its kind that uses filtering algorithm from the Chinese Academy of Sciences "based on keywords and combination of keywords" (Reporters without Borders 2004).

Free speech observers outside China are concerned about this new censorship system and the SMS surveillance technologies that can be sold and used worldwide. But within China, given the lack of media autonomy and the absence of a strong notion of privacy, such concern has been rarely expressed. Instead, the real issue most mobile customers care about across the board, including both the haves and the have-less, is not free speech or, for that matter, "rumors" or "indecency." It is spam, and the more sinister scams associated with it.[16]

The ubiquity of SMS spam in China stems from a systemic bias toward profit maximization under the circumstances of limited competition between the two mobile operators. Since 2003, landline operators have also started to play a role, with Little Smart phones being able to send and receive SMS. But the predominance of China Mobile continues, and there is little incentive to curb spam from the perspective of content and service providers as well as the telcos themselves.

Abusive spam has gone out of control in dramatic ways. A watershed event occurred during the 2005 October 1 National Day holiday week, when identity theft initiated by SMS affected thousands of mobile subscribers in Beijing (*Beijing wanbao* 2005). The deception was carried out by groups of spammers in South China who hacked the phone system and pretended to be bank employees and police officers in order to get personal account information and passwords from SMS users. Within a week, millions of yuan were lost, and the crime story made headlines, spurring a sense of crisis regarding spam. Yet the discussions bypassed the fundamental origins of spam rooted in the political and economic structure of the excessively commercialized mobile industry. Instead, the issue was framed to support further state control over SMS. A strict real-name registration system (*shimingzhi*) of all mobile users was proposed, and an opinion poll in Beijing found that 75.9 percent of randomly selected respondents endorsed the proposal (Beijing Statistics Information Network 2005). But despite overwhelming public support, real-name registration of mobile subscribers using their real-world identity has not been enforced, which stands in stark contrast to swift change in cybercafé regulation.[17] The critical difference is the structural positioning of the stakeholders. Whereas cybercafés are largely small, private businesses, SMS content and service providers are on a large scale, and the biggest chunk of profit is taken by publicly listed state-owned corporations. As prepaid services account for the bulk of user growth for both China Mobile and China Unicom, if real-name registration is implemented, a direct impact would be the reduction, or at least stagnation, in prepaid subscriptions. This is obstructed by the mobile operators, who cannot afford falling growth, which will be reflected in the stock markets.

Under such circumstances, a new type of ICP company has emerged that specializes in collecting mobile phone numbers and spamming, with support from the telcos. According to an investigative report by China Central Television, Focus Media is the largest of its kind. At the beginning of 2008, its database contained about half of all mobile phone numbers in China, and it sends out hundreds of million spam SMSs everyday (*Southern Metropolitan Daily* 2008).

How does all of the above relate to the information have-less and working-class network society? First and foremost, the rise of SMS demonstrates the power of an inexpensive wireless service to penetrate large parts of the Chinese urban society. This is not a high technology, but it nevertheless enjoys high popularity and high growth rates. Behind the boom is the fact that this business could attract talents from across social strata, including working-class groups, and give rise to a model that is more inclusive of have-less users.

Second, like Net bars, this working-class ICT appeals mostly to the younger generation. Although others, including senior citizens and the disabled, are also adopting SMS, youth remain the core user group. This demographic composition influences the ways in which SMS is put to use, for example, through young people's conspicuous consumption and public performance based on texting.

Third, a new industrial complex has materialized to expand the SMS market and deal with sociopolitical issues associated with this market expansion, for instance, during the SARS crisis. The process involves private and public sector actors, including the police. As for the have-less people, it on the one hand creates employment opportunities ranging from professional SMS writers to blue-collar workers manufacturing SMS surveillance technology. Yet on the other hand, there is underground use, as in the spam scam of October 2005, through which some marginalized members of the have-less population could defy the authorities and stage a temporary revolt.

Finally, as a result of industrial development, a structure of control has emerged to constrain the spectrum of SMS applications. The restrictions affect users in all social strata, although arguably they limit the have-less more than the upper classes in that the former benefit less from the status quo and are therefore more likely to initiate alternative modes of use. In so doing, the chances for independent horizontal networking and new class formation are seriously limited as well. Can SMS exist in something other than the purely commercial settings, as a true working-class ICT, free from spam and other abuse? For the moment, this cannot be answered.

Prepaid Services

Prepaid wireless services enhance user capacity in budget control while allowing mobile operators to reach the have-less population, who would be otherwise unable to afford personal phone service due to low income, the lack of a permanent address, or credit history. For this reason, prepaid services have spread across the world, particularly in developing countries, and become "arguably the most important form of appropriation that caters to the needs of those with lower income and education" (Castells, Fernandez-Ardevol, Qiu, and Sey 2006, 61). China is no exception in this regard. In 2000, its total number of prepaid subscribers was 14.9 million, or 34.6 percent of contract-based subscription. As 2007 ended, prepaid subscription stood at 360.9 million, or 2.1 times that of contract subscribers (figure 3.5).

Other than tremendous growth in subscription numbers, we know much less about prepaid services than other working-class ICTs. This is because of the highly decentralized structure of the market, which is far more complex than Little Smart provided by landline operators or SMS by mobile operators. The statistics in figure 3.5 show only the number of mobile subscriptions. We do not know how many of them are owned by the same individuals or shared among groups of friends. Moreover, besides China Mobile and China Unicom, many companies offer prepaid services, especially VoIP phone cards, such as *Jitong* and Railcom (*Tietong*), which operate nationwide, and numerous smaller regional and local firms. In addition, prepaid services are often sold with discounts, with the amount of discount

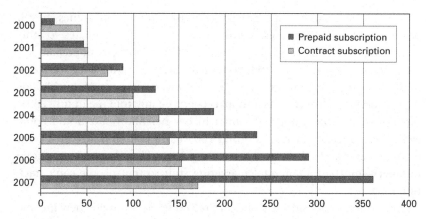

Figure 3.5
Year-end total prepaid subscriptions and contract subscriptions in China's mobile telephone market, 2000–2007 (million subscriptions). *Source:* Compilation based on *China Mobile Annual Reports* (2000–2007) and *China Unicom Annual Reports* (2000–2007).

usually negotiated on the spot. As a result, not only is it difficult to count the exact number of persons buying prepaid services, it is even harder to figure out the total value of the market.

But the flip side of immeasurability is ubiquity. Anyone arriving in any Chinese city cannot fail to witness the sales of prepaid services at all kinds of locations: post offices, newsstands, bookstores, convenience stores, restaurants, and sidewalk vendors. In summer 2002, in a bustling bar street of Chengdu in southwest China, a teenage boy biked past me shouting, "Phone cards! Phone cards!" He carried a schoolbag containing his inventory. Above his back wheel, a cardboard sign flapped, advertising his discount prices. Sales of prepaid phone cards have become a major grassroots ICT business in working-class neighborhoods such as migrant enclaves.

Both the consumer and the supplier aspects of this working-class ICT are important. Prepaid services are not necessarily convenient. In order to save money by using different prepaid packages, subscribers may need to take the SIM (subscriber identity module) card in and out, or they may have to press more buttons to make a call. Most important, the per minute charge may in fact be more expensive than a contract-based subscription. But the key is that this technology is use driven, and one can easily figure out the cost of a call. This mode of working-class connectivity suits the needs of the have-less, for whom income is low and life unpredictability is high.

Some of the urban elite also use prepaid subscriptions for business travel, privacy, and other purposes. We do not have precise estimates for this market segment. This, however, does not deny the centrality of prepaid services to have-less customers, who often have no other choice for service.

The heaviest users are spammers at the lower strata whose livelihoods depend on prepaid access. As a shopkeeper in Beijing told me in July 2005, for more than three months, a man in her neighborhood would come every week and buy at least a dozen 100 yuan mobile phone cards from her. "He never added funds to his accounts. He just kept buying new phone numbers—maybe for some telemarketing stuff so that people can't track him down."

As for the supplier side, the sales of prepaid services provide new income opportunities for have-less entrepreneurs. Unlike most other IT businesses, there is a lower entry barrier, and no license is needed. The wholesalers are ready to sell mobile prepaid cards to anyone interested—not only phone cards but also cards for landline-based VoIP service, dial-up Internet access, and online gaming, which are also sold in cybercafés. These cards are small and light, and therefore easy to store and transport. The retailers can buy as many or as few as they want, and user demands remain strong given that more than two-thirds of China's 547 million mobile subscriptions are prepaid. No wonder we see prepaid services being hawked on almost every street corner. Moreover, they create an immense number of jobs and a sizable amount of wealth, finally trickling down to those who have been laid off, migrants, and senior citizens, who tend to become vendors of prepaid cards more than other have-less groups in urban China.

Pagers

Narratives about ICTs in China have by and large excluded pagers, probably because, unlike the Internet or mobile phone, the service does not challenge the plain old telephone and the market has been shrinking. Yet a complete examination of wireless working-class ICTs must address the story of pager. As Hobsbawn wrote, "The destruction of the past, or rather of the social mechanisms that link one's contemporary experience to that of earlier generations, is one of the most characteristic and eerie phenomena of the late twentieth century" (1994, 3). To avoid this pitfall, it is essential to establish a historic tie between the declining pager and other wireless working-class ICT services. The pager is one of them.

China was once the world's largest pager market. The subscription figures grew from around 4,000 in 1985 to 447,000 in 1990. They then leaped to

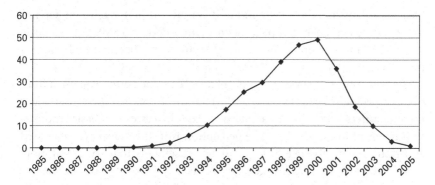

Figure 3.6
Year-end total pager subscriptions in China, 1985–2005 (millions). *Source:* MII (1985–2005).

17.39 million in 1995 and finally to 48.84 million in 2000 (figure 3.6). Until this point, pager service had gone through a process of diffusion similar to cybercafés and *shouji* in recent years, along a typical trajectory of transformation from an elite privilege to one with mass appeal, serving millions of have-less users and providing hundreds of thousands of low-rank jobs, most notably, female pager operators in this case.

However, the market of nearly 50 million subscriptions has been falling since 2000. The accumulation of pagers for more than a decade and a half basically evaporated within five years. By the end of 2005, total subscription had dipped below 1 million to 971,000. Now not only has the service disappeared from urban life in most parts of China, but it has also been stigmatized as unreliable and outdated. Even migrant workers look down on the technology and regard it as of poor quality and therefore not suitable for them.[18]

Unfortunately we do not have a solid basis to compare the level of customer satisfaction with pagers in the late 1990s in relation to newer technologies today. But the consistent growth of pagers throughout the 1990s suggests that they fulfilled what they promised to deliver. Even in the United States, the market base for pagers is quite stable. From 1998 to 2002, pager sales in the United States increased by 17.2 percent (Euromonitor 2003). Why, then, has the same technology so quickly become outdated in China?

A popular explanation is that pagers are technologically backward and therefore inevitably displaced by mobile phone and wireless services, especially SMS. Even if we accept that when a society gets wealthier (as China has), its members would demand and can afford better telecom service, there is little evidence that pager services are inferior to SMS or even Little Smart, yet another arguably outdated technology that in fact became a huge success after 2003.

The perception of pagers as an obsolete ICT can be better explained from the perspective of the telecom industry—the investors, advertisers, and manufacturers—rather than actual user experiences or the basic information needs of low-end users. The perception is in this sense manufactured as a result of the absence of pager in advertisements that try to sell more expensive *shouji* products. Pagers are viewed as "backward" not because of their technology but because of their low ARPU. Moreover, they are not fully automated; the female operators, as efficient as humans can be, are still no match for machines (as for SMS), and it remains an expense to hire, train, and manage these operators.

Such considerations made sense to companies under the pressure of the stock market to be lean and mean, while concentrating on high-end technologies. This is what happened to Unicom, which owns most pager systems in the country. Between 2000 and 2002, its strategic priority was building and marketing its new CDMA networks so that it could better compete with China Mobile. To do so, investment and personnel were shifted from the pager sector, a fundamental reason for the landslide decline of total pager subscription from 48.8 million in 2000 to 18.72 million in 2002, a startling drop of 61.67 percent within two years (figure 3.6).

While China registers some of the world's quickest growth figures, this is probably one of the largest falls in use in the history of world telecommunications. This is not just about blaming Unicom, although it does bear the most significant consequences of this decline. After spending heavily on CDMA, its market share climbed moderately from 26.7 percent in 2002 to 34.1 percent in 2005, although it still lags far behind China Mobile. Meanwhile, however, it has lost a market of about 50 million customers, or about 40 percent of its mobile subscription base. Not all pager users were upgraded to Unicom's new networks.

The decline of pagers was accelerated by another factor. The market structure was in a sense similar to that of prepaid services in that, under the umbrella of China Unicom, most services were carried out by a large number of regional and local pager operators. Financially they are independent, and each of them has its own team of female operators. Thus, in 2001, when it became clear that the pager market was set to plunge, many of them began to take flight, an act that soon had a network effect. As a result, there was a period of panic, especially among smaller pager companies. Some of them disappeared overnight as their owners decided to close down.

Female employees in the pager industry, mostly young migrant workers, lost their jobs. Working-class subscribers suddenly found that their pager companies had evaporated, taking with them the advance payments for six months or even a year that they had made. Those funds would never be returned. There was public anger, and indeed some local state agencies, like the Wireless Radio Regulatory Committee of Guangdong Province, attempted to intervene to prevent such irresponsible closings (Wu and Shi 2001). But it was too late, and the reputation of unreliable service, due to the wrongdoings of irresponsible operators rather than the technology itself, had already been slapped on pagers. If companies can act so selfishly and shed their contractual responsibilities so outrageously, which ICT, working-class or not, could be reliable after all?

The cautionary notes from pagers are clear. Networks of working-class ICTs can materialize rapidly due to strong market demand and clever entrepreneurialism. But the combination of the two cannot guarantee the continuation of the low-end service. At junctures of events, especially given the relentless drive for updated technology and higher profitability, working-class ICTs may decline at a speed faster than they had emerged. When this happens, it first hurts have-less subscribers and have-less employees. It also harms the telecom operators themselves with wounds that may not be immediately discernible but are nevertheless painful in the long run. Finally, without effective regulation by the state, the industry, or a third party, the market of a working-class ICT can be fragile. When it starts to dip, it may not just drop, but in fact collapse, and the damage is permanent.

The waxing and waning of pagers poses another important question. After a working-class ICT falls, what happens to its employees? Besides creating new jobs for the information have-less, the rapidly changing Chinese information economy also creates new groups of laid-off workers. Especially vulnerable are the more marginalized groups like female pager operators from the countryside, some of whom were forced into the illegal phone-sex business of "voice-information stations (*shengxuntai*)," as will be discussed in chapter 5.

Shaping Wireless Connectivity

We have discussed several aspects of China's low-end wireless market: the *shouji* handsets, Little Smart, SMS, prepaid services, and pagers. Each of these different businesses entails a unique mixture of technology, policy, and entrepreneurialism under a variety of institutional structures. They are, however, only the most obvious parts of the whole picture, which contains less quantifiable developments like the sales of used mobile phones and the use of SMS in underground activities, for example, among gangsters. Wireless working-class ICTs also exist in hybrid forms, both with each other (like using prepaid VoIP on top of Little Smart) and with other mediated channels, including mass media as in *Super Girl* and, increasingly, with the Internet. A recent vogue among female migrant workers in Beijing's service sector is mobile QQ service, which transforms *shouji* into a terminal for online chatting (Oreglia, 2007).

The ubiquity and hybrid modes of wireless working-class ICTs in the Chinese city indicate that there are many cost-effective solutions to meet the needs of the information have-less. Wireless communication has already offered innovative modes of connectivity from the bottom up, creating tremendous opportunities for low-end telecom markets to prosper in ways previously unimaginable. These wireless working-class ICTs have emerged over the past few years at the lower strata of the Chinese network society. In so doing, they have sent ripples across the information sector from equipment manufacturing to content provision to service delivery, causing structural change whose impact can be felt in the wireless market worldwide.

A notable feature across the board is the increasing linkage with the international marketplace in terms of not only technology transfer (Little Smart) and capital flow (SMS) but also large-scale imports and exports of manufactured equipment, especially *shouji* handsets. Without the overseas factor, wireless ICTs would have been less successful in providing working-class connectivity within China, as well as blue-collar job opportunities for new sectors like handset manufacturing, whose output depends heavily on export. Therefore, compared to the traditional model of telecom service under the state monopoly of MPS, an internationalized market mechanism with some internal competition proves to be much more responsive to the informational needs of have-less populations.

Nevertheless, only a fraction of China's telecom players are truly international. As a whole, the new industrial system of wireless working-class ICTs still depends on state support in significant ways. Although there are sporadic crackdowns on black *shouji* and SMS scams, the suppression is nothing comparable to what was inflicted on cybercafés. The low level of top-down intervention seen in this comparative light is a key reason behind the booming wireless sector at the local level.

But are wireless working-class ICTs guaranteed to succeed in a marketplace dominated by the commercial logic? The decline of pagers offers the strongest counterargument, while the crisis of market failure also looms, to a different extent, in the handset manufacturing industry with its huge surplus production capacity, the premature decline of Little Smart in recent years, and the incapacity of the market itself to eradicate spam. Commercial motivation may also play a conservative role by succumbing to systems of social control and the top-down imposition of upper-class interests, for example, by making SMS filtering and surveillance systems for censors in China and other countries. This ultimately narrows the range of possibilities for the social uses of wireless working-class connectivity.

Finally, a fundamental challenge comes from the drive of various telecom players to upgrade their technologies to high-end ICTs, more expensive value-added services, and ultimately higher ARPU. This is essentially what happened to Little Smart, SMS, and pagers. Thus, the wireless ICTs discussed in this chapter are not much different from cybercafés: both need an appropriate balance of public policy and commercial rationale in order to be sustainable. After all, working-class network society is not about the shaping of technology into instruments of accelerated capital accumulation. Rather, it is about the long-term well-being of people, now built on the materialized technosocial networks of working-class ICTs.

II   The People of Have-Less

4 Migrants

Migrants are people with high mobility. They constitute an essential part of the information have-less population that provides the basis for the formation of working-class network society in urban China. There are many kinds of migrants, from all over the country, in all walks of life. In recent years, especially since China's central government demanded fair treatment of migrant workers in January 2003,[1] there have been numerous books and reports on peasant workers (*nongmingong* or *mingong*) who leave the countryside to work in cities. For the discussion here, the term *migrants* more broadly includes a variety of industrial workers, service sector employees, and small entrepreneurs, including laid-off former state sector workers as well as other underemployed laborers in the Chinese informational city. Many of the jobless end up in informal and illegal economies, in China and abroad.

Because no agency keeps a full tally of the various kinds of migrants, an estimate of China's floating population ranges from 98 million to 200 million; a more precise figure from the National Statistics Bureau in 2005 was 147.35 million: 47.79 million interprovincial and 99.56 million intraprovincial migrants (*China Population Statistics Yearbook* 2006, 3). In comparison, the world's total number of international immigrants stands at roughly 96 million (ILO, 2002). In other words, there are more migrants within China than those migrating across national boundaries in the entire world.

Most of China's domestic migrants are have-less migrants: they are socioeconomically similar, have the shared experience of being uprooted, and hold common aspirations for human settlement and sociocultural recognition for what they achieve through long-term or temporary migration.

These migrants have come to rely on working-class ICTs for communication. These devices now constitute "the key technological development" in the context of China's "new urban mobility" (Cartier, Castells, and Qiu 2005). The spread of low-end technology services like Internet cafés and Little Smart, in turn, triggers, sustains, and conditions the ongoing migration process.

Working-class ICTs are not just gadgets; they also serve as a set of social, cultural, and political conditions running through migrant populations. ICT connectivity may empower migrants in pursuit of personal objectives. But it may also subject them to new systems of control, exploitation, and alienation and other ways of disempowerment by service providers, employers, or state actors, at work or at home.

Have-less migrants, however, are not only passive end users who are isolated from each other. They include small ICT business owners who know their neighbors well, as well as grassroots content contributors such as migrant worker bloggers, who have fans across the nation. Networked connectivity exists even for many poor migrants who can afford only public pay phones to keep old contacts while forging new bonds. This is a process that highlights the capacity of collective units like household, kin, and peer groups to survive social upheaval and remain functional through their translocal networks, now maintained and extended primarily by working-class ICTs.

Like middle-class social networks, the translocal network of have-less migrants forms an intermediary layer of negotiation, strategizing, and adjustment among its members so that they can act together in response to rapid change. Translocal networks are "networks that reflect multiple place attachments resulting from migratory lifepaths" and were "traditionally maintained through face-to-face communication, postal mail, and telegraph" but now "find convenient and more efficient expression via have-less ICTs" (Cartier, Castells, and Qiu 2005, 24). Translocality has been a central element in the social life of traditional China (Oakes and Schein 2006), and today the use of ICTs strengthens the existing propensity toward translocal networking. The result is not always socially uplifting because collective decision making may fail to yield practical results or produce unintended consequences, including in-group tension and conflict. Whatever happens, these are social processes with all the richness and complexity of human communication. Have-less migrants, thus construed, are interrelated human beings rather than isolated economic animals or rootless floaters (*mangliu*).

Working-class ICTs and translocal networks are also situated within macro social conditions, shaped and constrained by existing urban institutions. Urbanization and industrialization, both occurring in an era of globalization, have a direct impact on new mobility patterns. This chapter first provides an overview of these macrocontexts before examining the more specific relationship between have-less migrants and their working-class ICTs, focusing on the relationship between empowerment and networked connectivity. It then discusses variations among have-less migrants by gender, ethnicity, and regional identity and their translocal networking through working-class ICTs.

Besides secondary data and fieldwork, this chapter also draws findings from six survey groups conducted in 2002 and 2006. A survey group combines quantitative and qualitative methods with participatory empowerment design and action research (see the methodological appendix). It serves as an important empirical basis for this chapter and the next, which focus on relatively marginalized groups that cannot be studied adequately using conventional methods.

Urbanization and Industrialization in the Global Age

Cities are centers of flows—of people, goods, and information. The growth of cities necessarily boosts mobility, thus increasing the demand for information (Meiers 1962). Urbanization, especially in industrializing societies, is often characterized by the emergence of a working class that is seeking more inclusive means of communication. At times, this demand is answered by entrepreneurs who deploy new technologies and create new business models for cheaper modes of information delivery. Historically this was how the penny press emerged in mid-nineteenth-century New York and how television became a popular medium after the 1970s in industrializing Asian societies like Hong Kong. In China today, a similar process is under way as massive urbanization and industrialization are accompanied by the rise of working-class ICTs.

How does Chinese urbanization happen, and with what mobility patterns? Does the increase of migration suggest a retreat of the state, allowing more autonomous grassroots communication? China is late in experiencing urban growth. When Third World urbanization took place globally in the 1960s and 1970s (Castells 1977, Drakakis-Smith 1987), China was relocating people from cities to the countryside. During the Cultural Revolution, the urban population dropped from 17.86 percent of the Chinese population in 1966 to 17.44 percent in 1976.[2]

But in post-Mao China, urbanization accelerated at an extraordinary rate (table 4.1). Within a quarter-century, the State Council designated 469 new cities. The number of large cities with more than 1 million residents grew

Table 4.1
Urban growth in China, 1978–2005

	Total number of cities	Number of cities with more than 1 million urban residents	Urban population (millions)	Urban population as a percentage of total population (%)	Total territories of city areas (km²)
1978	192	13	172.45	17.92	—ᵃ
1990	467	31	301.95	26.41	120,800
2000	663	90	455.94	36.22	441,200
2005	661	113	561.57	42.99	580,055

Sources: Compilation based on *China Population Statistics Yearbook* (2006), *Yearbook of China's Cities* (1991, 2001, 2006), and *China City Statistics Yearbook* (1991, 2001).
ᵃ Data unavailable.

from 13 to 113. The urban population rose from 17.92 percent of the national population to 42.99 percent. Natural increase is only a small part of this. Given the one-child policy and declining birthrates in metropolitan areas, the additional urban population—nearly a quarter of all Chinese—is overwhelmingly from the countryside.

Urban growth also engulfs rural villages at the edge of cities, as shown by the expanding territories of city areas in table 4.1. Although the total number of cities has stabilized since 2000, still 138,855 square kilometers were added to urban territories by 2005, an increase of 31.5 percent. Therefore, these former rural areas being swallowed by cities are now large enough to accommodate new arrivals, thus creating migrant enclaves known as urban villages (*chengzhongcun*).[3] The expansion entails new infrastructures like roads, telecoms, water, and electricity systems, hence producing jobs for have-less migrants. Meanwhile, the enlarged city territories, overburdened with traffic and construction sites, are more difficult to traverse. This adds to the popularity of working-class ICTs among migrants, who need to retrieve information about jobs and housing, contacting families and friends, and coordinating everyday activities in the city.

The spatial expansion of cities precipitates the conversion of agricultural land into real estate, factories, parks, and reservoirs, hence forcing entire communities off their traditional land. The Three Gorges Dam alone will displace at least 1.5 million people by 2009 (*Yangtze River Archives* 2005). In other cases, land takings have caused so many conflicts and even bloodshed that it is not an exaggeration to call this a Chinese Enclosure Movement. In sum, Chinese cities have become more numerous, more populated,

Table 4.2

Distribution of urban employment by enterprise ownership (millions of employees)

	State ownership	Collective ownership	Private and individual ownership	Foreign ownership[a]	Other ownership[b]	Total
1978	74.5	20.5	0.2	—	—	95.1
1990	103.7	35.5	6.7	0.7	1.0	147.3
2000	81.0	15.0	34.0	6.4	13.4	149.8
2004	67.1	9.0	55.2	10.3	23.0	164.5

Source: Compilation based on Almanac of China's Population (2005).
[a] includes enterprises owned by Hong Kong, Macau, Taiwanese, and all foreign entrepreneurs.
[b] includes joint ventures, shareholding companies, joint shareholding companies, and limited liability companies.

and significantly larger than before, with the personal consequences of urbanization being disproportionately shouldered by have-less migrants.

An equally profound change is the restructuring of urban employment. As discussed earlier (see figure 1.2), the privatization of employment provides a key precondition for growing informational needs among the have-less. As shown in table 4.2, in 1978, almost everyone in Chinese cities worked for state or collective ownership work units (danwei), which provided stable jobs and benefits, taking care of workers and their families.[4] But the old socialist model has been decisively eroded, with more people today working for private and foreign enterprises.

Indeed, have-less migrants have gained more mobility, although state policy still matters. The privatization of employment is itself a result of state policy that ended up with more than 30 million laid-off workers between 1989 and 2004 (Hurst 2004), another large addition to the social category of have-less migrants. As table 4.2 shows, between 1990 and 2004, 63.1 million urban employees left the state and collective sectors. Some laid-off workers may be reemployed in their home cities. But to most of them, like those in the rust belts of northeast China, being laid off means the beginning of migration. Like rural-to-urban migrants, laid-off interurban migrants depend on working-class ICTs for information and networking, and in many cases for their own businesses because many of them become microentrepreneurs, selling inexpensive products like prepaid phone cards.

The role of state policy is manifest if we consider factors like the revocation of food rations (*liangpiao*, or food stamps that people had to use to buy food until early 1990s), the loosening of the *hukou* residence registration system that restricted population mobility to a single locale, and the opening up of coastal regions to both internal migration and foreign investment. Without these state decisions, both migration growth and urbanization would have been slower. Power was then decentralized, primarily to local governments and entrepreneurs with personal ties to local officials (Hsing 1997, Oi 1992) rather than to members of the working class at the grassroots level. It is essential to examine individual decisions about migration and ICT adoption in the context of urban transformation.

China's contemporary industrial revolution, like the one in England two centuries ago, has brought about a fundamental restructuring of the economic system and of society itself. This process of industrial growth has Chinese characteristics, of course, but it also epitomizes social transition in a global era when the entire world feels the impact of the transformation of a great nation.

Since China joined the WTO in 2001, we have heard much about the country's trade and investment issues and state policy. The picture is yet another East Asian economic "miracle" built on the joint forces of foreign capital, global trade, and China's unparalleled labor pool and enormous market. What is lacking in this portrayal is, first, the recognition of multiple ties between industrialization during the current phase and the earlier Maoist era. From 1949 to 1979, China's gross industrial output grew from 14 billion to 459.1 billion yuan, an increase of about thirty-two times over thirty years,[5] the result of the CCP's focus on industrialization.

Industrialization under Mao, characterized by central planning and the proletariat ruling class, of course differs from China's industrialization today. Industrial output during that period in history was primarily for domestic consumption, since China was much more isolated from the rest of the world. But there are notable legacies from Mao's era that have facilitated industrialization since 1978. The old socialist state trained large numbers of scientists and engineers, including China's strategic weaponry designers, organized through "open, flexible, networked-based management methods" (Feigenbaum 2003, 6), who played a major role in China's industrialization after the 1980s. Among China's power elite, almost everyone agreed that China had to modernize and go beyond its millennia-old agrarian economy. Industrialism took deep institutional roots, which explains the widespread focus today on high growth in manufacturing as well as the easy acceptance of informationalism as ideologically desirable.

Second, industrialization in the Third World context is nothing new. This is in fact a mirror process of postindustrialization in First World countries, through which blue-collar jobs are relocated to countries with lower labor costs. The relocation is, however, uneven and unstable. During the Cold War, many developing countries attempted to industrialize, usually with help from either of the superpowers. There were many such instances from Asia to Africa to Latin America; only a small number were successful, and most of them are adjacent to China.[6] These are the newly industrialized economies (NIEs) of Hong Kong, Taiwan, Singapore, and South Korea, all significantly influencing China's industrialization and forming a regional dynamic that continues to influence the path of industrialization in China today (Cartier 2001). A result of this regional dynamic, which reflects global restructuring, is the concentration of labor-intensive, export-oriented industries in coastal China.

Since the beginning of economic reform in 1978, China's secondary sector, consisting of manufacture and construction, grew faster than its national economy. Consequently, the percentage of people employed in the secondary sector increased from 17.3 in 1978 to 25.2 in 2006 (table 4.3). However, the GDP share of the secondary sector increased by only 0.5 percent over this period and its employment share by 7.9 percent. Although these are significant changes on top of the rapid expansion of the national economy, the patterns here are not the overall industrialization of the fundamental structure of economy. Still, manufacturing and construction account for only a quarter of China's total workforce.

Why are so many people around the world today feeling China's rising industrial power? Isn't the country actually becoming a "world factory"? There are several answers to these questions, including the size of China, for it simply takes longer to transform a large economy, and a single-digit change in China's labor distribution can have significant global ramifications.

Structurally, the impact of industrialization is most obvious in the primary sector (i.e., mostly agriculture in the Chinese context), whose share of employment decreased from 70.5 to 42.6 percent between 1978 and 2006. This means that more than a quarter of China's total labor force—the size of all employment in the United States—has migrated from the primary sector. After leaving agriculture, most of these overwhelmingly blue-collar laborers joined the tertiary or services sector, whose share in total employment almost tripled. Although the tertiary sector continues to absorb labor from agriculture, its GDP share has not been increasing at a comparable speed. This indicates that the new service jobs do not

Table 4.3
China's GDP and employment: Total amount and percentage shares of the primary, secondary, and tertiary sectors

	Total amount		Primary sector (%)		Secondary sector (%)		Tertiary sector (%)	
	GDP[a]	Employment[b]	GDP	Employment	GDP	Employment	GDP	Employment
1978	362.4	401.5	28.1	70.5	48.2	17.3	23.7	12.2
1990	1,854.8	647.5	27.1	60.1	41.6	21.4	31.3	18.5
2000	8,946.8	711.5	15.9	50.0	50.9	22.5	33.2	27.5
2006	21,087.1	764.0	11.8	42.6	48.7	25.2	39.5	32.2

Sources: Compilation based on *Almanac of China's Economy* (1981–2005) and J. Li (2005).

Note: The primary sector includes such economic realms as agriculture, forestry, fishery, and husbandry. The secondary sector encompasses all industrial activities, from manufacture and construction to chemical and energy industries. The tertiary sector, also known as the service sector, includes businesses like retail, entertainment, telecommunications, healthcare, banking, and legal services.

[a] In billion yuan.
[b] In millions of employees.

necessarily contribute to higher productivity. China now has more lawyers and engineers than before, however, they constitute only a small portion of the new tertiary-sector jobs. But when it comes to the majority of the new jobs for have-less migrants, most become waitresses, janitors, taxi drivers, security guards, or street vendors.

Most important, the growth of the service industry in China does not imply postindustrialization. Instead, it is a centerpiece in China's current phase of industrialization, which encompasses transportation, marketing, advertising, and telecommunications. These are not manufacturing jobs per se, but they were the weakest link of Maoist industrialism. These services allow Chinese firms and the new working class to participate in the global economy on a massive scale.

The composition of China's trading commodities demonstrates a clear pattern of industrialization (table 4.4). Today China's exports and imports are primarily industrial goods: raw materials, parts, and semiprocessed or fully processed products for the secondary sector. High ratios of industrial goods in both imports and exports mean that China's industrialization is highly dependent on external partners for both the input of resources and market output.

When foreign investments arrive in China, they concentrate on the most profitable sectors, thus giving rise to unbalanced development, which further alters the economic structure. One such sector is electronics, which has been remarkably transformed as industrial leadership has shifted from

Table 4.4
China's participation in the global economy: Imports and exports, foreign direct investment, and share of industrial goods

	Total imports and exports[a]	Exports value[a]	Trade surplus[a]	Foreign direct investment[a]	Industrial goods as a percentage of total exports	Industrial goods as a percentage of total imports
1980	38.1	18.12	−1.9	—[b]	49.7	65.2
1990	115.4	62.09	8.7	3.5	74.4	81.5
2000	474.3	249.21	24.1	40.7	89.8	79.2
2006	1,760.4	968.9	177.5	73.5	94.5	76.4

Source: China Trade and External Economic Statistical Yearbook (2007).
[a] Billions of U.S. dollars.
[b] Data unavailable.

Table 4.5
Transformation of China's electronics industry, 1985–2006

Ownership type	Industrial output (billion yuan)			Number of employees (thousands)			Export value (billion yuan)
	1985	1995	2006	1985	1995	2006	2006
State owned	70.0	37.4	11.7	65.9	58.9	275.3	27.0
Collective	19.9	12.3	6.2	29.2	19.9	138.4	14.6
Shareholding[a]	—	7.4	39.8	—	6.2	813.8	99.9
Foreign[b]	4.8	41.0	298.3	1.0	12.8	4,328.4	2,126.5
Other	5.3	1.9	21.5	3.9	2.1	708.0	42.5

Sources: Compilation based on *PRC 1985 Industry Census Materials Volume 7: Electronics Industry* (1988); *Collection of Data from the Third Census of the Electronics Industry* (1996); *Yearbook of China's Information Industry* (2007).
[a] Includes shareholding and joint shareholding enterprises.
[b] Includes all enterprises owned or jointly owned by Hong Kong, Taiwan, Macau, and all foreign companies.

state-owned enterprises (SOEs) to foreign-owned and Chinese-foreign joint ventures, as shown in table 4.5.[7] In 2004, these transborder network enterprises generated 91.9 percent of China's export value in electronics.[8] The percentage grew to 94.5 in 2006.

With the great leap in electronics exports, Chinese industrial products, including key ICTs like personal computers and mobile phones, have surged in their global shares, often playing a leading role in the market (table 4.6). Work in this globally oriented industrial system, occurring primarily in recently urbanized and still urbanizing regions, provides a concrete organizational foundation that sustains the flow of have-less migrants at the lower strata of China's enlarged network society.

Between Diffusion and Empowerment

How, then, are working-class ICTs being adopted and appropriated by have-less migrants, with what empowerment or disempowerment effects, and under the macrocontext of urbanization, industrialization, and globalization?

Fu is my hairdresser in Shenzhen. He comes from Sichuan and works in a salon owned by a Taiwanese boss. He goes online regularly because his workplace is equipped with online computers that he can use for free. Through the Internet, he learns the latest hair styles and techniques.

Table 4.6
Chinese global market shares of selected industries, 2005

Product	Global market share of Chinese production (%)
ICTs	
Personal computers	35
Mobile phones	37
Digital cameras	more than 50
Television sets	40
Others	
Air conditioners	50
Refrigerators	30
Microwave ovens	51
Marine containers	70
Cranes	50
Sewing machines	70
Ties	40
Toys	60
Lighters	70

Source: Compilation based on Zeng and Williamson (2007).

In March 2007, Fu asked me, "What is a search engine?" He asked the question as if it were an object, like the engine of a car. It turned out he always went online by typing in Web addresses and then just clicking from there, although he has been a regular Internet user for several years. He had no opportunity to learn about and use search engines as his upper-class clients do, and he thought that was fine. But in March 2007, he felt a strong need to learn about search engines because, after being at this job for a long time, he had decided to move on.

Anecdotes like this are seldom analyzed systematically. While scholars have long studied domestic migrants in Chinese cities, they usually attend to basic social, economic, and political issues like housing and the household registration system (Cheng and Selden 1994, L. Zhang 2001), employment and spatial mobility (Fan 1999, Y. Zhao 2003), and poverty alleviation (Huang and Domenach-Chich 2006). While some have looked at the role of communication in migration (W. Sun 2002), including the use of inexpensive mobile phones and SMS (Ma 2006, Law 2006), these are exceptions rather than the rule.

It is difficult to study migrants, especially have-less migrants in urban China, due to problems in data gathering. Most studies of migrants use qualitative methods like ethnography, in-depth interviews, and focus groups, which tend to be relatively weak in identifying general patterns across the population. Quantitative research is equally problematic because census and other official data usually do a poor job of including have-less migrants, especially their media communication patterns. Although researchers can carry out surveys, sampling remains a major challenge because probability sampling is often impossible (Manion 1994). Consequently, most surveys about migrants and media are based on a one-shot convenience sampling design (Cao and Liu 2006).

I tackled this problem using a survey group design that combines quantitative and qualitative methods with action research, which provides the basis for more general discussions about the diffusion of working-class ICTs and media empowerment among have-less migrants. Each survey group consisted of three to five young migrant workers whom I hired from the labor market as survey administrators. Over four days, we worked closely together on a survey about the uses and perceptions of ICTs. This process helped build rapport among team members and empowered migrants to become grassroots opinion leaders, who then spoke out in a focus group at the end of the survey period (see the details in the methodological appendix).

Six survey groups were held in two waves in 2002 and 2006, in Guangzhou, Shenzhen, and Zhuhai in the Pearl River Delta of Guangdong Province. Although this was not a national sample and was still based on purposive sampling, the design ensured quality data by empowering migrants and building up the group dynamics. Rogers and Singhal (2003), wrote that "the empowerment process fundamentally consists of dialogic communication. Individuals gain a belief in their power to achieve desired goals through talking with others, particularly peers . . . especially in small groups" (82). The result of this work was a rare data set that reflects change over time in this crucial region of South China that not only attracts the largest number of migrant workers but also plays a key role in China's export-oriented ICT industry.

Most survey group participants were young female migrants earning an average monthly income of 1,400 yuan (about $170) or no income because they had just graduated or were between jobs. After I cleaned up the data, the survey group consisted of 390 migrants (184 in 2002 and 206 in 2006), with about equal numbers of males and females. On average, these respondents were young (their average age was twenty-five), they earned about 1,350 yuan ($165) per month, and they had a high school education. They typically had lived in the city for three years, working in factories, at construction sites, or as sales personnel, clerks, and servers.

Table 4.7

Diffusion and monthly expenses of working-class ICTs among migrants in Guangzhou, Shenzhen, and Zhuhai

		Internet	Mobile phone	Home phone
Average monthly expense (yuan)	2002	108.8	242.0	157.5
	2006	96.2	111.2	27.9
Percentage change		*−11.6*	*−54.0*	*−82.3*
Diffusion (%)	2002	49.5	58.2	43.5
	2006	76.7	83.5	25.2
Percentage change		*27.2*	*25.3*	*−18.3*

Table 4.7 summarizes the trends about ICTs and have-less migrants. The overall change from 2002 to 2006 demonstrates two basic patterns. First, the cost of ICTs decreased significantly: the Internet fell by 11.6 percent, mobile phones by 54 percent, and homes phones (including landline phones at home and Little Smart) by 82.3 percent. Second, ICT diffusion greatly increased for most ICT services (the Internet by 27.3 percent and mobile phones by 25.3 percent) except home phones, which fell by 18.3 percent. This pattern of falling costs coupled with rising diffusion was identified in focus groups and field observations as well, although table 4.6 shows the specifics using comparable data collection methods in 2002 and 2006.

By 2006, large percentages of have-less migrants could use the Internet (76.7 percent) and had their own mobile phones (83.5 percent). If counting other forms of ICT connectivity such as landline phone at work, pay phone, and pager, only two respondents in 2002 had no ICT connectivity. In other words, the overwhelming majority (98.9 percent) of migrants surveyed in 2002 and everyone in 2006 had some form of connectivity.

The data reveal unique patterns of ICT diffusion among have-less migrants. Official statistics at the national level report home connection as the most important Internet access among Chinese netizens, followed by access at work (CNNIC, 2002, 2006). But in this sample, home access was used by only 17.5 percent of migrant Internet users, of whom 26.2 percent also went online at work. The most prominent method of Internet access was the cybercafé, accounting for 77 percent of Internet users in this sample.

While asked how they learned to go online, 46.5 percent of these migrant netizens identified the cybercafé, by far the most important place for first-time Internet users among migrants. Cybercafés are popular due to their low cost. Because most of these have-less migrants tend to have low incomes, little technical knowledge, a small place to live, and a highly mobile lifestyle, the cost of having their own personal computer would be prohibitive.

Cost has a similar effect for mobile phone diffusion. Between 2002 and 2006, the price for mobile handsets and per-minute charges dropped significantly. Have-less migrants could select from many more service packages in 2006 than they could in 2002, including prepaid services. Between the two phases of the study, the most significant change was the upsurge of SMS users from 13.1 percent of mobile phone owners in 2002 to 95.4 percent in 2006. On average, each respondent sent 12.5 SMSs every day in 2006. Price advantage was a main reason for this upsurge, which in turn drove up mobile phone penetration.

However, cost was not the only factor, as shown by the data on home phones. There was a dramatic price drop of 82.3 percent between 2002 and 2006 due to competition from low-end mobile services and the introduction of Little Smart wireless phone (counted as part of the home phone market in the official regulatory system). Yet the total uptake of home phone services still fell by 18.3 percent. As I learned in the focus groups, the decreasing popularity of home phones had to do with the poor perception of the service quality of Little Smart and the discriminatory treatment of migrant customers by the telcos. The increasing affordability of mobile services was another important reason for the decline of home phones. The focus groups revealed that home phones were used mostly for local calls; higher-income migrants tended to place long-distance calls on their mobile phones and lower-income migrants tended to do so using pay phones. As population mobility continues to rise, migrants have a greater need for long-distance calls rather than local calls only.

We can see that the diffusion of working-class ICTs is a complex process that involves both economic and noneconomic factors, above and beyond the technologies. While the general trend of falling prices and rising adoption can be observed, specific patterns vary depending on market dynamics as well as decision making by individual migrants.

After ICT adoption, how do have-less migrants use and appropriate these working-class modalities of communication? As mentioned in chapter 1, typical practices of working-class connectivity include going online at a cybercafé and using a pay phone, Little Smart, prepaid services, or SMS instead of mobile voice call. These distinct modes of networked connectivity are shaped to meet particular goals based on the broadly defined informational needs of have-less migrants as well as popular perceptions of ICTs that sometimes stem from the messages of advertising.

A common ICT practice among have-less migrants is the wide spread of QQ, a successful Chinese online chatting service. QQ can be accessed using computers and, increasingly, mobile phones. It is the most prevalent platform for online personal communication among migrants, most of whom do not have an e-mail address even after going online regularly for years. Unlike MSN Messenger, which is used more by white-collar professionals, QQ allows users to chat with strangers outside their existing social network. Yu, for example, is an office clerk from Guizhou and worked in Zhuhai for five years. In a 2002 focus group she was proud about the friends she had made through QQ: "My Net friends are all super. There are many questions about the Internet that I don't know. I go online to chat with them and they are always helpful. . . . The first time [I asked people questions online] was when I began to use QQ chatting, when I went home [in Guizhou] for the Chinese New Year. I was bored. So a friend got me started using QQ, which was actually quite simple. After I came back [to Zhuhai], I found out that many of my friends here were also using it [laugh]." In this case, existing social relationships functioned as a basis for the extension of Yu's network in cyberspace. The Net friends helped Yu learn more about the Internet. They also include Yu's friends in Zhuhai, thus facilitating her integration in the destination city.

Because survey group members were recruited from local labor markets, they were eager to discuss the role ICTs play in job hunting. A consensus was reached that the mobile phone is indispensable to finding a job. But when asked who actually received calls from future employers, most groups failed to give specific examples except one Guangzhou group. A participant in Zhuhai said, "Gee, I never thought about this. No boss ever called my mobile phone. But I always feel I can't find a job without it!" According to the survey groups, the most useful employment information still came from traditional interpersonal networks.

An unexpected but recurrent theme in discussing their job-hunting experiences was about the potential danger associated with ICT connectivity rather than the actual employment opportunities. In all six groups, participants talked about various ways of cheating—for instance, by posting fake information on human resources Web sites and sending scam SMS or QQ messages to job seekers usually asking migrants to pay a fee to secure a job. A Guangzhou migrant said, "They can cheat more people because now they no longer need to see people face-to-face [due to the technology]." Another respondent in Shenzhen who was victimized exclaimed,

"Shenzhen is full of cheats—in the job market, in the streets, and on the Internet!"

The most striking observation from these discussions is the high level of awareness among all survey group members of the potential dangers of ICT connectivity. Even those who appeared to be shy became articulate in talking about these dangers; knowing how to prevent a scam is essential for have-less migrants in labor markets.

Another prominent topic is the entertainment function of working-class ICTs, especially of cybercafés, which serve mostly young migrants. Why is entertainment content so important to have-less migrants? It in fact has little to do with their low income or low levels of education since entertainment is a basic media function, even for the upper classes. However, entertainment, especially commercial entertainment, is magnified by service and content providers. As one participant in Shenzhen disclosed in 2006, "I want to read more news but it's hard to find it on the Web sites I know. They are all full of commercials."

The general lack of news is only the tip of iceberg. Underneath the seemingly endless choices of entertainment programs and content, it is in fact difficult for have-less migrants to find a wide range of basic information that they need, especially if the information delivery is not profitable for the service or content providers.

Even so, the most frequently used adjective in all group discussions turned out to be *convenient*: "The Internet is really convenient." "Mobile phone makes everything convenient." "SMS, that's so convenient indeed." The perception of inconvenience is then used to discredit other "outdated" services such as pagers: "Who still uses the pager? It's so inconvenient!" This is a common response in discussing this outmoded working-class ICT.

The only exception was a female insurance representative. Responding to others' critiques on pager use in 2002, she said, "Pagers are in fact not that inconvenient. You can see who's trying to find you, and then you decide if and when you want to call back. It saves mobile phone expenses. It was quite helpful to me." This exceptional comment was buried in widespread perceptions among other members, not too different from elite perceptions, that the latest, more expensive ICTs are more "convenient" and the older ones needed "upgrading." While the practices of working-class ICT connectivity vary significantly from upper-class practices, the two may converge at the perceptual level.

The mismatch between practice and perception can best be found in the comments migrant participants make about the mobile phone. For most of them, the mobile phone is the most expensive item that they have ever purchased. It is also the most important status marker for their new-found urban identity. But the device and monthly expenses were expensive in 2002. In 2006, the handsets became more affordable, but the cost of calls was still very expensive for most migrants. One of them confessed, "We can buy a mobile but can barely feed it [can barely pay the phone bill]."

A more extreme pattern was disclosed by Xiao Wu, a male participant: "I know people who were broke in Shenzhen. They had to sell their phones to some private boss to have the money to go home." The mobile phone in this sense is not only an indicator for modern urban identity. It is also the last ticket for have-less migrants to get out of the city.

Empowerment can happen on multiple dimensions—economic, social, cultural, or political. For our purposes here, empowerment is "the process through which individuals perceive that they control situations" (Rogers and Singhal 2003, 67). To explore the effects of working-class ICTs on empowerment and disempowerment requires looking at three key variables. First, migrants' socioeconomic status (SES), measured by income and education, represents an internal stratification among have-less migrants. Second, ICT connectivity, taking into account the ownership and uses of Internet and telephone connection, represents empowerment because it indicates the inclusion of have-less migrants in an active network of two-way communication. Third, the percentage of migrants' monthly income spent on working-class ICTs represents disempowerment for those who lose control over their budget.

The results of correlation analysis, controlling for respondents' gender, age, and residential tenure, show that have-less migrants with higher SES enjoy higher ICT connectivity. The relationship is rather strong, with a coefficient of .53 ($p < .001$). This should be no surprise: migrants with more financial and educational resources tend to own more ICTs and use them most frequently and longer. However, better-educated migrants with more income do not necessarily have more control over their ICT budget. The relationship is very weak between SES and the percentage of income being spent on ICTs (coefficient = .04, $p > .05$). This is true for both males and females, in all age groups, and groups with different residential tenure in the host cities.

Finally, migrants with higher ICT connectivity tend to be more likely to lose control over their ICT budget (coefficient = .34, $p < .001$). This is in a way counterintuitive because those who are more empowered in ICT connectivity also tend to be more disempowered in terms of commercial alienation in using ICTs. However, it is also understandable because high-connectivity migrants, regardless of their SES, tend to develop more dependence on ICTs. This dependence may stem from their realistic needs, such as retrieving work- or family-related information, but also from perceptions promoted by advertising and marketing campaigns, imposed by peer group pressure, or internalized as personal desires for a "modern" and "urban" lifestyle, if not pure vanity. This means that while ICT connectivity creates openings for empowerment and upward social mobility, it also paves the way for alienation and disempowerment in the context of an overwhelmingly commercialized urban society.

Internal Variations

A basic finding from this analysis is that have-less migrants are not a single homogeneous group in terms of their socioeconomic positioning and ICT connectivity. Instead, there is significant internal variation, which this section examines more closely along the lines of in-group stratification, gender, ethnicity, and regional identity. Existing research on the internal variation of have-less migrants is uneven. Although many studies are concerned about peasant workers (*nongmingong*) and "working sisters" (*dagong-mei* or young female migrant workers), empirical data remain patchy and incomplete regarding the groups and subgroups. The purpose here is to explore the characteristics of differentiation among have-less migrants based on what is known from previous studies and my own fieldwork. Important is to note that scrutinizing internal differentiation here does not preclude the formation of a new working class among have-less migrants or imply that the divisions, all of which time honored, will exist only in the short run.

In-Group Stratification
The first basic variation is in-group stratification, which has to do with not only socioeconomic status but also the cultural and political positioning of have-less migrants. When China's massive migration began in the 1980s, the class composition of migrants was more homogeneous: the majority were rural-to-urban migrants who found jobs that city dwellers would not take. After twenty years, the situation has changed with the increase of interurban migrants, laid-off workers, and more internal stratification among rural-to-urban migrants.

Today we can find migrants in almost every stratum of the urban social hierarchy. A tiny proportion of them have worked their way up from the have-less position to the upper class, at least in a strict economic sense. These are usually diligent and entrepreneurial individuals who joined the market economy early on. In other cases, have-less migrants may have picked up skills in the destination city through training or self-learning and entered the white-collar world as clerks, technicians, salespersons, and managers. In Foshan, Guangdong Province, more than sixty thousand have become technicians and managers in local enterprises (Cui 2004a). In this and other cities with large migrant populations, night schools prosper by teaching word processing, foreign languages, and other skills for finding nonmanufacturing jobs. Although working in a low-end white-collar position does not guarantee a higher income, it does confer more prestige and more opportunities to move up the social ladder.

There are also self-employed migrants with small businesses who make enough just to feed their family. These are the average shopkeepers who run restaurants, convenience stores, and newsstands, selling all kinds of products, including domestic-brand handsets and prepaid phone cards. They make up a large proportion of the expanding tertiary sector. Although it is common for these microentrepreneurs to have some employees, most of them still do some manual work. Nevertheless, much of their income and social status are derived from their ownership of the business rather than the manual work itself.

Nevertheless, the majority of have-less migrants are still overwhelmingly laborers who rely on performing manual labor at low wages. This group is China's new blue-collar industrial workers, consisting mostly of migrants from the countryside and, to a lesser extent, state and collective sector workers, many of whom were laid off in recent years. In such industries as coal mining and urban construction, employees almost exclusively have rural origins. In manufacturing and transportation, the proportion of laid-off workers can be higher, although an even larger portion of them tend to enter the service sector by starting small businesses like cybercafés.[9]

Blue-collar workers are also internally stratified, with some of the more skilled ones becoming labor aristocracy, such as those who operate sophisticated machinery.[10] These skilled manual workers are usually well paid and may have a range of employment benefits. Despite the absence of unions, these benefits are likely to be maintained and perhaps improved because Chinese industries are becoming more capital intensive and skilled manual labor is in short supply.

Yet the great majority of blue-collar workers are highly exploited. Zhang Li's study in Beijing found that in small family-owned garment businesses, female workers commonly toil more than fifteen hours a day using a sewing machine (L. Zhang 2001). Pun's ethnographic research conducted in a computer factory in Shenzhen revealed that a day-shift "working sister" is usually on the production line from 8:00 A.M. to 9:00 or 10:00 P.M. except for short lunch and dinner breaks (2005).

At the national policy level, the most prominent issue is the delay in paying migrant workers. This was highlighted in 2003 when Premier Wen Jiabao demanded that all overdue wages be immediately paid (H. Lu 2005). The central government has taken important measures to protect workers' rights, although policy implementation at the local level remains uneven. Despite this increased attention to unpaid wages thanks to the prolabor policies of the Hu-Wen administration, other problems persist. Most migrant workers still have few employment benefits as required by law. Waitresses are often not allowed to use landline phones in restaurants. And assembly line workers are often forbidden to bring their mobile phones to work.[11]

In more basic terms other than the right to communicate, sweatshop owners often confiscate migrants' personal identity cards to prevent them from leaving. Even worse, some workers were fired when they become older and could not move so quickly or were disabled. According to a report by the Shanghai Academy of Social Sciences, each year about forty thousand fingers are either cut off or crushed in factories in the Pearl River Delta alone, mostly during assembly line operations for the export business (Barboza 2008a). Yet in this region, it takes an average of 1,070 days for workers to claim compensation for work injuries (China Labor Watch 2007). This is yet another manifestation of the personal consequences of industrialization and globalization that are disproportionately borne by have-less migrants. It has led to rising informational needs among migrant workers in order to seek legal protection. This demand provides a social basis for the formation of new working-class networks and the emergence of network labor.

Besides the traditional strata of white-collar and blue-collar work, the rise of China's ICT industry is blurring the division of labor between manual and nonmanual work, and between disposable generic labor and valued self-programmable labor as identified in the original framework of network society (Castells 1998). This recent development in Chinese informationalism is best exemplified by the growing importance of gray-collar (*huiling*) workers, including the so-called software blue-collar workers (*ruanjian lanling*) who do both manual and informational tasks at the lower-middle levels of the new industrial system.

Gray-collar workers are graphic designers, database operators, technicians, software testers, and others who engage in repetitive work procedures in the production process. The job often requires working with computers and some aspect of data entry and processing. The work procedure relies on the worker's hands as well as his or her mind. The SMS authors (*duanxun xieshou*) employed by China's ICPs belong to this category (Lan 2005). So do the online-game "gold farmers," organized as guilds or workshops to collect virtual property, to be sold for real-world currency to gamers in the United States, Japan, and Taiwan (H. He 2005). Since 2005, the business of gold farming has moved from coastal South China to inland provinces, where lower labor costs allow larger-scale operation and a higher profit margin.[12] In Wuhan, central China, there were more than two thousand so-called black gaming workshops in 2007 (Han and Yang 2007).

The supply of gray-collar workers lags far behind the demand of the growing ICT industry, which adds to the prominence of this new category of labor (L. Wang, Xu, and Huang 2004; D. Wang and Yang 2004). MII statistics showed that in 2005, China had about 100,000 software blue-collar workers, but the demand in the software industry was 460,000 (MII Personnel Bureau 2006). Shanghai, for example, needed 13,800 gray-collar workers in 2002, but the supply was only 3,800. The municipal government has therefore endeavored to train gray-collar workers in the city and attract them from elsewhere (L. Wang, Xu, and Huang 2004), thus expanding this lower-middle layer of workers in between the white- and blue-collar strata.

The income and status of gray-collar workers in China's new content business, such as SMS production and virtual property trading, vary greatly depending on the person's qualifications, skill level, and the overall market demand at the time of hiring. Yet these are similar structures of flexible and networked labor reorganization through which a new layer of informational workers, programmable labor, is added between generic and self-programmable labor.

The creation of programmable labor at the lower strata of the informational work process is more than an increase of gray-collar workers and the addition of another new layer in the production hierarchy. It is about complex cross-strata collaboration. As Zeng and Williamson (2007) argue, Chinese firms can outcompete companies in the global market not just because China has cheap labor, but because they can fundamentally restructure the production process based on the reality of Chinese labor and, in so doing, make a huge variety of products in an unprecedentedly cost-effective manner to meet rapidly changing market demands.

The best example of programmable labor working closely with self-programmable as well as generic labor is BYD, a battery manufacturer in Shenzhen, which by one account had about half of the world's market share for wireless phone batteries (Fishman 2005). Zeng and Willamson (2007) examined BYD's production model and found it has outcompeted Japanese firms like Sanyo and Toshiba, which dominated this market almost exclusively in 1995. But in the short span of a few years, the global market shares of BYD batteries skyrocketed to 75 percent in cordless phones and 28 percent in mobile phones.

The key to BYD's success is an innovative system of "process flexibility" that uses constantly trained and programmed migrant workers in the production process to replace standard machinery, which is expensive to purchase, maintain, and adjust to meet changing market needs (Zeng and Williamson 2007). A typical production line at BYD has a daily output of 100,000 nickel-cadmium (NiCad) batteries (a low-end battery for cordless phone):

It required about 2,000 workers, compared with just 200 needed to run a Japanese line with the same capacity. But the BYD line could be up and running for just 6 percent of the $100 million Japanese competitors would have to invest. One investment bank estimated that this meant financing and depreciation costs were slashed from 40 percent of total costs at Sanyo to 3 percent at BYD. Even with the extra labor required, BYD could produce a NiCad battery for a total cost of $1, compared with costs of $5 to $6 incurred by rivals in Japan. (Zeng and Williamson 2007, 74)

The BYD production model is impossible to use in industrialized economies like Japan due to its high labor costs. It is also impossible in other developing countries with a dearth of starting-level engineers and technicians, especially low-rank self-programmable and programmable labor involved in the manufacturing process. In this way, the BYD model is labor intensive not only in the conventional sense of blue-collar labor being deployed in manual work but in the constant training of assembly line workers, mixing them up with R&D personnel, and the adjustment of key equipment by skilled and semiskilled laborers collaborating with each other. Consequently, BYD can "switch to making a new product within weeks, compared with the three months required to retool a competitor's automated line," which "made BYD very attractive to the mobile industry, who are constantly under pressure to introduce new product ranges into the market quickly" (Zeng and Williamson 2007, 75–76).

The extraordinarily low cost of flexibility in this new Chinese model of labor reorganization refers only to the economic cost for the company and its corporate clients in the wireless phone industry. It does not reflect the full human cost incurred on the part of the low-end self-programmable labor, programmable labor, and generic labor being used as substitutes for computers and machinery. Describing the production process at Chint, which makes transformers and power supply units, Zeng and Williamson write, "These manual lines didn't even have a conveyor belt; when they finished a subassembly stage, the young workers simply snapped on a rubber band to hold it together, then someone else picked it up and delivered it to the next step in the production line" (2007, 77).

What is going on here is a twenty-first-century rendering in the electronics industry of Frederick Taylor's scientific management system that used "simplified unskilled jobs" to power the booming American auto industry in the early 1900s (Zinn 2001, 324). The persistence of simplified unskilled jobs in Chinese informationalism is not to deny the more innovative development of simplified skilled jobs or programmable labor as in the case of BYD's process flexibility. However, the underlying principles of labor management remain the same with respect to the division of labor among the hierarchical strata of employees and the treatment of bottom-level workers as standard parts, be they screwdrivers, conveyor belts, or computer chips, all attached to the assembly line.

This model of flexible yet labor-intensive production creates jobs for have-less migrants, but it also subjects them to dangerous working conditions, resulting in serious injuries. As discussed earlier, forty thousand fingers are lost each year in the Pearl River Delta, many in the process of making desktop computer cases. The problematic labor process is also responsible for occupational diseases like the chronic illness developed among workers in battery factories, for example, in the GP Battery International Ltd. (China Labor Watch 2007).

As in all other social groups, internal stratification among migrants reflects variations in education and gender. The class status of have-less migrants is also influenced by their geographical origins, especially if they are from the countryside. A migrant from rural Anhui and another from the rust belt in Liaoning may have a similar ability to work at the counter of an Internet café, but the former is likely to face more discrimination. Because of her accent and the way she dresses, people can tell whether she is of rural or urban origin, which will then influence the way she is treated as an employee.

While rural-to-urban migrants do not identify easily with interurban migrants, the gap is even deeper between them and the urban underclass of the host cities. In some places, this is due to the tension artificially created by local states, which frequently fire large numbers of migrant workers in order to create jobs for those who are newly laid off in the city (S. Zhao 2004). In other cases, underemployed urban youth from the local communities as well as others from nearby regions constitute a large portion of the urban control system, including not only the police but also a variety of security guard forces who often abuse and exploit have-less migrants, hence worsening the tension and conflict between locals and nonlocals (S. Zhao 2004, 2005a).

At the very bottom of the social structure of have-less migrants are the millions who seek livelihoods outside the formal and legal economic system. This includes the informal economy, which encompasses an army of unregulated laborers, as well as unemployed individuals and organized criminals. Counterfeit goods and products create their own production, transportation, wholesale, and retail jobs, usually involving poor migrants at each step (Booth 2000). Gangs and criminal groups often include rural-to-urban migrants and laid-off workers, not because they are by nature deviants but because society has failed to absorb them.

The criminal offenses are internally structured in a way that defies the typical stigma imposed on migrant workers. The overwhelming majority of crimes committed by rural-to-urban migrants have to do with property (theft and robbery), whereas more serious nonproperty crimes like fraud, drug dealing, and the trafficking of women and children tend to be committed more by interurban migrants and local residents (S. Zhao 2004, 357).

Even within this lowest stratum of have-less migrants, the spread of working-class ICTs is remarkable, as evidenced by the huge market of used handsets, many of which have been stolen and then pawned in exchange for food and shelter.[13] Meanwhile, any casual observation of downtown Guangzhou or the back streets of Shanghai cannot miss the many mobile phone numbers that are written, painted, or sprayed on pavements, walls, light poles, and phone booths. Most of these are for the sale of fake documents, especially personal identification cards, while others are for private detectives and professional debt recovery (by force and coercion). Each of these many phone numbers represents a have-less individual or a group of them who do not have a stable job but can afford a mobile phone.

As Castells and Portes point out, "The informal economy simultaneously encompasses flexibility and exploitation, productivity and abuse, aggressive entrepreneurs and defenseless workers, libertarianism and greed-iness" (1989, 11). It is thus not surprising that the Internet and mobile phones are already adopted to coordinate activities in both the informal economy and criminal networks. One such trade is the once prevailing blood business in Beijing, where the recruiters, known as blood heads (*xuetou*), use online advertisements to attract needy migrants who can access the Internet, most likely through cybercafés. The migrants then sold their blood for a small fee to blood heads, who made a profit by trading the blood at a higher price. In so doing, the migrants could be subjected to HIV infection, and there was a high risk of contamination of the blood products (L. Hu 2005). This underground trade continues and remains a major threat to public health, especially in central and northern China, despite repeated efforts to stop it at the policy level.

Gender

If we take internal stratification as a vertical system that goes from white collar to gray collar, from programmable labor to blue-collar generic labor to street-corner societies, then gender works on a less hierarchical and more relational dimension. Socioeconomic stratification is fundamental but not something that explains all variation within the have-less population. Gender relationship is ubiquitous and by no means a secondary factor in deciding migration patterns, migrant experiences, and the ways female and male migrants use working-class ICTs.

In traditional Chinese society, women were a dominated group. The CCP attempted to smash the Confucian family order in its early years, but Communist rule under Mao in fact reinforced patriarchal values, especially in rural areas (Stacey 1983, Johnson 1983, M. Yang 1999). A peculiar conse-quence of the Chinese revolution was reflected in the employment of Chinese women. According data from United Nations Development Program (UNDP), China was among the world's top countries in terms of its female employment rate. However, compared to their male counter-parts, the wages of Chinese women who were not in agricultural work were among the lowest in the world (Borja and Castells 1997).

With the acceleration of economic growth, gender relationship in China has become even more complicated with the increase of social mobility among the female population. What we see today among have-less migrant females is no longer submission to their fathers, husbands, and male super-visors. Overall, females have gained new autonomy while also facing new dangers of suppression. This complex process is both reflected and rein-forced by the recent adoption of ICTs among have-less migrant women.

Despite the huge amount of Chinese-language research on migrant workers and despite the vibrancy of the new feminist movement in Chinese cities, mainstream migration scholarship inside China has been wearing blinders on gender issues with only a few exceptions (Bu 2007). Many of these are well-established researchers who are keenly sensitive to social inequality in class and stratification. Yet they often implicitly assume that a prototypical migrant is a man, so therefore female migrants do not deserve separate attention. This attitude is also common among high-rank Internet policymakers in Beijing.[14]

In sharp contrast, among English-language publications, gender issues are central to mainstream scholarship on Chinese migrants. Besides volumes by C. K. Lee (1998) and Pun (2005) on working sisters (*dagongmei*) in the factories of Guangdong (not coincidentally, electronics factories in both cases), other studies, such as Zhang's, have emphasized gender problems within the families of microentrepreneurs in Beijing (L. Zhang 2001). There is also an edited volume by Gaetano and Jacka (2004) devoted to women from rural areas, who take up urban jobs ranging from bar hostesses to nannies.

Female have-less migrants have distinctive migration patterns independent of the movement of male migrants, as shown by three in-depth analyses of data from the 1990 census (Fan 1999, Y. Huang 2001, Liang and Chen 2004). According to Fan, although both males and females migrate to seek industrial and service jobs in China's coastal regions, on a national scale a much larger portion of females migrate to live with their husbands. Within Guangdong Province, the most favored destination of migration, females tend to be overwhelmingly concentrated in the more industrialized part of the Pearl River Delta, whereas the spatial distribution of male migrants is much more spread out in the province (Fan 1999). This is consistent with my observation that while most females live in large factory dormitories in the manufacturing zones, more males work on transportation and construction projects that require higher intraprovincial mobility. Besides this difference, Fan also maintained that when moving across provincial boundaries, females tend to travel longer distances than males. From another study, we learned that some of these have-less women emigrated to New York City and found work in the garment industry there (Bao 2001).

Given these findings, it is not surprising that females use working-class ICTs differently from males. In the general population, the gender gap in Internet access has been narrowing, with the male-female ratio declining from 7.13 to 1 in October 1997 to 1.34 to 1 in January 2008 (CNNIC 1997, 2008). Gender inequality, however, remains significant, especially among the have-less population. Visits to cybercafés in working-class communities almost always mean more encounters with males rather than females (Qiu and Zhou 2005). My female focus group participants in Sichuan and Guangdong explained that they wanted to save money, and a number of them do not know how to surf the Web. Even among those who visit Internet cafés, whereas males tend to play online games, females like to chat through QQ or spend time in chatrooms. Research findings from several studies also suggest that SMS and mobile communication have started to assume an important role in shaping the identities of female working sisters in both Guangdong (A. Lin 2005, Ma and Cheng 2005) and Beijing (Oreglia 2007).

Have-less female migrants tend to find jobs mostly in manufacturing (for example, as assembly line workers) and services (waitresses and nannies, for example) rather than male-dominated occupations like construction worker, taxi driver, and security guard. Searching for jobs often involves "gendered sorting," by which the spectrum of jobs available to females is narrowed for both gender groups, but especially for women (C. Fan 2004). Those who can settle in the city with a residence permit (*hukou*) have a good chance of finding a low-level professional job (for example, as an accountant) or joining the expanding ranks of gray-collar workers in the ICT industry. But the majority of migrants from rural areas still find it difficult to rise above the status of manual laborer. Hence, overall, the average occupational attainment of female migrants remains significantly lower than that of males, as evidenced by official statistics about migrants in Shenzhen (Liang and Chen 2004).

Women also play an irreplaceable role in the burgeoning ICT industry by supplying manual labor on assembly lines of electronics under stringent factory floor management.[15] For ICPs, they are the majority of low-rank service and content providers working in call centers in Beijing and Shanghai to serve, for instance, domestic customers of online travel Web sites. There is a wide spectrum of similar informational gray-collar jobs now occupied primarily by have-less migrant women.

Structural inequality conditions a special mode of gendered industrialization by which a large number of females are entering low-income jobs while becoming part of the myth of docile Chinese women, a critical cultural factor that attracts investors to China's coastal regions (Cartier 2001). The new export-oriented manufacturing industries rely on gendered ways of social control. The entire industrial system, insofar as the rapidly growing coastal regions are concerned, is patriarchal, from the larger urban institutions to the workplace, now reshaped to control the work and life of female migrant workers using the newly available wireless technologies, as chapter 6 will discuss in detail (Qiu 2007b).

But it is erroneous to deny the liberalizing effects of social mobility on women who back home were controlled by their fathers and husbands. Despite the terrible work conditions they face at their migration destination, being in a factory offers young women escape from the traditional family hierarchy, at least for a few years. They can control their lives with some economic freedom and, above all, choose their own male partner. These are ways by which migration helps empower females within the family structure, which in part explains why females accept their exploitation.

Gendered industrialization takes place in two additional ways. One way relies on the feminization of the agricultural labor force, which releases more male than female surplus labor from agricultural work (Cartier 2001). The other is a key link in the emerging services sector consisting of massage girls, bar hostesses, and commercial sex workers. This is, of course, not just a new "service sector" in an economic sense by catering to the physical and emotional desires of domestic and transnational businessmen and working-class men as well. It also provides a crucial social context for the industrialists to entertain and develop ties with local officials.[16] Hence, without migrant women offering intimacy services, this "ultimate form of male bias in the development process" (Cartier 2001, 201), many deals would not have succeeded as parts of China's industrialization miracle today, a phenomenon systematically discussed by Xin Liu (2002a).

A recent emerging business is telemarketing call centers in selected coastal cities. A large number of female migrants in Zhuhai, for example, have been trained—again, as programmable labor—to speak Mandarin with a Taiwanese accent so that they can place telemarketing calls to Taiwan each day.[17] Similar call centers have also mushroomed in the former Manchurian region of northeast China in cities like Dalian, where have-less migrant women are recruited and trained to place long-distance calls to or answer calls from Japanese customers (Young 2005).

"Telephone service lady" is in fact an old occupation in China's telecom industry. Up to the 1980s, most phone calls in China needed to go through human operators, typically working-class urban women at the time. With the rapid adoption of automatic program-controlled switchers, these phone operators were among the first to be laid off from the state sector. In their place during the 1990s was a new army of pager operators who were behind the market of nearly 50 million customers by the end of 2000. Unlike the phone ladies, these are overwhelmingly female migrant workers hired by private employers. They no longer have the health care and other benefits provided to the earlier phone operators. Since 2000, their jobs have silently evaporated with the pager business.

In the beginning years of the new century, the profession of phone service ladies continued to buttress new ventures in e-commerce, offering everything from customer service to telemarketing messages. But their public image worsened around 2002 with high-profile campaigns against the so-called audio-information station (*shengxuntai*), the Chinese euphemism for phone sex. These are high-cost telephone content services offered by business partners of local phone companies to a predominantly male market. Women employees in this case, known as voice information station mistresses (*shengxuntai xiaojie*), are migrants from the countryside as well as laid-off urban residents, including former schoolteachers and pager operators (Xinhua News Agency 2002, *Modern Life Daily* 2002).

The official crackdown on phone sex was triggered, quite similar to the cybercafé campaigns, by sensational mass media coverage on how youth were being corrupted by phone sex services. This was yet another moral panic created by the commercial media, which reflected little on its own sensational and gendered way of newsmaking. The sentence was squarely laid on the dubious ethics of the powerless voice information station mistresses rather than their male employers or male customers. No one was asking the right questions: Why were so many females unemployed? What are the alternative job opportunities available to them under these male-dominated urban institutions that have expanded through working-class ICTs?

Ethnicity and Regional Identity

The view that socioeconomic stratification explains everything about working-class ICTs can be also put to rest by considering the ethnicity and regional identity among have-less migrants. While the Chinese population is predominantly of the Han ethnicity, there are fifty-five minority nationalities that receive official recognition. These include more famous ethnic groups like the Tibetans, Mongolians, Uyghurs, and Manchurians, as well as lesser-known ones such as the Yis, Tujias, and Drungs. Although geographically most minority nationalities tend to concentrate beyond city limits in their more traditional forms of nomadic, farming, and fishing communities, their lives are nonetheless affected by China's urbanization and industrialization. Increasingly, ethnic minority groups are migrating to major metropolitan centers such as Beijing (Iredale, Bilik, and Su 2001; Iredale, Bilik, and Guo 2003), while the number of Han settlers soars in traditionally minority areas (Hansen 2005). The two interwoven processes produce new dynamics of interaction among the ethnicities.

Within have-less migrants of the majority Han nationality, region-based differentiation also plays a significant role in their everyday opportunities in ways similar to the functioning of ethnicity. Regional identifications like northerner (*beifangren*), southerner (*nanfangren*), and Shanghainese (*Shanghainren*) are so commonly used that they serve as quasi-ethnic social categories. These regional labels, like ethnic labels, sort migrants into groups and subgroups according to the way they look and speak and their cultural habits, which in turn determine their patterns of migration, occupational development, and communication and the distribution of life chances.

Since the beginning of economic reform, the proportion of China's minority population has been rising. According to official census data, this percentage increased from 6.7 of the total population in 1982 to 8.41 in 2000. This is a result of intermarriage and preferential state policies such as looser implementation of the one-child policy in minority communities. Meanwhile, the minority population has also been assimilated into the mainstream Han society.

Still, many ethnic groups are left out of the general modernization process. These are people in remote areas with crumbling public infrastructure and living in desperate poverty. Those who remain in these areas are strictly have-nots because their villages lack reliable electricity and water supply. Even if some of the richer families have a TV or radio, many of them do not understand the official Mandarin language because their village schools have had no teachers to teach them Mandarin since the end of the Maoist era.

Their deteriorating living conditions explain why, in recent years, more ethnic-minority migrants have appeared in the streets of large cities creating, for example, notable ethnic enclaves in urban areas (Iredale, Bilik, and Su 2001). From Beijing to Chengdu, more Mongolian restaurants are now served by migrants from Inner Mongolia. Muslim noodle shops are appearing in Guangzhou and Tianjin, and Tibetans now sell herbs and silverware in the streets of Shenzhen and Shanghai.

Although researchers have turned their attention to the migration experience of various minority groups (Iredale, Bilik, and Guo 2003), overall there is little research on social networking among China's ethnic-minority migrants, in part because ethnic tension and discrimination remain politically taboo. But these people, like have-less migrants of Han ethnicity, have also started to use prepaid mobile phone services and other working-class ICTs for migration decision making and coordination. Among ethnic minorities in southwest China, the mobile phone has become a common communication tool, especially for village seniors and local businessmen, who used it to organize cultural and religious activities.[18] Buddhist monks are reported to have been the first group to adopt mobile phones in Tibet (Roudanjia 2007).

The obstacle facing many of the migrant ethnic groups is deep suspicion from the urban Han population. Muslim migrants from northwest China, for example, are often discriminated against in Beijing due to their skin color and accent and are equated with criminals (Iredale, Bilik, and Su 2001). Yi nationality cadres in Sichuan also complained about incidents of ethnic hatred against poor members of their ethnic group that have occurred in the cities of Xichang and Chengdu.[19] As a result, an enclave economy became the typical solution: ethnic migrants either specialize in certain service sectors like ethnic restaurants or they become absorbed by the informal and criminal economies because of the lack of decent employment opportunities. Semilegal and illegal associations perform more than simple economic functions. To marginalized people, they may also provide social support, a sense of belonging and trust, and a taste of power and respect, although in the final analysis, these may turn out to be illusions and disguise more profound in-group exploitation.

Regionalism within the Han majority group works in ways comparable to the ethnicity-based processes of social sorting. As documented by the classic work of Honig (1992) regarding Subei people in prereform Shanghai, the local origins of migrant populations within the Han ethnicity function as a powerful basis for urban prejudice and discrimination. The most basic distinction here is the north/south division, which is relatively easy to tell based on physical characteristics like height, face shape, and, above all, dialect and accent.

Regional stereotypes result from long historic lines of representation that continue to govern daily life in Chinese cities (Cartier 2001). Like Shanghai residents who used to despise those from Subei, it is common in the industrial zones of Guangdong for northerners to be seen as rude and unsophisticated. In particular, the derogatory name "northern sisters (beimei)" is used to designate uneducated female laborers in low-pay manufacturing jobs or sex-related service sectors.

In Beijing, region-based discrimination more often targets selected migrant origins, especially people from Henan. A common myth is that all Henan migrants cheat. Thus, a number of computer companies in the Zhongguancun area, Beijing's IT hub, once posted signs on their entrances saying "Henan people and dogs are not admitted" (S. Ma 2002). Similar discrimination happened in Shenzhen in 2005 when a local police bureau put up a banner against "Scam Gangs from Henan" (XinhuaNet 2005).

Both incidents spurred widespread criticism and debate among Chinese netizens, although there is no sign that region-based discrimination will be put to an end anytime soon. Migrant workers from Henan continue to be singled out as not suited for urban employment and Henan entrepreneurs are considered untrustworthy for business partnership. The consequences of this bias are quite similar to the discrimination against minority ethnicities, like Muslim migrants from Xinjiang, or the unequal treatment of migrant women, all feeding into the spiral of prejudice and constraining the life chances of have-less migrants.

On March 14, 2008, a devastating outburst of ethnic tension raged through Lhasa. Five female shop attendants, four Han and one Tibetan, were trapped in their store and burned to death. All were migrant workers around twenty years old, who had come from Henan, Sichuan, and elsewhere in Tibet. Minutes before they died, they sent SMSs to their families in Lhasa and in their home villages (Barboza 2008b, 6): "Don't go outside. We are hiding in the store," texted Cirenzhuoga, the Tibetan victim. Liu and Chen, two of the Han victims, texted: "Mom, don't go outside. Be careful. Some are killing people." "I am safe at the store." These final words sent from the burning store shall be remembered as some of the most emblematic texts for the persisting problems of class, gender, and ethnicity, for the internal stratification and confrontation among have-less migrants, now inscribed in history through low-end wireless phone.

Translocal Networking beyond Boundaries

A translocal network is a flexible structure that spans two or more places. It consists of localities like villages or factories or businesses by migrants. It includes, more crucially, all forms of connectedness among the localities, like those through working-class ICTs. Altogether the people, their relationships, and the tangible and intangible flows of goods, services, information, and emotions constitute an expansive space of mobility and meaning. The migration streams, following family, kinship and kin-like connections, are not floating blindly, but are purposively to selective places of shared experience. In this way, the spatial scope of translocal networking is expanded while the core logic of social bonding, like that surrounding migrant families, is strengthened (Cartier, Castells, and Qiu 2005).

As Eric Ma critiques, too often researchers of contemporary culture focus on transborder "global/local flows" at the expense of better understanding of "local/local dynamics" (2002, 132). The problem is more serious in China ICT studies, which have almost completely ignored issues of translocal connectivity, as shown by researchers' focus on global and national issues (Qiu and Chan 2003). But it is precisely the networks of connectivity that have immediate effects on opportunities for the information have-less. It is also an oversimplification to see have-less migrants as merely individual consumers of ICT services. For them, much more so than the elite, working-class ICTs serve collective purposes of decision making and coordination—above and beyond individualistic pursuit for personal goals—in the process of migration.

Translocal networking is nothing new in Chinese history. Networks of family, kin, and friends have been always critical to migrant experiences, as can be learned from migration studies worldwide. Traditional Chinese society particularly emphasizes the Confucian family order in its translocality. The era of Mao also created its own translocal networks, for instance, among cadres, soldiers, and the sent-down youth (the generation of teenagers sent from urban to rural areas during the Cultural Revolution). Hence, as Oakes and Schein maintain, "While the current translocal boom might appear to be an artifact of the marketization and liberalization of Chinese society, a straightforward causal relation between the two is belied by the occurrences of translocality earlier in Chinese history" (2006, 2).

In the post-Mao era, translocal networks have played a central role in directing the flow of migration from the countryside and the rust belts to the urban, urbanizing, and industrializing areas. A survey of 818 migrant workers at the Beijing Railway Station found that 76.8 percent of them found their first job in the city through family members, relatives, friends, or fellow migrants from their places of origin. Half of the employed migrants relied on such networks of acquaintances for their current job (S. Zhao 2004).

A probability sampling survey done in Jinan, Shangdong Province, in 1995 included 1,504 migrants registered with the local police bureau.[20] Overall, 81 percent of them depended on translocal networks in their decision making in rural-to-urban migration through such ties as relatives, friends, and same-origin migrants (*tongxiang*). For interprovincial migrants, the ratio is 88.3 percent, significantly higher than intraprovincial migrants. In contrast, news media were seen as helpful by only 2.7 percent of intraprovincial migrants and 4.9 percent of interprovincial migrants. The failure of traditional media to meet the informational needs of have-less migrants is a basic reason for the continued centrality of translocal networking, which explains the surging popularity of working-class ICTs in recent years.

Indeed, some telcos have been more locally oriented, as shown by the development trajectory of Little Smart. This is also the case for domestic-brand handset producers like Bird, which used rural counties and market towns as its main launching pad. Most important, landline phones have made significant inroads in the countryside, thus enabling more have-less migrants to call home. The ratio of villages equipped with landline phones was 45 percent in 1985, 75 percent in 1999, and 85 percent in 2003 (Harwit 2004). By the end of 2007, telephone access was available in 99.5 percent of villages in China (MII, 2007).

Since 2004, impressive growth has been observed in the rural areas of West China. While single-digit growth rates were recorded for urban landlines and landlines in East China, it was 16.4 percent and 15.6 percent for the countryside of West China in 2005 and 2006, respectively.[21] Improved connectivity in ethnically diverse western regions means that minority ethnicity migrants now also have a stronger motivation to adopt working-class ICTs such as low-end mobile phones and prepaid services in order to place voice calls to their families back home.

There is a wide variety of migration trajectories. Have-less migrants, some with their families, others by themselves, may go from city to city for an extended period of time. Or they may go home regularly and become seasonal workers. The journey may end up in the provincial capital, a factory zone in coastal China, or overseas destinations, as in January 2007, when five migrant workers from Sichuan Province were abducted while working on a rural telephone project in southern Nigeria (Xinhua News Agency 2007).

Along the migration journey, numerous have-less ICT entrepreneurs and telecom service providers have established cybercafés and newsstands that sell prepaid cards. These businesses usually do not have access to bank loans or state subsidies, which means that microentrepreneurs have to rely on family savings and, quite frequently, funds borrowed through translocal networks, for example, among fellow villagers. If the business succeeds, the investments strengthen migrant networks translocally.

This was how Zhang, a Shenzhen cybercafé operator, brought his entire extended family from the northern rust belt zone of Benxi, Liaoning Province. After being laid off in 1998, Zhang used informal borrowing to start his cybercafé in a neighborhood of blue-collar and gray-collar service industry workers. As his business steadily grew, his brother joined him, followed by his parents and cousins. Some of them helped at the cybercafé, and others started their own business nearby, following a typical pattern of migrant enterpreneurship.[22]

Translocal networks thus perform multiple functions in directing migration flow, providing social support, and sustaining identity formation among newcomers in the city. A widely expected result is upward social mobility, by which migrants gain new skills, higher income, and more prestige. This is the case for migrants from poor inland provinces, who are found in large numbers working in coastal industrial zones. Most of them could earn little cash back home. But taking jobs in big cities allows them to be financially independent and able to send home billions of yuan that can exceed the total fiscal income of the local governments at migrant origins (table 4.8).

What can be observed here is but one result of massive migration and translocal networking: the flow of wealth that should be among the most effective ways to alleviate poverty. These are much more than strictly monetary resources in the economic sense because they also bring dignity to migrants and their families, a real uplifting with tremendous social value. Because these flows could not have been coordinated without long-distance communication, they powerfully testify to the relationship between migration and translocal networking, which was well under way in 1999.

After the wide spread of working-class ICTs, translocal dynamics have intensified, taken on new modalities of communication, and led to new

Table 4.8
Local fiscal income and remittances from migrant workers in five provincial-level administrative units, 1999

Province or municipality	Fiscal income (billion yuan)	Total remittance from migrant workers (billion yuan)
Anhui	17.4	21.7
Chongqing	7.7	12.0
Sichuan	21.2	21.0
Hunan	16.7	15.9
Jiangxi	10.5	9.9

Source: Compilation based on Cui (2004a). Data collected by Research Center for Rural Economy, PRC Ministry of Agriculture.

empowerment effects and cultural expressions on the basis of networked connectivity. One example is the temporary labor shortage since 2004 in many Guangdong factories, where managers found it increasingly difficult to hire employees, especially low-wage ordinary workers (*pugong*), an unprecedented problem of migrant dearth (*mingonghuang*) (Chua 2005, S. Yang 2006). The underlying reasons were stagnant wages, poor benefits, and rising living costs in the southern region, which made Shanghai and the nearby Yangtze River Delta more attractive to have-less migrants than Guangdong. But how could migrant workers learn about employment information in other places?

Migrant worker networking often started with face-to-face communication during the Lunar New Year festival, when have-less migrants went home and exchanged job information using working-class ICTs and made their collective decisions from there. The common use of SMS to coordinate collective reposition has been recorded in the industrial zones of Dongguan, Guangdong (Law 2006). The network effect of migrant dearth then takes place quickly because have-less migrants are informally organized according to their home origins. The translocal ties can therefore empower them in their bargaining with employers. Despite the absence of labor unions, network labor can nonetheless gather and exchange job information through SMS or long-distance phone bars and then vote with their feet.

Have-less migrants have begun to use blogs to foster horizontal communication among themselves (see the Internet Resources at the end of the book). One of them is Han Ying, who left home in rural Sichuan at age sixteen and lived in Chengdu, a large city, where she worked for five years as a waitress and hairdresser. She began blogging in November 2006. By March 2008, her blog has attracted a million visits.

Han Ying's blog chronicles her life as a migrant worker. She had many jobs—street cleaner, construction worker, security guard, foot massage girl, factory worker, and others—including some she took just for the experience so that she could blog about it. Her writing is usually brief but reveals her personal emotions: homesickness, childhood memories, and aspirations for the future. It contains more than a thousand photographs showing her daily activities, such as the one in figure 4.1, which was taken when she bought goods for her new online clothing store at Taobao.com, a popular low-end e-commerce Web site. Images like this attract new friends, especially other have-less migrant bloggers. By March 2008, Han Ying has 2,269 blogger friends whose blogs were cross-linked with hers.

Figure 4.1
A blog by Han Ying, a migrant woman from Sichuan. *Source:* http://hybh3399
.blog.163.com (accessed March 29, 2008).

Sun Heng is a migrant from Henan who used to work as a porter
and salesperson in Beijing. On May Day 2002, he founded the New Labor
Art Troupe and began to provide nonprofit musical performances and services for other migrants. Initially the group was not well known. But in
2004, the troupe produced its first CD, *All Workers Are Family* (*Tianxia
dagong shi yijia*), which was uploaded to their Web site for free trial
listening (www.dashengchang.org.cn). In 2007, they produced their
second CD, *Singing for the Labor!* (*Wei laodongzhe gechang!*) including a song
written by Sun Heng entitled "Coal" that describes translocal ties among
have-less migrants:

Coal

When it's cold outside
A man from my village
Brings me a cart of coal
That blackened face grinning wide
Warmed my heart and soul

Snow is floating in the sky
Those two black hands
Are his pride
The hands bring his grain, his child's toys, his wife's clothes,
And the whole family's happiness.

I have wondered more than once
How to pass these long cold nights
But now I finally understand
What real light and warmth is.

By the end of 2007, the New Labor Art Troupe had performed in more than a hundred concerts in eighteen cities all over China, including Hong Kong. Everywhere they went, they tried to mobilize performance art resources in the local migrant worker communities, using e-mail and mobile phones. They held training sessions for labor activists and sang their songs—always straightforward and down-to-earth like "Coal"—together with their working-class audiences. They also adopted Creative Commons-Mainland China, using the Attribution-Noncommercial-No Derivative license to distribute their content online and via CD albums.[23]

Han Ying's blog and the New Labor Art Troupe reflect increasing efforts at the grassroots level to use working-class ICTs for cultural expression and networking. A similar development is *Migrant Poets* (*Dagong shiren*), a magazine based in Guangzhou now using the Internet actively, for example, by calling for poetry submissions by migrant workers nationwide.[24] As Zhan (2006) discovered, writing poetry has become increasingly common among migrant workers, especially domestic helpers who work and live in solitude in upper-class families. *Migrant Poets* provides a platform for these literary expressions on the Net and in print.

Despite these bottom-up cultural formations of network labor, there is a limit to what they can publish under China's censorship regime. They can talk about the forty thousand fingers lost each year in the Pearl River Delta, but they cannot write about collective actions and labor-capital confrontations within mainland China. Otherwise their blogs and Web sites will be closed down or sanitized.

As a result, discussions about industrial actions outside mainland China and international labor movements become popular. For example, during the iron workers' strike in Hong Kong in 2007, poems by working-class strikers in Hong Kong were widely circulated and discussed in online forums of migrant poets within the mainland. This is polemic poetry that criticizes the unequal distribution of wealth and power in Hong Kong's capitalist system, dominated by the corporate elite. In this case, the transcendence of social boundaries is not a reflection of increased physical mobility among have-less migrants. Rather, it is a strategic way for independent cultural expression at the grassroots of the Chinese informational city.

The Mobility Multiplier of the New Century

While examining media and modernization in the Middle East during the 1950s, Lerner coined the term *mobility multiplier* (1958, 59) because he found the radio and, to a lesser extent, film allowed communication beyond face-to-face interaction, thus fostering understanding across space and time. People's horizons were broadened, and they could imagine how social change might be possible.

In many ways, working-class ICTs can be seen as the twenty-first-century equivalent of mobility multipliers because they facilitate the expansion and acceleration of mobility patterns created by urban growth and industrialization in a global context. Surging mobility leads to more informational needs among migrants that are now met primarily by working-class ICTs. This is a process that changes millions of information have-nots into information have-less, which is inevitable due to the disappointing role of mainstream mass media in serving have-less migrants. The result is increased networked connectivity and more prominent translocal dynamics that feed back into the erosion of traditional economic sectors like agriculture and state-owned enterprises (SOEs) and into population mobility, from rural areas to cities, from small towns to metropolises.

Working-class ICTs also differ from the radio Lerner observed. One may argue that the new digital communication tools are more powerful because they are two-way and interactive. They are more in the hands of the have-less, allowing them to talk directly to each other and share their own user-generated content like image-loaded blogs, which would be impossible in elite-dominated mass media. Working-class ICTs are, in this sense, microsolutions for macroproblems faced by have-less migrants by directing migration flow, disseminating job information, and providing badly needed social support.

But these are not yet the core differences, which should be understood in three more profound ways. First, the decentralized network structure of cybercafés and low-end mobile communication means more complexity in the direction of social change, of which modernization is only one possibility. The diffusion of working-class ICTs into the hands of have-less migrants may empower them by providing more connectivity, but may also subject them to commercial alienation, gangster activities, and stricter means of control at work or at home. The smaller scale of the operation, often in personal and small-group settings, means a close match with traditional translocal networks, thus suggesting a process of retraditionalization rather than a one-way journey to modernity.

Second, while physical mobility has increased with the spread of working-class ICTs, it remains disputable whether there is real social mobility at the system level toward more equality across strata and class. This is due to the trend of decentralization and the predominantly translocal ways of networking, based on the fact that have-less migrants are not a single homogeneous group in their composition and ways of adopting and appropriating ICTs. Migration does create openings for upward social mobility. But translocal networks cannot by themselves erase existing inequality and prejudice. Instead, the translocally networked nature of migration and communication means that the life chances for different migrant groups are still structured in drastically dissimilar ways. Some may be marginalized more than others. Some, due to their gender, ethnicity, or regional identity, tend to be locked into particular enclaves of migrant businesses. Still others are more likely to be absorbed into informal economies in order to survive.

Third and perhaps most fundamental, the rise of working-class ICTs is a harbinger of new class dynamics, whose centerpiece is the emergence of network labor in not only occupational but also cultural and political terms. Essential to China's urbanization and its ascendance as a global industrial power is its burgeoning electronics manufacture and IT services provision sector, whose structural transformation toward cost innovation would have been impossible without a systematic reorganization of Chinese migrant labor. This process reflects the peculiar historical juxtaposition of industrialization and informatization in the Chinese context. It produces gray-collar software testers, SMS authors, and call center ladies, all in the expanding category of programmable labor. They collaborate with low-rank self-programmable labor and generic labor, as not only in the case of BYD but also the networks of migrant-worker bloggers and Internet poets, who use working-class ICTs to organize themselves in flexible networked ways horizontally and from the bottom up to resist the top-down challenges of network enterprise. This emerging network labor, still in a formative stage, is a defining feature of Chinese informationalism in the new century.

5   Young and Old

The information have-less are not only people on the move but also those with lower mobility. In contemporary China, immobility may result from a lack of financial and social resources. Or it may reflect the inertia of old lifestyles, which is, however, increasingly difficult to sustain given the pressure of China's urbanization and industrialization. In all this, age makes a huge difference by limiting mobility at both ends of the age spectrum. The young and the old need care. Their dependencies—some biological, some social; some enjoyed, some imposed—prevent them from leaving the family, which constitutes a distinct part of their vulnerability in coping with the transformations, using the limited means at their disposal, including working-class ICTs.

Relative immobility creates and intensifies localized informational needs in the family unit, which is now characterized by only children and aging. This is most prominent in China's newly commercialized education and health care systems, which are referred to, along with for-profit housing reform, as the new "three mountains" that weigh down the Chinese people (Gu 2007, D. Yang 2005, 2007).[1] Dealing with surmounting insecurity and the existential issues of life is essential to the shaping and "domestication" (Silverstone and Haddon 1996, Haddon 2003) of ICTs among the main subjects of this chapter: the have-less young and have-less seniors.

This chapter focuses on the young and the old among the information have-less, who are also critical to the formation of the new working class in the Chinese informational city. The core issue at stake is the family—the disparity between families and the inequality within them—which determines the life chances for the young and the old, empowered or disempowered through the deployment of working-class ICTs. The social scope of the have-less needs to be broadened here to include even some upper-class families where the young and the old are disempowered, neglected, or even abused. This broadening of scope does not dilute our attention on young people and seniors in working families. Instead, it highlights the need to look at more general trends of inequality and ICTs concerning the young and the old, for the information have-less are an integral part of Chinese society. Socioeconomic stratification is but one dimension in the notion of the have-less, whereas power structure, cultural expression, and autonomy in the family are equally important elements in the overall conception.

What are the basic living conditions of have-less young people and have-less seniors? Why do they need working-class ICTs? How do the processes of change, like the one-child policy and education reform, affect the younger generation and thus condition the diffusion of low-end technologies among them? What role do working-class ICTs play for the elderly, who face the challenges posed by health care reform and the lack of social security? Can new services such as SMS and Little Smart create opportunities for equality? To what extent are the new means of communication being usurped in ways that disempower lower-mobility groups, for example, through aggressive promotion of commercial products? What policies can enhance the social services function of working-class ICTs for the young and the old? This chapter tackles these questions.

The Young, the Old, and Working-Class ICTs: An Overview

First, let us briefly examine demographic change regarding these two groups of have-less people and how they are related to working-class ICTs in general terms before looking at the more specific structural conditions that shape the technosocial emergence of the young and the elderly. Because this is an overview designed to provoke questions, I use more inclusive definitions in order to fully capture the internal diversity of these people and their dynamic relationship with the technologies.

By *the young,* I mean all children, adolescents, and young adults through age twenty-four, which corresponds to the age breakdown of official demographics on the Internet user population (CNNIC, 1999–2008). China had 355.5 million young people between ages six and twenty-four in 2004, accounting for more than a quarter of the national population (table 5.1). If we look only at registered city dwellers, in 2004 there were 77.9 million young people within this age range, representing 24.1 percent of the total urban population (*Almanac of China's Population* 2005). These statistics encompass wealthy households and dispossessed communities. Overall in urban China, young people from working-class backgrounds account for a

Table 5.1
Population change of the younger generation and the elderly, 1982–2004

	The younger generation, ages 6 to 24		The elderly, ages 60 and over	
	Number (millions)	Percentage of total population	Number (millions)	Percentage of total population
1982	422.8	42.12	76.6	7.63
1990	419.5	37.38	97.0	8.58
2000	396.2	31.88	130.0	10.46
2004	355.5	28.37	154.9	12.36

Sources: Compilation based on Almanac of China's Population (1985, 1993, 2005); Tabulation on the 2000 Population Census of the PRC (2001).

large proportion of this age group, which includes the children of manual laborers, laid-off employees, and migrant workers.

In urban areas, not only colleges but all middle schools and primary schools are also required to offer courses on information technology (xinxi jishu bixiuke) according to Ministry of Education (MoE) guidelines.[2] Hence, students have been a prominent group of Internet users in nationwide surveys. Since 2000, official CNNIC reports show consistently that about a quarter to a third of Chinese netizens are students, and more than half of all netizens are aged twenty-four or younger, almost doubling the percentage of youth in the general population (table 5.2). The percentages were even higher in surveys by CASS during the Spring Festival in five large cities (Beijing, Shanghai, Guangzhou, Chengdu, and Changsha), which found that students accounted for 42.6 percent of all netizens in 2000 and, in 2005, 87.8 percent of young people aged sixteen to twenty-four went online regularly (Guo and Bu 2000, Guo 2005).

School dropouts, including boys but more often girls, also can be haveless young people, which also encompasses diverse types of unemployed youth, child laborers, and juvenile delinquents. These young people at the margins of society may be deprived of formal education. But for a variety of reasons, they are also becoming members of the information have-less and adopting a range of working-class ICTs whose uses often go beyond classroom instruction.

As learned from my fieldwork and research, teachers and parents often complain that young people regard Net bars as more magnetic than schools. In China as in other countries, youth are the leading force in shaping a

Table 5.2
Youngest people and seniors as a percentage of China's Internet user population,
1999–2007

	Students	Below age 18	Ages 18 to 24	Age 24 and under	Over age 60
1999	21.0	2.4	42.8	45.2	0.4
2000	20.9	14.9	41.2	56.1	1.3
2001	24.1	15.3	36.2	51.5	1.1
2002	28.0	17.6	37.3	54.9	0.9
2003	29.2	18.8	34.1	52.9	0.8
2004	32.4	16.4	35.3	53.5	1.1
2005	35.1	16.6	35.1	51.7	0.8
2006	32.3	17.2	35.2	52.4	0.9
2007	28.8	19.1	31.8	50.9	4.2[a]

Sources: CNNIC (2000–2007), year-end data.
[a] more than 50 years old.

"mobile youth culture" (Castells, Fernandez-Ardevol, Qiu, and Sey 2006), which includes young migrant workers. Like have-less young people raised in urban families, these young migrants, many with only a junior high school education, have become mobile users as a result of the availability of domestic-brand handsets, second-hand markets, SMS, and prepaid services.

In contrast to young people, senior citizens are often latecomers to the diffusion of new media technologies. As in many other societies, the growth of the number of aging people in China has accelerated since the 1990s. In 2004, there were 154.9 million seniors at or above age sixty, making up 12.36 percent of the country's population. But the proportion of older people using the Internet has been flat, at around 1 percent of all Internet users in China, since 2000 (table 5.2).

Overall, when it comes to Internet access, the age gap identified by Harwit and Clark (2001) persists. But given the rapid growth of China's total Internet user population, the absolute number of senior-aged netizens has also increased significantly, from 35,600 in 1999 to 1.23 million in 2006. This means, importantly, that the age gap has not widened and the growth of elderly Internet users has kept pace with that of the general population. So far, most of these senior citizens are urban residents with relatively high socioeconomic status, many of whom nevertheless retain their old lifestyle and consumer habits including, for instance, frugal spending patterns.[3] They go online to search for information, especially medical information, and to keep in touch with their children in other cities or overseas. With Internet penetration approaching saturation among urban youth, have-less seniors are among the potential groups that will benefit from the next wave of Internet diffusion.

Meanwhile, senior citizens, including those from lower socioeconomic groups, are catching up much faster in the wireless market. According to a 2004 report , 11 percent of Chinese mobile phone consumers were between the ages of fifty-five and sixty-five,[4] which slightly surpasses the share of this age group in the total urban population.[5] Voice telephony over wireless phone is much easier to handle than Web surfing. Handsets are less expensive than desktop computers and more portable than laptops. They are also more likely to receive these as gifts for staying in touch with their adult children or keeping up with their social activities and networks.

From a broad perspective, have-less seniors include pensioners, who are living on a fixed income, as well as those who retired without a pension or were forced into early retirement in layoffs. While young people are affected by the industrialization of education, the elderly face the commercialization of health care. For these reasons, they go online for medical information and stay connected with families and friends through low-end mobile phones, for example, using Little Smart and prepaid services.

At a time of increasing uncertainty, when the safety net is yet to be woven, when sons and daughters are moving to other towns or the other side of the ever-expanding city or even the world, it is understandable that seniors would turn to ICTs to preserve their cherished social bonds. Working-class ICTs are popular among have-less seniors because few of them need the latest multimedia technology or high-end mobile services. What they need is something simple and affordable, which is the case even for those who enjoy a sufficient retirement income and benefits or have wealthy children.

Due to their relative dependence on the family, the young and the old are both affected by the one-child policy, aging, and changes in household structures. When rural-to-urban and interurban mobility rise among the adult population, the fate of the two lower-mobility age groups is often closely tied to each other. Grandparents take care of grandchildren when the parents are away, while the reverse is also true for young people, who provide their company and support to the elderly. According to Duan and Zhou (2006), there are approximately 22.9 million children under age fourteen who are left behind by at least one of their parents. These left-behind children (*liushou ertong*, mostly left behind by migrant-worker parents to live with grandparents or other relatives for several months of the year) are highly concentrated in six provinces, such as Sichuan, Jiangxi, and Anhui. These six provinces have 55.2 percent of all left-behind children in the country. These children live with other left-behind family members, especially the elderly (Bu 2008).

Among migrants, the rising demand for ICTs is a direct result of their sociospatial movement. Both the young and the old need information and connection to the world surrounding them, which is going through rapid change. Have-less young people and have-less seniors must acquire new means of communication in order to survive, adjust to the environment, and hold on to the things they value. In a transitional society like China today, immobility does not guarantee life stability.

It is under the circumstances of profound structural change that the value of informal networks, sustained by working-class ICTs, should be understood. In this sense, low-end ICTs are also microsolutions for macroproblems for the young and the elderly, just as they are for migrants. Although there are different levels of mobility, the function of working-class ICTs is not different in kind.

When it comes to specific technology, these two groups make notably different choices that set them apart from migrants and from each other. Some working-class ICTs have a strong appeal to groups with lower mobility rather than those on the move—for instance, Little Smart, the limited-mobility wireless technology. Other low-end services like cybercafés are socially constructed almost exclusively for young consumers. SMS is predominantly for youth because of the physical challenge of the interface. Although in theory adequate technical support can make Internet cafés and SMS user friendly to senior citizens, in practice this has not happened, leaving the challenge of the aging society largely unanswered.

When the young and the old begin to use working-class ICTs, they extend existing social ties among family members, friends, and relatives. This reinforces their social networks, communities, and their collective values. But can have-less young people and have-less seniors enjoy more autonomy and forge new connections using these new communication tools? How can they appropriate working-class ICTs for new goals under unforeseen circumstances, which may impinge on the family unit in flux? The lack of mobility may constrain the process of technology deployment, but it may also bring about unexpected applications and liberate the have-less from the immediate environment that can make them vulnerable.

"Little Emperors" and Have-Less Young People

Why do Chinese young people adopt ICTs? At a general level, the reasons are not too different from what we have learned in other countries: they need to get information, socialize, and be entertained. The three Internet applications most popular among Chinese urban youth were online gaming, chatting, and e-mail in 2000; in 2003 they were Web browsing, online gaming, and content downloading (Bu and Guo 2000, Bu and Liu 2003). These seemingly universal ICT functions for the younger generation, however, emerge from specific Chinese conditions. One of the most noteworthy and most distinct factors is China's one-child policy, "the most aggressive, comprehensive population policy in the world" (Short, Zhai, Xu, and Yang 2001, 913), which impinges on all aspects of young urban lives, including their connections with working-class ICTs.

The one-child policy, formally promulgated in 1979, affects everyone, especially the urban population. As a result, the nation's birth rate dramatically dropped from nearly 6 percent in 1969 to 2.7 in 1979 and 1.87 in 2006 (Tien 1991; *China Statistics Yearbook* 2007). The fertility rate is generally lower in cities than in the countryside. Shanghai, for instance, became the first to see death rates exceed birth rates since the 1990s (XinhuaNet 2004a). The family planning policy effectively creates a distinct generation that accounts for the overwhelming majority of urban youth below their mid-twenties.

Known as "little emperors (*xiaohuangdi*)," only children are often spoiled by the older generations, who devote their undivided attention and resources to the upbringing of their youngsters. Empirical research confirms that Chinese parents are now more involved in child care than in the past (Short, Zhai, Xu, and Yang 2001). One important effect of this change in urban areas is the elevated status of girls, who can "enjoy unprecedented parental support because they do not have to compete with brothers for parental investment" (V. L. Fong 2002, 1098).

But more care also means more control and less autonomy. Excessive protection leads to dependent personalities, while it may also trigger rebellion. In most urban families, Chinese parents tend to maintain significant control over their children's Internet behaviors, although not always successfully. As Bu and Liu found in their seven-city survey, 51.3 percent of the parents exerted "some control," 12.9 percent imposed "a lot of control," and another 6.4 percent had so much control that "it is almost impossible to go online when parents are home" (2003, 27).

Parental control is also a prominent issue in wireless communication, as in the case of a Shangdong family in East China, where the father used the mobile phone to maintain surveillance over his teenage daughter. Her wireless phone was a so-called subunit (*ziji*), meaning that her father could see every SMS she sent or received, as well as the phone number every time she received or placed a wireless call. According to the informant, a class-mate of the daughter, she was very upset with this arrangement but had to live with it until she entered college, when she switched to regular mobile service.[6]

The most obvious consequence of the one-child policy is the elimination of siblings, at least in cities, where the policy is more successfully imple-mented than in the countryside. Care from parents and grandparents, however attentive, cannot replace the company of brothers and sisters. Loneliness therefore has become a major issue, especially at a time when most urban families have moved away from traditional communities based on *hutong* alleys and *danwei* (work unit) housing. In the new environment of high-rise buildings, where most neighbors are strangers, children have to conduct more "microcoordination" (Ling 2004) than ever before in order to conduct social activities. With the help of working-class ICTs, have-less young people can reach out to their peers. Their collective activities may be conducted over the Internet, like chatting via QQ, or they may go through SMS. There may also be an offline component, such as the commonly observed pattern of teenage boys collectively patronizing Internet cafés (Qiu and Zhou 2005). For these junior netizens, the time spent together is a precious part of the shared experience, which becomes all the more important for only children precisely because it is not purely online.

What kinds of families do adolescent Internet users come from? Table 5.3 summarizes findings from two surveys conducted by researchers at CASS in 2000 in five large cities and the other in 2003 in seven large cities. It shows that although up to a quarter of China's adolescent netizens come from the families of professionals, managers, and cadres, more of them have parents who are workers, clerks, and sales and service personnel. There are also a notable number of them whose father or mother (or both) are unemployed.

Most important, between 2000 and 2003, more children from low-income families had become Internet users. In 2000, 36.1 percent of all adolescent user families had a monthly income not exceeding 2000 yuan. The percentage, however, grew to 47.2 percent in 2003. Although families with higher incomes are still more likely to have Internet-capable children, have-less families are catching up (Bu and Guo 2000, Bu and Liu 2003).

Table 5.3

Distribution of selected professions for the parents of adolescent Internet users in Chinese cities

	Fathers		Mothers	
	2000 (N = 725)	2003 (N = 3036)	2000 (N = 726)	2003 (N = 3089)
Information have-less	*25.8*	*50.1*	*34.0*	*59.7*
Workers	15.6	18.1	14.6	14.4
Sales and services	10.2	8.5	20.4	14.8
Clerks	—[a]	19.7	—[a]	21.5
Unemployed	—[a]	3.8	—[a]	9.0
Upper class	*25.7*	*27.1*	*12.0*	*22.0*
Professionals	10.5	18.0	—[a]	18.1
Managers and cadres	15.2	9.1	12.0	3.9

Sources: Compilation based on Bu and Guo (2000) and Bu and Liu (2003).
[a] Data unavailable.

Bearing in mind the family background of these young people, the one-child policy makes a critical difference because even though the families are not wealthy, the "little emperors" may still have adequate means to get what they need using the meager income of their parents and grandparents. This, however, cannot alter the basic financial conditions of working-class families. While have-less young people seek self-identity under the pressures of China's new consumer society, the funds available to them are still limited. Hence, there is a market boom for preowned brand-name mobile phones and laptops, some stolen, some refurbished, to meet the needs of have-less young people.[7]

This pattern of young people spending excessively on working-class ICTs can also be observed in the three-city survey group project conducted in 2002 and 2006.[8] We found that migrants with higher ICT connectivity are more likely to lose control over their ICT budget. After probing several social demographic indicators including income, education, gender, residential tenure, and age, the strongest factor turns out to be age.[9] This means that compared to those older than twenty-five, young have-less migrants are more likely to lose control of their spending on ICT products and services. This is because they are seeking personal identity against the backdrop of the market economy. They are more targeted by advertising and marketing campaigns while also being prone to conform to collective norms set by their peers in their social networks, now increasingly connected by working-class ICTs.

A dramatization of the larger social problem can be found in the movie *Beijing Bicycle* (*shiqisui de danche*), directed by Wang Xiaoshuai and released in 2001. In the film, a Beijing teenager stole the savings of his father, a laid-off worker, to buy a mountain bike from the second-hand market so that he could join his biker friends and be cool. The plot can be easily rendered as about a teenager longing for a mobile phone. But the movie has another equally important character: a teenager from the countryside, the original owner of the bike, who depended on it for his livelihood as a new employee of a package delivery company. Given traffic unpredictability, bikes prove to be the most reliable transport in the city. But his bike was stolen and sold to the teenager from the working-class urban family. The two adolescents fought over the bike. At the end, they had to sympathize with each other and accommodate each other's needs by using the bike alternately. The ending expresses hope that only children may grow up and learn to compromise, something that they may fail to learn in the family.

Important to note here is that it is very common for young people to lose their mobile handset, often their most valuable possession. Theft is a main reason, and it happens in crowded public spaces like buses, cybercafés, and shopping districts, or in other settings like factory dormitories. Where public security enforcement is lax, there are also more robberies targeting have-less youth with expensive mobile phones. Liang, a twenty-three-year-old graduate student in Guangdong, for example, reported that he was robbed twice of his mobile phone on a bus route that he took frequently. "It happened in broad daylight. Several of them [robbers] surrounded me, asking to see my *shouji*. I had no choice. They took it and went off at the next stop. No one dared to say anything." This security problem will be further discussed in chapter 7. But here one should wonder: Where do these stolen or robbed phones go? First to the second-hand market, then to other have-less young people?

The Consequences of Education Reform

If the one-child policy is a unique component of the Chinese situation, the reform of the education system is more universal. It forms another essential social condition facing have-less young people in the evolving network society of urban China. In recent years, the privatization of education and subsequent rise in tuition fees have caused much tension and discontent around the world, particularly among have-less young people in higher education. In May and June 2006 alone, there were major student protests in Chile and Greece against the commercialization of education (Franklin 2006, Labi 2006). Also following a neoliberal route, China has reformed its education sector since the mid-1990s, which has led to serious disruptions such as the June 2006 student uprising in Zhengzhou, Henan Province (Kahn 2006).

Throughout much of China's history, education has usually been regarded as a public sector and a social equalizer. Beginning in the Han dynasty, Confucian learning offered opportunities for members of the lower class to rise through civil examinations. Until the 1980s, the Communists had broadened the scope of education to peasants and the proletariat working class. Has the equalizing role of education continued into the information age? Or has education been turned into yet another system that reproduces inequality?

A look at the general trend of registered school enrollment shows that overall, the scale of education in China has increased (table 5.4). The one-child policy has led to the declining number of children, which explains the decrease in the number of primary school students. But secondary schools and colleges are gaining pupils. Between 1982 and 2006, the number of middle school students more than doubled. The fastest growth is in higher education, indicated by college enrollment that skyrocketed from 1.15 million in 1982 to 5.86 million in 2000 and then to 27 million in 2006.

While the youth population fell between 1982 and 2004 (table 5.1), total school enrollment climbed from 187.9 million to 239.88 million. As a result, students as a proportion of those aged six to twenty-two rose from 48.3 to 74.2 percent (table 5.2). A small fraction of this increase is from

Table 5.4
School enrollments at the three levels of education, 1982–2004 (in millions)

	Primary school enrollment	Secondary school enrollment	College enrollment	Total school enrollment	Students as a percentage of the population ages 6 to 22
1982	139.72	47.03	1.15	187.90	48.3
1990	122.41	51.05	2.06	175.52	46.9
2000	130.13	85.03	5.86	243.84	68.1
2004	116.30	102.25	21.33	239.88	74.2

Sources: Compilation based on *China Population Statistics Yearbook* (1996) and *Education Statistics Yearbook of China* (2000, 2004).

the expansion of educational services to adults over twenty-two years old. The bulk of growth comes from the sharp rise in technical programs for late teens and those in their early twenties. Be they vocational high schools (*zhiye gaozhong*) or colleges, these programs offer technical qualifications for gray- and blue-collar jobs as well as starting white-collar jobs, including those who become network labor in China's ICT industry.

In a sense, the formal education system promotes equality in ICT access because the MoE required all urban secondary schools to offer ICT courses by 2001 and all urban primary schools to do so by 2005 (MoE 2003). At the level of higher education, the China Education and Research Network (CERNET) plays an indispensable role by bringing the Internet to some of the most isolated regions, such as Tibet, where CERNET was the only service provider in 2003 (Harwit 2004). Without these efforts, millions of young people would have been unable to learn about ICTs, whether over online computers or through book-based traditional pedagogy.

While most high schools in China have computer classrooms, the percentages are significantly lower in terms of campus networks and among primary schools (table 5.5). Unsurprisingly, computers and networking resources are concentrated in urban areas (Bu and Liu 2003). In most schools, especially in primary and junior high schools, students need to

Table 5.5
Ownership of computer and networking equipment in China's primary and high schools, 2003

	Primary schools	Junior high	Senior high	Full high schools[a]	Total[b]
Number of schools	396,665	62,272	5,910	7,398	472,245
Schools with computer classrooms	61,584	38,070	4,950	5,541	110,145
Schools with campus networks	13,215	7,576	2,567	2,968	26,326
Number of students per computer	52	27	14	15	33
Investment in computer and networking per student (yuan)	173	408	590	612	291

Sources: Data based on *National Comprehensive Statistics on Education Equipment in Primary and High Schools* (2004).
[a] High schools that have junior and senior highs.
[b] Includes primary and high schools.

share computer resources, as can be seen in the number of students per computer terminal. ICT access at school is therefore also in a collective mode as in cybercafés. It is in this sense less exclusive as compared to private ownership, although how to best use these shared computer resources remains an open question.

The expansion of computers and connectivity among secondary schools and colleges does not equate to equality. On the contrary, China's education system, especially after the profit-oriented reforms since mid-1990s, has increasingly become the opposite of a social equalizer. First, in order to privatize education and transform it into an education enterprise (*jiaoyu chanyehua*), tuition fees have skyrocketed, especially in public schools that make up the bulk of the education sector, causing school dropouts that otherwise would have not happened. The problem has been most acute in rural areas, although there has been some improvement since 2006 when the Chinese government endorsed the policy of free nine-year education in the countryside. Expensive education fees, however, remain a critical issue beyond nine-year education, for rural families as well as those in low-income urban communities, especially children whose parents are laid-off workers (H. Zhao 2005).

Second, the schools themselves exist in a discriminatory environment. It is difficult to ensure equality among the schools or even within them. The distinction between key schools (*zhongdian xuexiao*) and ordinary ones is a typical system of inequality that privileges schools with more resources and students with higher scores (Yang 2005). Another case in point is schooling for the children of migrant workers in Beijing, which triggered a controversy in 2003–2004 (W. Wang 2003). These children—about 20 million of them at the national scale (D. Yang 2007)—are not registered residents in the city, although their parents have lived and worked there for a number of years. Most of them could not enter schools formally recognized by the education authorities because they lacked residential status. The parents subsequently organized their own schools, although they faced threats of being closed down. The struggle for education, formal and informal, is continuing for have-less young people, particularly those from rural backgrounds who now reside in cities (Huang and Cheng 2005, L. Wang 2006).

Third, as a social institution, schools may play a discriminatory role against working-class ICTs because these are low-end services associated with less wealthy communities and the values embedded in have-less grassroots networks can be at odds with the high-end elite orientation that dominates formal ICT curricula. The most obvious example is teachers' frequently speaking out against the negative influences of cybercafés as can be seen in news reports. In other cases, some high schools banned the use of Little Smart among students (W. Li 2004). Before they dismiss working-class ICTs, school authorities rarely consider why their students want these ICT services. Does this suggest inadequacy in the school's ability to provide sufficient connectivity to young people? Should they open their computer labs for longer hours and be less authoritarian in managing students' online activity? Should a broader and more practical vision of ICTs be integrated in their teaching?

This is also the case with female Internet dropouts, an odd phenomenon in the affluent Nanhai area of Guangdong Province.[10] Since the late 1990s, Nanhai has been a national model for informatization: all of its local schools offer IT classes using computers beginning in the third grade. However, in 2002, most female members of my focus groups still held the misperception that technology is a male thing. Even teenage girls graduating from high school became Internet dropouts because, as one of them said, "It's impossible for us girls to get a job in the IT business." "The Net is just something for boys to play." It is obvious that their IT classes dealt only with technical issues. The curriculum needs to fill a significant gap in order to counter misperceptions about gender and technology. Here, the disparity between boys and girls was perpetuated through the socialization process, and a large number of the female population became excluded.

The most serious problems facing have-less youth exist in higher education, by far the most rapidly expanding segment of education (table 5.4). The expansion of universities—almost all of them public universities—is a process of "deformed industrialization" (Zhong, Liu, Liu, and Mo 2005, 48). Until the early 1990s, undergraduates not only paid no tuition but also received a modest stipend from the government. The situation began to change after 1998 as universities transformed into for-profit enterprises, charging increasing amounts of tuition and fees for room and board. Concomitantly, large-scale land seizures also occurred to meet the needs of university expansion, thus creating university towns (daxuecheng) in remote suburbs. This is a peculiar spatial component of the new urban landscape, whose market value often rests more on the commercial real estate development at the fringe of these clusters of universities.

The result of such education reform is that college administrators and professors are better paid than in the past, but more students and their families are in debt. Increasing class size leads to a decrease in quality education, at least with regard to the undergraduate programs that account for the bulk of the new college student population. Although more financial aid has been allocated among students from poor families, this measure is far from sufficient to reduce inequality on the campus.

Moreover, the job market is unprepared for the tremendous upsurge of college graduates. State-owned sectors, which used to provide secure jobs for young graduates, are shrinking. Private enterprises and foreign companies are hiring, but they prefer those with experience. According to the National Development and Reform Commission, at least 60 percent of China's 4.1 million college graduates in 2006 had difficulty finding jobs (Kahn 2006). Hence, the saying that "graduation means unemployment (*biye jiushi shiye*)," which makes life particularly difficult for those from working-class backgrounds who need to repay student loans (Zhong, Liu, Liu, and Mo 2005).

The problems facing new college graduates epitomize the dilemma in China's education reform. On the one hand, insufficient government funding pushes schools into the marketplace, where public schools and the newly emerged private schools compete for students in order to make more money rather than giving every child an equal opportunity through education. On the other hand, class sizes are much larger, thereby compromising quality learning. More students have to take part-time jobs to pay their bills, meaning that they are spending less time studying. On graduation, many of them can find only semiskilled or gray-collar jobs, and so they join the ranks of network labor.

It has also been reported that certain schools forced students into internship positions that essentially exploit child labor for profit, for example, by requiring computer majors to work long hours in online game "gold farms" in Xinjiang, as discussed in more detail in chapter 6 (*China Youth Daily* 2007). In other cases, needy students from low-income families or new graduates without stable jobs may also be tempted to join the team of network commentators (*wangluo pinglunyuan*), for instance, in Shanghai (Wu 2007), whose task is to post politically correct messages in Internet discussion forums. This new type of network labor results from the expanding Chinese network state. They are also called "five-mao party (*Wumaodang*)" because allegedly they are paid 5 mao (a half yuan or 6 cents) for each progovernment post they put online (Li 2007).

Finally, high tuition, substandard teaching, poor job prospects, and the accumulation of discontent build up to major breakdowns unwittingly ignited by critical incidents of mismanagement by school authorities. This was what happened on the campus of Shengda College in Zhengzhou,

Henan Province, in June 2006, which was probably the most violent university uprising in China since 1989.

Shengda was a privately run college founded by a Taiwanese entrepreneur under the state-run Zhengzhou University, a top university in Henan Province. Shengda charged students $ 2,500 a year, which is five times the tuition for Zhengzhou University, in part because Shengda students generally had lesser qualification but would pay extra to be affiliated with Zhengzhou. Money became the equalizer here because Shengda students were promised they would receive diplomas bearing the Zhengzhou University stamp. When the graduating class found out in June 2006 that their diplomas were issued in the name of Shengda College instead of Zhengzhou University, they pillaged campus buildings, clashed with police, and, in a powerful symbolic act, toppled the statue of the college's Taiwanese founder (Kahn 2006).

Shengda was not the only incident of student rage. In December 2005, a similar but smaller-scale protest took place in Dalian involving students in the EastSoft Information Institute (Kahn 2006), one of many newly founded colleges for training software engineers. While MoE officials have publicly denounced turning schools into for-profit enterprises, it remains unclear how, after several years of market-oriented practices, the damages can be undone and how a reasonable level of trust in the education system can be restored among have-less young people and their families.

On the morning of June 16, 2006, right after the revolt in Henan, more than a thousand police sealed the Shengda campus and prevented students from leaving. But the news had spread through students' mobile phones, especially SMS, at the same time as the protest took place in the early morning hours.[11] Media censors quickly clamped down on online discussions about the demonstrations, and Baidu.com, the popular Chinese-language search engine, erased all traces of the event in its search results. But on the Hong Kong-based Google traditional-Chinese search engine, the combination of keywords "Shengda," "student riot," and "blog" generated more than 2,500 results.[12] These include blogs maintained by overseas Chinese students as well as those hidden in domestic Web sites based in mainland China.

To a great extent, have-less young people are deprived of their access to low-cost education and subjected to gloomy job prospects. Yet at the same time, we see the spread of ICT knowledge to a greater portion of society and the formation of grassroots urban networks among have-less youth through the very same institution of schools. The problems triggered by for-profit education reform also force angry youth to roar together—not only in Zhengzhou and Dalian but also online and in the blogosphere—to protest the unfair situations that they are thrown into. This time, their voices are heard.

Commercializing the Health Care System

As education reform affects have-less young people and their families, the commercialization of China's health system impinges on the lives of everyone, including the younger generation but particularly have-less seniors. Old age, fixed income, and the absence of an effective social safety net make the elderly most vulnerable when health services are privatized. Overall, the conditions for public health in urban China are deteriorating, caused in part by detrimental change in the physical environment as a result of industrialization and urban growth. Factory pollutants are in the soil, car emissions in the air, health hazards in waterways. The environmental consequences of industrialization have a human health cost.

Pollution created by industrialization and urbanization is only one reason for the decline of health conditions. A more immediate reason is the marketization of the health care system, a process that exploits the have-less groups and creates more demand for alternative information and grassroots communication among the information have-less. In China today, "public [state-run] hospitals dominate the market of health services yet they have become for-profit organizations" (Gu, Gao, and Yao 2006, 450).

Consequently, although China's economy is booming and the society is more affluent than in the past, the general conditions for public health are deteriorating and average Chinese are feeling increasingly insecure when faced with disease and accidents. This trend constitutes what Hu Angang (2005), a leading public policy scholar in Beijing, calls a paradox of development (*fazhan beilun*) . He maintains that the Chinese government has to react to a critical report from the World Health Organization (WHO) based on a study conducted in 2000. In this report, China is ranked number144 in terms of the overall performance of its health system among all of WHO's 191 member states. In regard to social equality in the health system, China is number 188, fourth from the bottom (Liu 2005).

Medical expenses have been increasing at a much faster pace than personal income since the 1990s in both urban and rural areas (Gu, Gao, and Yao 2006). According to the Ministry of Hygiene (MoH), depending on the type of hospital, average fees for seeing a doctor increased eight to ten times between 1993 and 2003 and the expenses for hospitalization six to nine times (*China Hygiene Statistical Yearbook* 2005). At the same time, public funds are decreasing as a proportion of total investment in health care, although most hospitals nominally remain state-owned public institutions. The number of for-profit clinics has increased and now surpasses those in the nonprofit category. In 2004, only 12.8 percent of hospitals' budgets, even for state-run hospitals, was from the government, whereas a staggering 40.3 percent was from the sales of medicine and another 44.6 percent from fees charged for medical services (*China Hygiene Statistical Yearbook* 2005). In other words, the more that doctors can sell expensive medicine and overpriced services, the more profit they can contribute to their hospitals and, ultimately, to their own salary, following the model of "provider-induced over-consumption" (Gu 2007, 5).

Admittedly the absolute amount of government funds for health care has increased, but the distribution of funds is highly uneven. Most of the additional money goes to the pharmaceutical industry and hospitals rather than disease prevention, although it has been proven that to prevent disease is a much more efficient and economical solution for public health problems than efforts to cure them (Liu 2005). With the outbreak of SARS and the AIDS pandemic, China has given more priority to epidemics. But overall, preventive measures remain the weakest link because they require a lot of input but yield little revenue.

Another set of problems in China's medical system has to do with the waste of scarce health care resources. This is evident as the proportion of occupied hospital beds decreased from 80.9 percent in 1990 to about 60 percent between 1997 and 2001 (Zhou 2005). The average number of patients each doctor treats has also decreased significantly. This does not mean that the health of Chinese people has increased and they do not need to consult doctors as much as in the past. Rather, increasing numbers are deterred by skyrocketing costs for medicine and medical services. The percentage of urban residents who choose not to see a doctor even when they are sick increased from 1.8 percent in 1993 to 16.1 percent in 1998 and then to 20.7 in 2003.[13] Although many hospital beds lay empty in 2003, about 41 percent of low-income urbanites chose not to be hospitalized even though their doctors advised otherwise (Hu 2005). Patients and their families no longer trust information provided by doctors, whose personal interests are too closely intertwined with the medical bill.

China's new pharmaceutical industry also plays a central role in elevating the cost of medicine, especially through pharmaceutical representatives (*yiyao daibiao*) (Zhang 2005). These are employees of the pharmaceutical companies, both multinationals and domestic Chinese firms, who promote medical products using a combination of kickbacks, personal favors, and interpersonal *guangxi* networks to influence hospitals. Due to these organized legal and "underground" activities, doctors are tempted to prescribe more expensive treatments. In Beijing alone, there were at least ten thousand pharmaceutical representatives in 2005, whose main task was to inflate the cost of medicine in the city (Zhang 2005).

Could there be an organized force to counter the alliance between profit-seeking hospitals and the pharmaceutical industry? Official bodies like the National People's Congress and the State Development and Reform Commission have paid attention to the problem (Pei 2006). High-level MoH cadres have spoken out against the for-profit behaviors (L. He 2005). It has also become common practice for the mass media to carry out investigative journalism reports on the commercialization of the health care system. These are notable improvements compared to a few years ago, but it remains unclear how effectively the price of medicine can be lowered by these measures.

Medical insurance can be an effective structural counterforce to restore checks and balances in the health system. As an industry in itself, insurance companies need to work to prevent the abuse of prescriptions in order to protect their own interests. Yet as shown in table 5.6, overall only a small portion of urban residents have medical insurance. The counterbalancing effect of the insurance companies is therefore minimal, particularly for have-less seniors, most of whom lack insurance coverage.

As of 2003, the largest portion of urban residents (44.8 percent) paid medical expenses from their own pockets. The second largest group (34.4 percent) used social medical insurance (*shehui yiliao baoxian*), a general term for copayment among employee, employer, and the government.

Table 5.6
Percentage of urban residents using different payment types for medical expenses

	1993	1998	2003
Self	27.3	44.1	44.8
Social medical insurance	1.1	4.7	34.4
Cooperative medical insurance	1.6	2.7	6.6
Commercial insurance	3.6	3.7	5.6
Labor-protection medical insurance	48.2	28.7	4.6
Coverage by public funds	18.2	16.0	4.0

Source: *National Survey on Hygiene Services* (1993, 1998, 2003), cited in Gu, Gao, and Yao (2006).

Together, self-pay and copay cover 79.2 percent of the urban population. Compared with 1993, the most significant change is the decline of labor protection medical insurance (*laobao yiliao*). This is a state-run insurance plan, a legacy of the socialist era, designed for blue-collar workers, like those working in mining, railway, and telecom work units. Labor protection insurance used to be the single largest category, protecting nearly half of China's urban population in 1993. But by 2003, its share had fallen to 4.6 percent. Meanwhile, public funds also plummeted from 18.2 percent to 4.0 percent.

Although insurance covers only a fraction of the total population, the situation is even gloomier for the elderly. According to official statistics, only 33.59 million retirees in 2004 had medical insurance (*Almanac of China's Population* 2005), which represents less than 27 percent of China's 155 million populations above age sixty. In other words, the majority of China's senior citizens had no medical insurance. Yet they have to cope with the reform of the health care system. No wonder have-less seniors look for more trustworthy information, online or through interpersonal networks extended by mobile phones. Using ICTs to seek health information is, of course, a worldwide phenomenon with the spread of Internet (Rice and Katz 2001). But to have-less seniors in China today, rapid commercialization of health care and the collapse of traditional social security system have created a unique set of imperatives for them to seek medical information themselves.

ICT Solutions for the Elderly

The commercialization of health care is having a strong influence on the elderly, although this is only part of the more profound changes in the pension system and the delivery of social services in general. Although more resources are available in the cities for the support of senior citizens than in the countryside, the urban social security system remains fragmented and often ineffective when it comes to have-less seniors in working-class families, for instance, the parents of laid-off workers. The problem of this social deficit has to be solved at the level of public policy given the restructuring of Chinese family. While filial piety (*xiao*) remains a relevant notion, the combination of the one-child policy and rising labor mobility means that during China's transition to a market economy, "the trend of forming nuclear families instead of multigenerational families under one roof runs counter to the needs of the elderly" (England 2005, 45).

A telling indicator is the increase in the number of so-called empty-nest households (*kongchao jiating*): households with only senior citizens who either do not have children or do not live with their children. This type of household accounted for 16.7 percent of Chinese families with elderly members in 1987 and 26 percent in 2000 (D. Yang and Zhao 2004). Up to 2004, there were 23.4 million senior citizens living in empty-nest households nationwide.[14] Because of the rising number of seniors living by themselves, there is an urgent need for more supportive measures in the medical system, the pension system, and the social services system overall (R. Huang 2005).

How should this social services system for the elderly be built so that it can perform some of the most crucial functions of the traditional multigenerational family? So far most studies have stressed the physical and economic needs of senior citizens, which explains the abundance of information on the health and pension status of the elderly. In contrast, communication needs are insufficiently emphasized; however, they are at least an equally fundamental service provided by the traditional family for the social and psychological well-being of the senior population. Can this communication function be taken over by working-class ICTs? If so, how?

It is important to note that not just in China but in other countries as well, research findings have indicated that communication is critical to health for the elderly and the process of "successful aging" (Hummert and Nussbaum 2001). Not only could ICTs be used in telemedicine and caretaking for seniors with disease, but they could also strengthen family ties across space and thus function as an important preventive measure for physical and psychological disabilities. After his analysis of Chinese empty-nest households, Huang Runlong provided two policy recommendations that have communication components: establish community-based mutual help groups among the elderly and install telephone lifelines in these empty-nest households so that seniors can call for help in an emergency (Huang 2005). Some local state agencies in Shanghai, Liaoning, and Hubei have provided more support than others in helping foster mutual-help activities on the Internet. However, at the national level, there is no policy structure for ICTs among the elderly, especially among have-less seniors.

We have seen the spread of working-class ICTs among the senior population in Chinese cities, which results largely from bottom-up entrepreneurialism. Most obvious in this trend is the ability of the mobile phone market to better serve elderly users. The diffusion of mobile phones is faster than the spread of Internet among the elderly. This process began a few years ago when senior family members inherited used mobile phones from their adult children (Xi 2004). More of them are getting new handsets now with more choices in the market. As in the early years of mobile phone diffusion, it used to be the case that one could find only imported models suitable for senior citizens. A popular model among seniors in Shanghai was the Samsung T208, originally launched in the Chinese market in October 2002 to target the upper class. But by the end of 2004, its price had dropped from more than 3,000 yuan ($362) to 1,850 yuan ($223), and it had become a favorite choice for elderly users in the city because it was easy to use (*PC Online* 2004).

Domestic brands have been catching up in the elderly market. One example is Huali's Old Companion (*laoban*) handset, costing about 600 yuan ($73) in December 2006. It has big buttons, a large display, amplified sound output, amplified vibration alerts, and an audio reader for time and phone numbers for easy handling of senior citizens, especially those with some health problems. It is also equipped with a radio. This phone has a special key to send emergency information simultaneously to multiple family members and social service organizations. This not only frees them from the trouble of remembering or searching for phone numbers but also helps them save critical time in an emergency. The design and production of this handset was based on the estimate that the elderly market can consume potentially 7 million mobile phones, and the low-end market niche had yet to be tapped (China New Telecom Network 2006).

At the same time, Little Smart handsets makers are marketing products specifically for seniors. For instance, the UT190 handset by UTStarcom has big buttons, a large display, and loud alerts. It also has an FM radio and a red button for emergency calls (*China Netizens Daily* 2006). Moreover, Little Smart service providers like China Netcom in Qingdao, Shangdong Province, have begun to provide location service that allows subscribers to trace the physical location of their Little Smart handsets. The information can be retrieved by SMS, voice call, or on the Internet. This Little Smart service is reported to be much cheaper than GPS and more precise than similar service through GSM (Xu and Yu 2004). It is particularly popular among seniors with Alzheimer's disease, who may otherwise frequently go astray (Dong 2006). In Qingdao, this location service costs as little as 3 yuan ($0.36) per month, and it can also be used to trace small children or anyone else carrying the handset (*Qingdao Morning Post* 2006).

This location service is yet another indication that working-class ICTs for the elderly are often appropriated and domesticated in a family setting.

Mobile handsets and services targeting the elderly market have often been promoted as gift items from children to their elderly parents or between senior-aged couples. The spread of these ICT objects itself is likely to be a process that strengthens existing family ties even before the actual use of the technology.

In my own research trips, I have quite commonly encountered seniors using working-class wireless services in various Chinese cities. These include average senior citizens I met on the streets and on public transportation from Beijing to Guangzhou and in small cities as well. They are people like the pensioner in Ningbo who used Little Smart as his only phone line in winter 2004 and my retired uncle with a hearing impairment who bought his SMS-only handset in spring 2006 in the southern city of Ganzhou. My parents who live in Wuhan had also used prepaid GSM service for a few years until they switched to Little Smart in 2005.

Finally, have-less seniors may also use landline phones at home in distinct ways that allow them to stay in touch with their mobile-equipped family members for free. One of them is the practice of beeping: seniors in working families can call someone (usually their adult children in the city) and immediately hang up. This allows the receiver to know who just called and can then return the call. Beeping is quite popular in Africa (Castells, Fernandez-Ardevol, Qiu, and Sey 2006, Donner 2007), but is seldom reported among Chinese user groups except have-less seniors. According to my survey group participants, the elderly in low-income families who have limited technical know-how prefer this practice; some of them do not know how to dial phone numbers correctly, so they just press the redial button to beep their children, and others want to save paying the phone bill.[15] These low-end uses of ICT allow formerly excluded have-less seniors to start enjoy networked connectivity, however limited it may be.

With regard to the Internet, users who are older than sixty account for about 1 percent of all netizens in China (table 5.2). The proportion has been rather stable since 2000. But because the elderly group constitutes more than 12 percent of China's total population and the aging of society is accelerating, it is evident that much remains to be done for the Internet to fully serve senior citizens, especially have-less seniors. Currently, not only is the Internet less popular among the elderly than among the younger generation, but it is also adopted mostly by those who are better educated. The physical challenge of old age is but one of many reasons for this pattern of adoption. Other reasons include the general absence of social

148

support systems, whether technical or educational. Unlike the younger generation, few have-less seniors belong to any school where they may learn about computers. Even fewer go to cybercafés because they see these places of collective Internet access as something for young consumers only.

However, these seniors generally read newspapers and magazines, and they have been targeted by a number of popular TV programs (for example, *Gorgeous Sunset* or *Xiyanghong* by China Central Television) regularly covering a variety of topics that concern them, such as health, cooking, and family life. As a result, the mass media in general do a better job for have-less seniors than for have-less young people, which at least partially mitigates the informational needs for alternative communication channels among the elderly.

This does not mean that the senior population has not found any use for the Internet. A survey in seven Chinese cities in 2002 discovered that the elderly have been particularly active in searching for medical information on the Internet.[16] This corresponds with my own observation that my parents go online because one of them has a chronic disease and they need to learn as much as possible about prescriptions and treatments for it. It is especially so given the context of the commercialization of the health system, under which it is a routine for them to see multiple doctors whose prescriptions may or may not agree with each other. They always take doctors' advice with a grain of salt and cross-check it with information online.

Even seniors who do not own or do not know how to use computers may ask their children to go online to search for medical and other information for them. The information can then be shared either face-to-face or in phone calls. In this way, access to the Internet is sustained in a collective mode based on the family unit, which has also been extended locally and translocally due to the diffusion of working-class ICTs.

Beyond the family level, we have begun to see organized efforts to bring the elderly online, such as the North China Seniors Network and Honggen Seniors Place in Hubei, Central China. The best-known Web site for elderly users is probably Old Kids (*laoxiaohai*) in Shanghai, the city with the highest percentage of old-age residents in China.[17] Founded in 2000 by three graduates of top universities in the city, the Web site endeavors to help the elderly go online. This dot-com works closely with the Commission for the Elderly (*laolingwei*) under Shanghai Municipality.[18] Its activities are both on and off the Net, including Internet schools that have trained more than 50,000 senior netizens (Y. Zhong 2004). In addition to serving the elderly, they also bring together the young and the old through Internet-related activities.

At the beginning, Old Kids was exclusively for highly educated retirees, such as those belonging to the Association of Elderly Science and Technology Workers in Shanghai, an institutional partner of the Web site since October 2000. But since June 2001, the site has entered Shanghai's ordinary residential communities to promote Internet knowledge among a wider scope of senior citizens. It has collaborated with Shanghai Oriental Radio Station in launching two popular programs, Senior Classroom (*laonian xuetang*) and 792 Internet Time-Space (*792wangluo shikong*), so that average members of the elderly population can learn about Internet technologies. As of July 2006, Old Kids was sending out approximately 12,000 monthly newsletters to its members, who need to contribute only 2 yuan ($0.24) each month as the membership fee.[19]

ICTs as Welfare? Chances and Challenges

Lower-mobility people have begun to adopt the Internet and mobile phones in order to adjust to the rapidly changing network society of contemporary China. This presents an equally pivotal process as the adoption and appropriation of low-end ICTs among higher-mobility members of the information have-less. In the first process, as discussed in chapter 4 and visualized in figure 5.1, migrant workers and laid-off workers join the ranks

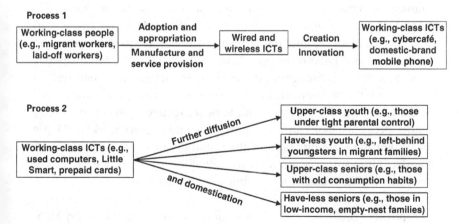

Figure 5.1
The information have-less and working-class ICTs: Adoption, appropriation, innovation, and domestication.

of network labor in creating and shaping working-class ICTs. In the second, and equally important, process, the further diffusion and domestication of working-class ICTs transcend its initial technosocial basis of the urban underclass to a much wider scope of families across class and strata. This is a crucial development because it extends networked connectivity to the formerly excluded young people and seniors in both upper-class and have-less families. This spread enlarges the social demographic reach of working-class ICTs and, in so doing, creates more working-class jobs. It also highlights structural changes in the family unit itself, which functions as another micro, yet collective, mode of problem solving amid macro social transformations.

With the passing of the traditional multigenerational family and the overall commercialization of social services, both the old and the young have become more vulnerable than before, for the public institutions that used to provide shelter, such as education and health, have now been turned into for-profit organizations. Microlevel solutions, however effective they are in the grassroots networks of individuals and families, cannot fundamentally alter the status quo at the system level. A similar process of commercialization also characterizes the ICT sector.

In order to solve these problems, and include rather than exclude the have-less, it is essential to rethink and reform education, public health, and social services, at the very least to prevent them from further marginalizing the less powerful and less affluent. In terms of ICTs and urban communication systems at large, the most profound challenge starts with rethinking and reimagining the basic social roles of the technologies. Can we conceive of an information industry that takes services for the young and the old as a pillar of its operation, not just for profit, but for public good as well? A network society based on the inclusion of have-less as much as it relies on the haves and have-mores? Currently the market value of the young and the old has begun to be recognized. Some of them have joined network labor, such as underaged online game workers (H. He 2005). But these are just signs of the beginning that may or may not be translated into autonomy, power, and self-efficacy—and may even lead to the further subjugation of less mobile populations.

In September 2005, the Zhengzhou Institute of Aeronautical Industry Management declined applications for student loans on the ground that the applicants possessed mobile phones (Wu 2005). In October 2006, the Jinan Bureau of Civil Affairs issued a new procedure that would disqualify two types of people from applying for low-income welfare: those who had purchased computers in the previous year and those who used a mobile phone regularly (Qiao 2006). Both incidents triggered nationwide public debate, in print and broadcasting media as well as online forums and the blogosphere.

This was the first wave of serious discussion regarding welfare provision and the information have-less, signaling that it is time to reconsider the social role of ICTs in a different light—not as a tool of profit making but as welfare, a mechanism of equity and social inclusion beyond computers in the classroom, beyond telemedicine, beyond conspicuous consumption, or any short-term uses of ICTs for economic development. Many of the basic issues here have been discussed in international forums such as the World Summit on the Information Society (WSIS). In the context of urban China, it is imperative to address the problems at a system level that takes the needs of young people and the worries of the aging society as a fundamental dimension of its long-term operation.

The loaded term *welfare* of course entails a few caveats. First, the idea of ICTs as welfare foregrounds communication as a basic human right, thus calling for welfare policies for the less mobile and more vulnerable populations as a basis of a more inclusive network society. While basic life necessities like food and shelter remain important in the welfare system, in the contemporary world characterized by the wide spread of ICTs, the notion of welfare has to be expanded to cover the informational needs of have-less people, particularly the young and the old.

Second, fundamentally different from the past passive welfare policies imposed from top down, ICT welfare policies need to be built from the bottom up. Participation is the key for the have-less to take part in the decision-making process through their working-class ICTs as well as more traditional involvement. Good welfare relies on what the people need, whether the have-less are treated with respect in program design, and to what extent they are involved as actors or even providers rather than mere consumers of information services—so that have-less young people and have-less seniors are socially uplifted in addition to the purely instrumental benefits they receive.

Third, the notion of ICTs as welfare should include all stakeholders in both the public and private sectors following the multistake holder approach proposed by WSIS (Padovani and Nordenstreng 2004). In urban China today, successful involvement of the government, especially at the local level, is fundamental to the long-term sustainability of any welfare program. It is true that in certain cities, predatory local officials have posed threats to working-class ICTs, and in general they are more concerned about upper-class than lower-class interests. But this does not mean that local government is always hostile to have-less people. On the contrary, if we look at the places with the most vibrant working-class ICTs, the local governments are almost always central to their local structure of policy support, for example, in the case of the Old Kids Web site in Shanghai, with its close ties to the Municipal Commission for the Elderly, as well as the social support group for left-behind children in Hunan, sponsored by the Provincial Committee of the Communist Youth League (Bu 2008).[20]

The central role of the local state is evident in the prospering of cyber-cafés in Shenzhen and the growth of Little Smart wireless service in China's second- and third-tier cities. It is important to note that the local government is seldom involved as the sole ICT service provider in any of these cases, whose success depends on the involvement of the business community. In other words, the local state is central in that mayors and local telecom authorities are in the best position to motivate the private sector by providing supportive policy. After this initial stage, it is up to entrepreneurs to decide what the information needs are, where the next site of service delivery should be, and how to conduct their business: via Internet or mobile phone or other local and translocal networks.

The consortia behind successful ICT welfare delivery can create working-class jobs in local communities, bringing income, respect, and sustainable lifestyle to the young and the old who are now at the margins of society. Low-end ICTs like SMS and cybercafés can be used to deliver new types of social services. Or they can help enhance existing services through shared access that is inexpensive yet convenient, for example, the distribution of information for preventive medicine through SMS. In so doing, public institutions like universities and hospitals can be reconfigured into crucial platforms on which working-class ICTs are developed for have-less populations with lower mobility. For instance, in Norway, SINTEF (the Foundation for Scientific and Industrial Research) at the Norwegian Institute of Technology organized a workshop in 2006 designed to facilitate the creation of ICT systems that "seek to improve elderly peoples' access to social services."[21] In other Western countries, the Internet has helped hospitals in delivering and improving their services through the use of Web sites, mailing lists, and online databases (Rice and Katz 2001).

The issue is particularly imperative for the elderly population because China already has 1 million Internet users above age sixty; throughout the country, but most typically in the rust belts of the northeast, the aging working class of the Maoist era has been suffering greatly from the

commercialization of medical services. Not only is the level of technopho-
bia high among this age group, but they also have little access to technical
support and training in accessing alternative information. Even for
the better-educated seniors, we do not know how well they are using
online information, especially given findings in the Western context
that online health information may also mislead and cause hazards
if patients and their families are not provided with proper guidance
(Cline and Haynes 2001).

To develop a full-fledged ICT welfare policy for the elderly is not just
about the technology. Helping seniors to go online, providing them with
quality health information on Web pages or SMS requires organized efforts
from not only the ICT industry but, more important, traditional social
service providers in the government, nongovernmental organizations, and
local communities. Fundamental to all these is how a rapidly changing
country like China should handle the human cost of modernization and
how the industrializing society can prepare itself for aging, using working-
class ICTs as a more efficient means for content and service delivery to the
family and as a more effective means for community participation.

Unlike the elderly, have-less young people face another set of challenges.
Most of them are acquiring ICT knowledge and skills thanks to schooling
as well as advertising that targets them. These advertising and marketing
campaigns are a major factor behind the contemporary Chinese youth
culture sustained online and through mobile phones. It has been quite
common for China's younger generation to use working-class ICTs to
strengthen and extend their interpersonal ties, thus forming informal
networks of information and technical support that are supplementary to
the key institutions of education and family.

According to a survey conducted in Fujian Province in 2001, the Internet
has become an essential information source for college students to learn
about sex and sexuality (Q. Chen 2001). But what kinds of informal sex
education are young people receiving in cyberspace? The answer is com-
modified body images, sexist jokes, and the online promotion of adult
products that reflect and reproduce existing social inequalities of gender,
class, and ethnicity. Much of these come through mainstream Internet
portals and telecom service providers, who exploit the curiosity and sus-
ceptibility of young people to maximize corporate profit.

In more general terms, Chinese young people today are vulnerable to
excessive commercialization, which is particularly true of those from
working-class families because they are overwhelmingly spoiled only

children. At the beginning of new semesters, they often spend a lot, purchasing expensive products including the latest models of handsets, some even spending the equivalent of their living costs for an entire semester within a few days (Pang 2003). If the notion of ICTs as welfare can be introduced to social policies for have-less young people, the first challenge is how ICTs can be separated from conspicuous consumption and how the dissemination of ICTs can become a process that promotes equality rather than the exclusion or demeaning of the less affluent and less powerful.

The challenge of commercialization is not only a problem facing young people. The basic living conditions of low-mobility groups are changing because the old safety net and traditional social equalizers have disappeared and the new ones have yet to take shape to deliver badly needed public good. It is therefore a fundamental task to bring the notion of welfare back in for both the young and the old. In retrospect, most problems facing have-less young people and have-less seniors are rooted in the lack of wider social participation and the domination of elite opinions. The power imbalance explains the hasty commercialization of public institutions as well as the prevalence of consumer culture, both influencing the development of working-class ICTs. Although domestic companies and multinationals have recognized the market value of have-less users, the recognition stays at the level of consumption that carries only superficial and temporary commitments to the information have-less. In this sense, the most fundamental driving force for the rise of have-less people and working-class ICTs is not commercial interests or state policy. Instead, it is the bottom-up informational needs of people, young and old, to deal with their existential issues at the grassroots level of the enlarged network society.

III   A New Working Class in the Making

6 Places and Community

Working-class ICTs and the information have-less are two essential components of China's evolving network society. But what happens to the city after the technology meets the people? We have seen that the spread of low-end ICTs produced new markets and jobs. But how do these technological and economic developments influence the transformation of China's urban places and the rise of new working-class communities in the Chinese informational city?

Urban places are sociospatial structures that sustain the city's daily activities and collective memories. They are based on tangible infrastructures such as architecture, roads, signs, and the telephone grid. Yet places are also intangible because they exist in people's minds, maintained through social organization, enacted by an image of the street, a smell of the factory, or a conversation with a neighbor. Behind each urban place is an invisible array of power relations, economic ties, and interpersonal networks. And it is often these invisible parts that ultimately define the flavor of an urban community.

Place making on the local level is crucial to the technosocial emergence of working-class network society. Cybercafés, Little Smart, the sales of prepaid phone cards and used handsets: these are primarily local, small-scale, grassroots businesses. The subsequent networks operating on these low-end ICT infrastructures—among migrant workers, laid-off workers, the young and the old—are also largely local and translocal sociospatial structures: family, residential community, friendship, and coworker networks. Some of these are instances of local resistance against the encroachment of neoliberal globalization—efforts to protect local culture and local identity using networked connectivity. Others are more explicit efforts to strive and thrive within the larger framework of the "space of flows" (Castells 1996) as shown by the "gold-farmer" guilds of the online gaming industry.[1]

What kinds of places arise when have-less people adopt working-class ICTs as an ordinary part of their everyday life in the city? What social structures support or constrain technological applications at the grass-roots? What are the opportunities, problems, and challenges in these spa-tialized processes of class formation? This chapter deals with these questions by focusing on the concrete urban places where the information have-less live and work. These are, first, the urban village (*chengzhongcun*), a lower-class community that mixes have-less migrants with lower-mobility indig-enous villagers, a topic examined through interviews, focus groups, field observations, and a sociospatial census of working-class ICTs in a typical urban village in Guangzhou. Second, we discuss the most important places of production: factories. Place making in factories consists of assembly-line management and resistance as well as life in the dormitories, including not only domains dominated by the employer but also spheres created through workers' collective action, online and offline. These contemporary urban places, essential to the lives of the have-less, would lose much of their distinctiveness without working-class ICTs.

Beyond Hukou and the Work Unit

How are decisions made as to which people belong to which place? Who are the "locals" entitled to urban social services and citizenship rights? Answers to these questions are quickly changing given China's soaring population mobility and increasingly globalized economy. Nevertheless, Chinese cities inherited from the Maoist era two important ways of urban organization that are fundamental to place-making and community-building processes today: the *hukou* residential registration system that decides urban resident status and the subsequent distribution of state-provided benefits and services (Cheng and Selden 1994, Solinger 1999); and the *danwei* work unit system that governs the domain of work and employment (Lu and Perry 1997, Bray 2005). During the Maoist period, the two mechanisms were combined to manage nearly all aspects of work and life in the city, from political mobilization to consumption, from education to entertainment. Since the 1980s, both systems have been significantly eroded, reformed, and partially dismantled. Neverthless, they continue to function materially, organizationally, and culturally, reinforc-ing old prejudices and causing new discrimination, thus becoming two basic conditions in the transformation of working-class communities (Cartier, Castells, and Qiu 2005).

The *hukou* system, established in 1958, has two major effects. First, it restricts the movement of population by requiring everyone to register with the authorities as the resident of a particular place. In the Maoist years, this residential status was the precondition for obtaining employment, food rations, and social services. The *hukou* system therefore effectively curbed population flows into the cities until the 1980s. Since then, with the transition from the planned economy to a market economy, the *hukou* system has loosened. Migrants can now find jobs and purchase food and services as long as they can pay, although without local *hukou*, they usually have to pay more for health care and education (Cheng and Selden 1994, Solinger 1999). Despite notable efforts at reform, especially since 2003, have-less migrants still face barriers. For example, someone who did not hold *hukou* status in Guangzhou in 2007 had to pay to obtain a temporary residential card in order to become a taxi driver in the city.[2]

The other impact is that the *hukou* system splits society along a rural-urban dichotomy, thus maintaining an inferior category of "peasant workers" by institutional measures even though millions of these people now live in cities. The system has two categories: agricultural *hukou* for people in the countryside and nonagricultural *hukou* for city dwellers. Due to proindustrialization state policies, rural communities are often left to take care of themselves, whereas the cities receive more public investment to develop infrastructure and provide a wide range of services not available in rural areas (Chan and Zhang 1999, Solinger 1999, MacKenzie 2002). With massive rural-to-urban migration, the dichotomous *hukou* structure forms a fundamental dimension of inequality that underlies the urbanization process. Often only migrants holding agricultural *hukou* are willing to take low-paying blue-collar jobs that are essential to the growth of the city, whereas long-term city dwellers, even if they are jobless, enjoy the social status of local residents because they are regarded as permanent members of the urban community rather than dispensable parts.

This inequality structure based on *hukou* has a profound impact on the formation of urban places as an integral part of working-class network society. It artificially separates locals from migrants and magnifies the social schism between them. As a result, while lower-class long-term residents demand neighborhood improvements, they usually exclude those without local *hukou* even though some of these people with rural origins have lived among them for decades. In other cases, long-term residents may also look at rural migrants as intruders and build up walls of segregation, physically or through discriminatory measures in the job market, residential housing market, or school system. Consequently, migrant enclaves appear, adding to the discontinuity of the sociospatial landscape in have-less urban communities.

While *hukou* decided individuals' residential status, *danwei,* or the work unit, was the main organization determining people's official residential neighborhood through employment-based housing provision. A typical work unit, like a state-owned factory, a government unit, or a university, was a small society in itself. Central to the system is lifetime employment, known as the "iron rice bowl." But besides organizing work, a *danwei* community contains the facilities to support its members' needs: housing, education, health care, a pension, and entertainment. Until the 1980s, most of China's urban population was attached to such work units, which dictate people's income, social and political status, and citizenship rights (Lu and Perry 1997, Frazier 2002, Bray 2005).

Now, with the decline of the state-owned enterprises (SOEs), work units no longer play the central role in urban life that they once did. Although the term *danwei* is still in use, the work unit has lost many of its social roles other than its core function as the workplace. Services traditionally provided by the work unit, such as housing, schooling, and health care, have been transferred to other social organizations, particularly commercial ones, discussed in chapter 5. Accompanying this transformation is the fading away of the *danwei*-based urban community, where employees of the same work unit and their families live together, usually adjacent to the workplace.

Despite the withering of traditional *danwei*-based communities, work units still matter given their continued economic role in shaping urban society. This is especially the case when the notion of work units has been broadened to include private companies, Sino-foreign joint ventures, and multinational corporations. Income inequality within and among these broadly defined work units is tremendous; so are the employment benefits they provide.

A key continuity in the transformation of work units is that most *danwei* organizations remain top-down hierarchical structures, as in the case of Beijing's high-tech companies.[3] The top leaders can be senior CCP cadres, as in the Maoist years. Or they can be a private entrepreneur, a member of China's new rich, a Taiwanese investor, a Japanese businessman, or someone from Silicon Valley. Regardless of the types of *danwei* leaders, management maintains control over employees, which is often more stringent than elsewhere due to the weak power of labor unions. It is precisely this power imbalance within the *danwei* that has made it easy for work units to shed the welfare responsibilities that they used to carry a few years ago. In so doing, the Chinese work units are becoming "lean and mean" while strengthening their role in exploiting and subjugating the information have-less.

The retreat of *danwei* from the domain of social services provision leaves employees and their families to take care of themselves. This adds to population mobility, freeing people from the control of their employers while exposing them to the whirlwinds of the market. Heightened instability then contributes to the adoption of working-class ICTs because grassroots communication has become a life necessity for all city dwellers, especially the information have-less, as *danwei* withers away.

Across the country, similar work units tend to form clusters that reflect the characteristics of the regional economy. In the rust belt areas of the northeast, there are more state-owned factories; in the energy-rich western regions, more mines and refineries; in the export-oriented industrial zones of the southeast coast, more multinationals and trade firms. By drawing different types of people together—people of different ages, different education attainment, different professions, different *hukou* standing, and different regional identities—these clusters of work units define the tone of local working-class communities and set in motion the multiple processes that are essential to the formation of new urban places—places to which the information have-less belong.

In the following we examine these grounded processes of place making and the typical communities they generate by focusing on the urban village (*chengzhongcun*) and the factories. For the people of the have-less, these are arguably the most important urban places, where the birth of new working-class communities is most likely—and most contested. Emerging beyond the traditional *hukou* and *danwei* systems, these new spatial formations bring us closer to the technosocial reality: a working-class network society in the making.

Urban Villages: Communities between Past and Future

The urban village (*chengzhongcun*) is a working-class community and a most intriguing element in China's urban landscape. In other countries, the phrase *urban village* may invoke different images, ranging from revamped traditional quarters in developed countries to impoverished slums and ghettos at the margins of large Third World cities (Epstein 1973, Aldrich and Sandhu 1995, Bell and Jayne 2004). But *chengzhongcun*, meaning literally "village in the middle of the city," is distinctly Chinese in several ways.

Although urban villages in China do not exclude the upper class or the extremely poor, life in these communities generally falls somewhere in between. Most residents here are not affluent, but neither are they in dire poverty. Even if some of them earn more money than the city average, they are still looked down upon for their accent, the way they dress, and their lack of cultural sophistication. These are communities of the under-class—mostly migrants, but also lower-mobility have-less people, such as elderly indigenous villagers. To outsiders, the place may look shabby and chaotic. But anyone who spends time in these neighborhoods would be hard-pressed not to see the networks that hold the have-less community together. These networks are increasingly sustained by low-end ICTs, offering us a rare window to observe and understand the Chinese informational city from the perspective of the have-less.

From Rural Village to Migrant Enclave

The land in China's urban villages is owned by the village collective, unlike other urban properties directly managed by the city government (P. Li 2002). This collective ownership originates from state policy allowing rural villages to distribute land to rural households. Following the rapid expansion of cities, many rural villages adjacent to the cities were encircled by urban land. In Guangzhou, for example, there are 139 urban villages including those in distant or adjacent suburbs and some right in the middle of city proper (P. Li 2002).

As the surrounding environment changed, internal transformation became inevitable. The village economy shifted from agriculture to more lucrative urban businesses such as retail and rental housing services. The rental business of inexpensive apartments is often by far the largest source of income for indigenous families with long-term *hukou* residential status. Large numbers of have-less migrants move in, changing these villages into the most prominent mode of migrant settlements in large Chinese cities (Wu 2002).

Rent is much more affordable here than elsewhere in the city because there is no land cost for villagers to add several stories of rental space above their private house. Since most real estate projects in China are directed at the upper class, demand far exceeds supply in the low-end rental market, thus giving rental housing in urban villages a crucial role (Qian and Chen

2003). In Guangzhou, the average rent in urban villages was one-fifth to one-tenth the cost of commercial apartment leasing nearby (J. Li 2004). Besides affordability, it is more convenient for migrants without local *hukou* to rent residential and commercial space in urban villages because the landlords usually require little or no paperwork while allowing more migrants to share rooms (M. Liu 2000). The popularity of urban village rental thus reveals the failure of the Chinese government to provide housing for the have-less, especially migrants. As a result, private solutions—individual tenants renting privately owned housing—become the most likely choice. This was confirmed in a survey conducted in Dongguan and Guangzhou in 1999, which found that most migrants (33.2 percent) rented privately owned housing, followed by employer-provided dormitories (25.3 percent) and self-built shelters on construction site (9.9 percent) (Zhang, Zhao, and Tian 2003). Given the enormous size of the migrant population, it is common for tenants to outnumber indigenous villagers, as shown in table 6.1.

A typical urban village in Guangzhou is characterized by "cement monsters *(shuini guaiwu)*" (P. Li 2002). These are private houses, usually seven or eight stories tall, lined up on both sides of a narrow alley. In order to maximize living space, the buildings from the second floor up are built out

Table 6.1
Ratio of migrants to indigenous residents in selected urban villages

City	Urban villages	Year	Number of migrants	Number of indigenous residents	Ratio (indigenous residents = 100)
Beijing					
	Wabian	1997	2,162	2,086	104:100
	917 district	1997	287	318	90.3:100
Guangzhou					
	Shipai	2000	42,000	9,234	455:100
	Sanyuanli	2000	11,000	4,200	262:100
	Tangxi	2000	9,534	4,656	205:100
	Ruibao	2000	60,000	2,000	3,000:100
Dongguan					
	Shangyuan	1998	8,000	2,842	281:100
	Yantian	1998	70,000	2,877	2,433:100

Sources: Zhang, Zhao, and Tian (2003); Shipai Village estimates based on Zheng (2006).

as far as possible. The space directly above the communal alley is often completely occupied, thus transforming the street into a dark tunnel. Locals call these buildings *woshoulou* (handshake building) or *qingzuilou* (kissing building), for residents on both sides of the alley can literally shake hands with each other or kiss each other from their windows (M. Liu 2000, P. Li 2002). In such overcrowded neighborhoods, the density of buildings can be overwhelming. In the Shipai Village of Guangzhou, 3,656 private residences are crowded together on the village's 0.6 square-kilometer land (Lan and Zhang 2005).

Despite efforts to clean up, modernize, and upgrade urban villages, many of these have-less places have survived and even prospered. In this sense, the Chinese informational city is not complete without urban villages, just as an industrializing society cannot continue without the working class. Researchers have therefore argued that policymakers must acknowledge the long-term importance of urban villages "on the Chinese road to urbanization" (Zhang, Zhao, and Tian 2003, 913).

Although urban villages are physically located within cities, these working-class communities are in important ways half-urban and half-rural. The large tenant population includes many rural migrants from the country-side. Indigenous villagers, including those who have prospered with their rental businesses, hold on to some of the centuries-old traditional social and religious practices (P. Li 2002).

Two basic types of urban villages exist according to the heterogeneity of the migrant population (Wang and Huang 1998). A heterogeneous urban village is one with migrants from different parts of China, working at a variety of jobs that require different skills and education levels, ranging from blue-collar laborer to gray-collar worker, from low-rank clerk to sex worker (table 6.2). These migrants are usually loosely organized, and they seldom identify with each other due to their internal diversity. Shipai is a typical heterogeneous urban village, located in Guangzhou's new city center. It is the most intensively studied migrant settlement in South China (C. Liu 2000, Qian and Chen 2003). In this village, less than 30 percent of tenants are from within Guangdong Province; the others come from all over China, including Tibet and the Islamic Xinjiang region (C. Liu 2000).

The other basic type is the homogeneous urban village, consisting of migrant tenants primarily from the same place of origin, engaging in identi-cal or highly-related economic activities, following a classic pattern of enclave "migrant entrepreneurship" (Light and Bonacich 1991, Light and

Table 6.2
Characteristics of residents in urban villages in Guangzhou and Dongguan
($N = 459$)

		Percentage
Gender	Male	67
	Female	33
Education	Illiterate	5
	Primary school	14
	Secondary and high school	71
	University	10
Occupation	Industry	17
	Self-employed	14
	Construction and services	38
	Other	31
Origins	From many parts of the country	
Ethnicity	Han dominance, but also multiethnicity	
Business	Grocery store, hair salon, household services, commercial sex, and others	

Source: Zhang, Zhao, and Tian (2003).

Gold 2000). The most famous village in this category is Zhejiang Village in Beijing, where migrants from Zhejiang play a leading role in shaping the community and leading business activities, predominantly in the garment industry in this case (Xiang 1999, Zhang 2001). In contrast to the more loosely structured heterogeneous villages, homogeneous urban villages usually have a clearer hierarchical organization defined by people's places of origin, economic resources, and social status. Zhejiang Village, for instance, includes migrant entrepreneurs and their families from Zhejiang; landlords, that is, long-term indigenous villagers in southern Beijing; and laborers, including mostly migrants from the countryside of Hebei, Henan, and nearby northern provinces (L. Zhang 2001). Homogeneous urban villages also exist in South China, for example, Guangzhou's Shahe Village, which attracts mostly migrants from Chaozhou (Liu 2000).

A most remarkable enclave with homogeneous business activities is Dafen Village in Shenzhen, known as "China's No. 1 oil painting village" (figure 6.1). This village with fewer than one hundred indigenous villagers now hosts more than one hundred oil painting companies and seven hundred art galleries, according to the village Web site.[4] The English version of this Web site, targeting overseas customers, advertises:

Figure 6.1
A gallery in the Dafen Village of Shenzhen, "China's No. 1 oil painting village,"
September 2007. Photo courtesy Carolyn Cartier.

China's low wages and hunger for exports are now changing world of art for the
masses as more and more skilled artists graduated from Chinese art colleges are
willing to work cheaply and produce tens of thousands of assembly copies of famous
Western painting. The oil painting market has become more competitive than ever.
Dafen art village [with] its oil painting (original and reproduction) [have] gained its
great reputation both at home and aboard, and a great deal of its oil painting (original and reproduction) [have] been sold to many countries in North America, Europe,
Australia, and Asia.

We represent the best painters and galleries at Dafen art village and promote their
art works to the global market of oil paintings. To our customers, we provide with
the most extensive selections of art works from Dafen art village and offer oil painting reproduction of various categories and the best price of oil painting.

The labor structure of Dafen's art industry is another manifestation of
Chinese informationalism that applies the model of cost innovation and
competition to the transnational market of oil paintings. Compared to the
wireless phone battery production at BYD (discussed in chapter 4), these
oil painting businesses are smaller in scale, yet still based on the essential
elements of network labor and process flexibility, now synchronized with
the global flows of trade and information.

When I entered a gallery in Dafen Village, the owner, Zhu, was working on a painting for a newly married couple in France who had e-mailed their wedding photo to him. For an oil painting measuring 40-by-40 centimeters that is based on the picture, Zhu charges 600 yuan ($75) if he does it. But it can be much cheaper if one of his students, who work in a crowded studio upstairs, does the painting. These students, or apprentices, are the gray-collar network labor in this case. They are almost exclusively in their late teens and early twenties and are paid a few yuan for each painting they produce. At the time of my visit, they were busy working on a large order from New Zealand, Zhu's main export destination.

Following a well-documented pattern of patriarchic control over youth labor in homogeneous urban villages, Zhu acts toward his students as a demanding father figure, which is standard practice in Dafen Village as it is in the garment industry in Beijing's Zhejiang Village (Zhang 2001). Some of these enclave economies may be connected to global and transnational flows. But by subjecting the workers to long hours and specific job duties, they hinder the assimilation of migrants into the city (Liu 2000), thus adding to the urban landscape of being "globally connected" but "locally disconnected" (Castells 1996, 404).

In contrast, heterogeneous communities like Shipai Village more often serve as a transitional zone for newly arrived migrants before they move on to take up jobs elsewhere. However, both homogeneous and heterogeneous urban villages build on migrant social networks in providing bottom-up solutions for problems in housing and employment. In so doing, they reduce the risks and uncertainties that come with migration, and new urban places start to emerge (Zhao 2000). In many cases such as the Zhejiang Village in Beijing and the Shipai Village in Guangzhou, migrants and their families have begun to self-organize to provide essential social services such as kindergartens, restaurants, barber shops, clinics, and schools (Liu 2000, Qian and Chen 2003). These represent a critical breakthrough because they show that, although inequality and exploitation widely exist, migrants are also engaging in collective community building and bottom-up place making.

Long-term indigenous residents constitute a privileged stratum in urban villages because of their landownership and membership in the village collective. They are entitled to subsidies, welfare services, and even stockshare benefits provided by the village, which has considerable revenue from the prosperous rental market and other businesses (P. Li 2002, Lan and Zhang 2005). Generous offerings from the village collective such as pensions, senior care, and education allowances, however, do not ensure population stability or equality. The emergence of the landlord stratum means these people no longer need to work to earn a living. They may lease out all rooms in their house and move to an upscale neighborhood outside the village. Others invest their earnings and capitalize on their local connections to make even more money. Still others may eat and drink all day, gambling, becoming drug addicts, and squandering everything away in no time. In the matter of a few years, internal differences within indigenous villagers can be striking.[5]

Traditional practices of place making are of special importance to indigenous villagers, who are often seen as culturally inferior by average urbanites. These new landlords, now economically well off, were peasants with little education who were working in agriculture fairly recently. A distinct cultural identity is therefore cultivated, especially in South China, among indigenous villagers given the local tradition of strong family and kinship networks. Age-old clan organizations and lineage networks soon resurface. In many cases, village committees often act quickly to reconstruct the communal sites of cultural significance such as ancestor halls or village gates, thus boosting the pride of long-term villagers and their families. While urban planners may dislike these relics of the past in the middle of modern cities, some scholars maintain that these ancient practices and traditional social networks are likely to persist (Q. Sun 2003).

Finally, although most urban villages are characterized by a two-layer social system of locals and migrants, the two groups are not completely isolated from each other. Distinctions between them generate tension and a sense of inequality, which may end up in violent conflicts. But in most cases, both groups are adapting to each other in an effort to improve the quality of communal life. Village committees often invest heavily in kindergartens and primary schools, whose buildings are almost always among the most prominent in urban villages along with ancestor halls and senior centers (P. Li 2002). Due to the large population of migrant tenants, especially those who have raised their families in the village for many years, it is not infrequent for the children of tenants to attend the village schools, thus creating new opportunities for social integration.

The services delivered to all residents in the urban village are another opportunity for network building. These are mundane but significant jobs essential to the operation of the community. For instance, the Tangxia Village of Guangzhou, a community of six thousand indigenous villagers and more than thirty thousand migrant tenants, employs more than a hundred security guards, more than thirty cleaners, more than twenty garbage collectors, fifteen market management personnel, and six family planning personnel (P. Li 2002). These are working-class jobs for the have-less within the have-less community. Some of them are more labor intensive and carried out by migrant workers; others are better paid and managed by indigenous villagers. Together, both groups try to maintain and improve their shared community.

Places of Connection
Urban village is also a concrete place for working-class ICTs to materialize. When wired and wireless technologies take root in the village, they both reflect the ways in which residents are organized and extend the social fabric of the community into the city, the country, and overseas. Studies have mostly focused on the social structure of the urban village and its role in economy, especially in the low-end housing market. While these are indispensable aspects of the community, a more complete picture of the urban village is in order that emphasizes the underlying cultural and communication system. To consider this largely unaddressed facet of urban villages, we need to address some fundamental questions. What is human settlement? What makes a place meaningful? What produces a real community? Finding a residence, getting a job, supporting a family: these are all part of the settlement process. In order to meet bottom-up informational needs in such a process, there has to be a social construction of places of connection, for communication is a human necessity.

The rise of working-class ICTs in urban villages results from the general failure of the mass media to address the informational needs of the have-less. As discussed in chapter 4, less than 5 percent of migrants surveyed in Jinan reported that the news media were useful for their migration decision making.[6] A survey in Shanghai reveals that 58.9 percent of migrants regard mass media as of little or no use at all (Tao 2005). Mass media usually target upper-class audiences only, neglecting issues that are important to the have-less. It therefore comes at no surprise that a peculiar ecology of informational services has taken shape in urban villages, differing significantly from the rest of the city, just like the distinct economic and spatial growth of the community itself.

Here we examine commercial informational services in Shipai Village based on data collected from April to December 2007. Besides conventional fieldwork skills like participant observation, interviews, and focus groups, a census of all commercial informational services was carried out through sociospatial mapping (see the methodological appendix). I selected Shipai because it is the most researched urban village by anthropologists, sociologists, geographers, and urban planners, few of whom have studied the informational structure of the community. Shipai also has Guangzhou's largest concentration of IT malls selling new and used computers, repairing mobile phones, and conducting other working-class ICT businesses. Among IT marketers, there is a saying comparing Shipai or Shipaicun with Beijing's Zhongguancun, the main IT hub of China: "Zhongguancun in the north, Shipaicun in the south" (Du, Chen, and Chang 2005).

Shipai is densely populated and full of migrant businesses. On its 0.6 square-kilometer land, there are more than 2,000 stores (Lan and Zhang 2005). Our census identifies 481 businesses providing 46 kinds of commercial informational service, mostly working-class ICTs but also a much smaller number of traditional informational services (table 6.3). In this community of more than 50,000 residents (Zheng 2006), there is no locally based print or broadcasting media service and only one post office. There are 21 bookstores (figure 6.2) and 31 newsstands scattered throughout the community. Their main business is, however, not the sales of books or newspapers. Rather, the main revenues are generated by selling prepaid phone cards and mobile phone accessories while renting out books and magazines to migrant tenants, yet another shared mode of access—to print media in this case.

Table 6.3
Selected commercial informational services in Shipai Village, Guangzhou, October 2007

Type of service	Number of locations
Post office	1
Bookstore	21
Newsstand	31
Cybercafé	8
Computer parts business	31
Content download	34
ADSL cooperative	71
Mobile operator shops	4
Mobile number sales	106
Long-distance phone bar	110
Prepaid phone cards	124

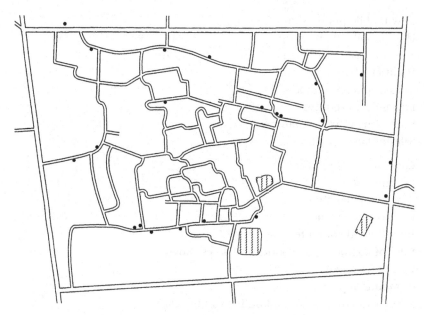

Figure 6.2
Spatial distribution of bookstores in Shipai Village, Guangzhou, October 2007. Line
drawing by Kitty Chen.

These are diverse services, each with its own market logic, all trying to
meet the broadly defined informational needs of local residents, from
social networking to entertainment, from basic connectivity to work. They
include formal businesses like cybercafés, mobile operator shops, handset
repairs, the sales of mobile phone numbers (SIM cards, but some with
numbers considered lucky, like 888, which are more expensive), and
the rental of digital cameras at the price of 5 yuan ($0.63) per day for
domestic-brand cameras. There is also a wide variety of informal businesses: vendors selling pirated DVDs and used books or purchasing mobile
phones and used printer cartridges. They often sit right on the pavement
with a cardboard sign, placing their commodities in a small box or on a
piece of cloth. And there it is—their makeshift store.

This is, in short, a rich and diverse array of informational services (table
6.3) Some of these are formal and legal:

Telephone-related services
Long-distance phone bar
Small-scale pay phone service
Telecom operator shop

New mobile phone shop
Used mobile phone shop
Sales of used phone parts
Handset repair
Sales of phone numbers
Prepaid card services
Sales of handset decorations
Sales of landline phones

Computer-related services
Internet café
New computer shop
Used computer shop
Sales of used computer parts
Sales of computer accessories and access lines
Computer rental
Computer repair
Sales of Internet access and online gaming card
Home Internet access network enhancement
E-mail access service
Video chat service
Computer training sessions
Storage room for computers and accessories

Other information services
Post office
Bookstore
Newsstand
Sales of used TV and home appliances
Pawnshops for handsets and computers
Content download service
Digital camera rental
Digital camera sales
Typing and photocopying
Signage and ads production
Fax sending and receiving
Disk burning
Image scanning service

There is also the informal economy:

ADSL cooperative and broadband rental
Sales of pirated disks (videos and games)

Rental of pirated disks
Handset unlocking and program updating
Street-side purchase of used handset
Street-side purchase of used computer
Street-side purchase of computer accessories
Street-side sales of handset accessories
Production of fake IDs and documents

A good example of these services is the ADSL cooperative, the most prevalent informal-economy Internet service in Shipai; seventy-one of them were identified in the census. It allows neighbors to share a single ADSL broadband connection, much like the old party-line phone system, which is prohibited by the ISPs but popular among urban village residents. Low-end ADSL costs about 100 yuan ($12.60) a month. If three neighbors share the connection, each pays only one-third the cost. ADSL cooperatives are advertised by handwritten or printed signs, some on stickers, all including phone numbers for people to call. This suits the physical environment of urban village because the neighborhood is densely populated, with "kissing buildings" standing right next to each other. Although the authorities have tried to crack down on ADSL cooperatives, they can still be spotted all over the place, demonstrating their central role for Internet access in this working-class community.[7]

ICT businesses are quickly changing. When I first visited Shipai in 2002, it had many cybercafés. But in October 2007, we identified only eight of them, including licensed ones and unlicensed black Net bars (figure 6.3). The decreasing number of cybercafés is due in part to the falling price of new and used computers and alternative ways to get inexpensive Internet access, for example, through computer rentals (about 50 yuan, or $ 6.30 per month) and ADSL cooperatives. The remaining cafés have become bigger, with better computers designed to meet the entertainment needs of mostly young males. In order to get cheaper rent and avoid frequent inspections, they have moved to the second floor or higher in buildings at the edges of the village because only there can they find large enough space, which is also more accessible and closer to public transportation.

A more telling case of rapid change is the content download business, which is usually offered in a tiny shop operated by a single attendant with an online computer. The shopkeeper helps customers download ring tones to their mobile phones or music to their MP3s, charging half to 1 yuan for each download. When I started fieldwork in April 2007, the business was

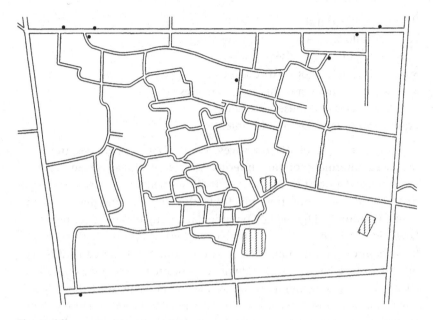

Figure 6.3
Spatial distribution of cybercafés in Shipai Village, Guangzhou, October 2007. Line
drawing by Kitty Chen.

booming. But by October, many content-download shops had shut down,
leaving only thirty-four of them (table 6.3).

Despite the pace of change, across the board these are relatively small-
scale working-class ICT services provided by have-less migrants for local
consumption. Although many of these businesses are owned by long-term
indigenous villagers or housed in commercial space rented from them,
invariably the labor supply comes from migrant tenants living close by,
who also constitute the overwhelming customer base.

The most important and prevalent informational facility in Shipai Village
is the long-distance phone bar (*changhuaba*), where attractive rates are
offered for people to place phone calls across the country. Calling it a bar
(*ba*), like a Net bar (*wangba*), indicates that these are venues of modest
consumption designed to meet the basic human needs of relaxation and
social networking. These are workers' bars—a commercial, but still shared,
collective place of working-class connectivity.

While cybercafés tend to be located closer to the village border at sites
of more convenient access, most phone bars operate in the depth of the

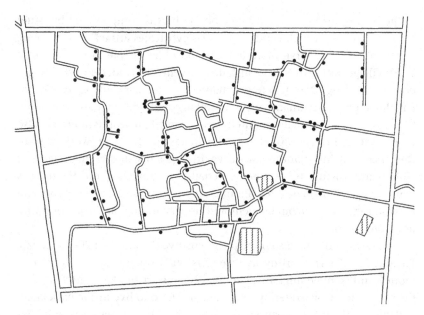

Figure 6.4
Spatial distribution of long-distance phone bars in Shipai Village, Guangzhou, October 2007. Line drawing by Kitty Chen.

alley labyrinth, usually underneath the "cement monsters" where migrants dwell. In 2002, there were only a few phone bars in Shipai. But in October 2007, 110 of them existed in this have-less community (figure 6.4). The demand for long-distance phone service is much larger than for Internet access, as the former requires less technical know-how. Phone bars offer more attractive rates than mobile services because fixed-line operators have to compete to maintain their customers, for instance, by using VoIP. Moreover, GSM and CDMA signals in the urban village are quite unreliable. Following a pattern observed in small cities, mobile phone reception is the worst for China Mobile customers, better for China Unicom customers, and the most reliable for those who use Little Smart.[8] Consequently, although many residents have mobile phones for use outside the community, they still prefer to patronize the phone bar in their neighborhood. At the end of the day, for most migrant workers, old-style voice telephony is the simplest way to keep in touch with their families and friends. The fact that more members of the have-less are adopting low-end wireless phones enlarges, rather than reduces, the market for phone bars because now there are more people to call.

The wide spread of long-distance phone bars is compounded by issues of safety and, above all, gender. Whereas cybercafés attract mostly young males, phone bars serve more females and older people. Although since 2000, village authorities have installed surveillance cameras in the neighborhood (Zheng, 2006), safety remains a major concern, especially for females and predominantly when walking at night in dark alleyways. Compared to their male counterparts, young female migrants are also more systematically exploited and suppressed, both at work and in their personal life planning with regard to such issues as marriage and child care. Facing these tougher challenges imposed on them at a younger age than males, female migrants need more social support and networking, more encouragement and understanding, and someone who listens to them.

Female migrants are also more price sensitive (Bu and Qiu 2002a, 2002b; Bu and Liu 2004). Starting as teenagers, girls usually try to save more money, unlike male migrants, who may soon start smoking and frequenting cybercafés. Consequently, more females tend to live in the back alleys and the depth of the urban village, where rent is cheaper than in better-located housing near public transportation. The price difference—50 yuan ($6.30) per month, for instance—may appear to be inconsequential to outsiders, but it is significant to many female migrants. This gendered residential pattern is another reason explaining the prosperity of phone bars in the depth of Shipai Village.

Lao Zhang has been in Shipai's phone bar business since 2000. Before then, he and his wife, both from rural Henan, worked as janitors in a dormitory in a nearby university in Guangzhou. They entered this market first as helpers for a long-term resident with local *hukou*. But soon they started their own shop, which looks like the long-distance phone bar in figure 6.5. It has six booths, separated by glass, each containing a landline phone and a stool. It has a prominent sign outside, advertising the price: "*Changtu yijiao* [0.1 yuan or 1.3 cents for a long-distance call]."

Opposite the phone booths is the service counter, which has a computer that tracks each call and calculates the charge (figure 6.6). Lao Zhang or his wife sits behind the counter, which contains a range of working-class ICTs: prepaid phone cards, used handsets, low-end accessories like batteries and chargers, and shiny mobile phone ornaments that female customers refer to as flashlights (*shanguangdeng*). On the counter, a stack of paper shows the mobile phone numbers on sale. Behind the counter and on the wall, more accessories are displayed. Lao Zhang also repairs mobile phones if the problem is not too complicated. They sell newspapers

Figure 6.5
Street view of a long-distance phone bar in Shipai Village, Guangzhou, March 2008.
Author photo.

Figure 6.6
Inside view of a long-distance phone bar in Shipai Village, Guangzhou, March 2008.
Author photo.

and rent used magazines in small quantities. This tiny shop is typical of phone bars in Shipai in offering a wide range of informational services and products.

A ladder in the corner of the shop leads to the family bedroom upstairs, which sits on top of the phone booths (figure 6.6). The kitchen in the back is so small that it has no room for a refrigerator, and it is next to the bathroom, which is even smaller and has only a shower over a squat toilet. This is a combination work and residential space of about 300 square feet for Lao Zhang, his wife, and their nineteen-year-old son, who was an apprentice for about a year in a large mobile phone repair shop three blocks away and is now ready to set up his own business. The family pays close to 1,000 yuan ($126) for rent and makes about 2,000 yuan each month. They work from 8:00 A.M. until 2:00 A.M. After paying for their expenses (electricity, water, maintenance, food, and clothing), they may be able to save 200 to 300 yuan ($25–38) each month. They use these savings to go to family reunions in Henan during the Lunar New Year, for sickness, and other unpredicted expenses.

In Shipai, as in other urban villages, working-class ICT businesses involve long-term indigenous villagers as well. Young people frequent the cybercafés and use SMS, as do have-less young people in other parts of the city. Although some members of the older generation have become affluent in recent years, they remember how hard peasant life can be. They therefore patronize working-class ICT stores, although their purchases account for only a fraction of the total revenue of these businesses, most of which comes from migrant tenants.

The indigenous villagers control the rental market, which allows them to shape the spatial development of working-class ICTs at a structural level. Indigenous residents are not only acting as individuals renting out a small space for phone bars or content download shops. They are organized under the village collective, which in Shipai used to be the Village Committee, China's smallest administrative unit in the countryside. But in 1997 the Shipai Village Committee was transformed into the Shipai Sanjun Group, a collectively owned shareholding company (Lan and Zhang 2005). This collective entity of indigenous villagers invested heavily in real estates, including skyscrapers, on the edge of the village (figure 6.7). In a few years, these high-rise buildings have formed the most famous concentration of IT complexes in the city.

In 2000, these IT malls in Shipai accommodated about fifteen hundred companies and shops selling computers, parts, software, and telecom

Figure 6.7
A view of Shipai Village: High-density housing and high-rise IT complexes (October 2007). Author photo.

products and services. The businesses did so well that the rent increased five times in five years (Liu 2000). The most important complex is the Pacific Computer City, whose sales influence computer prices throughout Southeast Asia (Feng 2005). These IT malls sprung up because Shipai offers inexpensive housing for migrant workers in its high-density residential area. The Pacific Computer City, for example, has more than 50,000 blue-collar, gray-collar, and low-rank white-collar employees, of whom 80 percent live in Shipai.[9] Considering the much higher rents outside the urban village and Guangzhou's notorious traffic, it would have been impossible to move these migrant tenants elsewhere without significantly raising labor costs in the IT complexes.

There are also larger dynamics behind the rise of Shipai as the main regional hub of IT businesses. Since the mid-1990s, many computer factories have appeared in the Pearl River Delta, especially in the nearby cities of Dongguan and Shenzhen, given the influx of Taiwanese and Hong Kong manufacturers into these cities. Their products are shipped to Guangzhou before being sold to wholesalers coming from the rest of China and overseas. They need storage at a place easily accessible to highways and railroads, and Shipai meets these requirements (Zhang 2006). Consequently, Shipai West Road, the main border street to the west of the community, is now lined up with basement-level storage rooms for computers and accessories. Strolling down this road in the summer evenings in July 2007, I often counted more than twenty cargo trucks waiting for computers to be loaded. Their license plates revealed that these trucks came from different cities of Guangdong and different provinces such as Guangxi and Hubei.

The goods being traded here include used computers as well. A few blocks from the upper-class IT malls that advertise the latest-model laptops and online games is Guangzhou's most prominent clustering of shops in the used IT product market. One of them has an entire floor for cybercafé operators to purchase, trade, and repair Net bar computers. Another has an extensive network of used computer traders in not only Guangzhou but also Shenzhen, Beijing, Shanghai,, and several other large cities, which is claimed to be "the most authoritative professional website of second-hand computers in China."[10]

The effects of these IT malls are multifaceted. They give a localized spatial expression to China's new ICT industry while allowing some economic benefits to trickle down to network labor and working families. They push up land prices around the community, thus empowering the village collective to extract maximum rent. Although the collective helps create jobs at the IT complexes and keeps the high-density housing from being eliminated by more powerful state agencies or real estate developers, it is also a conservative force that reaffirms the social schism within the urban village. Indigenous villagers are often appointed to senior positions that enjoy special power and benefits. In contrast, migrant tenants have to work harder but earn less, with few or no employment benefits. When business slows, migrants will be the first to go, whereas indigenous villagers almost never need to worry about losing their jobs.

Shipai Village officials proudly claim that the booming IT sector has a positive impact on the indigenous population: "Those who had not even seen a black-and-white TV in the past now are familiar with computer operation. They are taking part in the management of the science and technology computer malls or helping run the 'electronic eyes' (surveillance cameras) in the village."[11] It is remarkable that such narrative by the officials completely excluded migrant tenants. Without basic guarantees for equal rights and responsibilities among all members of the community, ICTs may also be abused, particularly with regard to the surveillance system.

Factories: Production, Discipline, and Human Life

Factories are places of economic production. In the Maoist years, they were among the most powerful urban institutions, representing the celebrated proletariat working class, who had tenure, full employment benefits, and high social status. Workers and their families lived in the *danwei* community next to their factory, enjoying a relatively stable life, to the envy of other city residents. Although China has since gone through a new stage of industrialization and earned the title of "world factory," old-style factories, mostly SOEs, have lost their previous economic and political status. More than 30 million workers were laid off with little or no severance pay between 1989 and 2004 (Hurst 2004). Factories have been moved to city outskirts and *danwei* residential communities dismantled. The work units have become lean and mean and competitive in the global market, now powered by network labor.

Workshops without Borders

China's economic reform since 1978 has changed the spatial characteristics of Chinese plants, including their location, landscape, and internal structures. Twenty-five years ago, smoking chimneys used to dominate the urban skyline. Now they have either disappeared or been moved elsewhere.

The remaining ones stand in the shadows of commercial skyscrapers. Entire factories have been erased on city maps to make room for financial districts, shopping malls, upper-class real estate projects, and IT complexes. The proletariat industrial city has been literally driven to the margins of the Chinese informational city.

But despite the declining status of factory workers, the spatial significance of factories is greater than ever before. This is because, with the dismantling of traditional *danwei*-style factories, units of industrial production have found infinite ways of new spatial expression, thus giving rise to a large variety of factory places throughout the urban landscape. With this vital transformation, the concept of factory as a place of physically concentrated manufacturing activities has to be opened up to include networked ways of production, on-line and offline.

First, within the city proper, although big state factories have significantly declined, there are numerous types of small-scale workshops. These include family businesses run by migrant entrepreneurs, for example, in the enclave economy of Beijing's Zhejiang Village, whose main economic activity is based on hiring female migrants for garment production (Zhang 2001). The oil painting workshops in Shenzhen's Dafen Village, operating on the back of young art "students," are a bit larger in scale. They are, however, still a variant of locally based factory production—in this case, more reliant on ICTs such as e-mail. These small-scale factories are crowded and typically contain living and production spaces under one roof. Many of them, like garment studios in migrant households, are invisible to outsiders under the guise of residential housing. Yet they constitute an essential part of the enlarged network society, for without the support of translocal, regional, and transnational networks, few of them would exist.

Second, today's more visible large-scale factories tend to be located on the outskirts, including urbanizing areas newly incorporated into the city. Industrial pollution is one reason for relocation from the inner city; so is the increasing value of land in old working-class neighborhoods. More important is the creation of state-sponsored industrial zones at city peripheries, designed to accommodate a cluster of factories. The Chinese authorities, especially local state agencies, have played an active role in planning and building industrial zones in all key cities in coastal and inland regions. At the beginning, most factories engaged in traditional industries, producing goods such as clothing and toys. But since the 1990s, a large number of high-tech parks have emerged, and electronic products such as computers, mobile handsets, and switchers have claimed a large share of China's total exports revenue.[12] These are the spatial materialization of state efforts to attract capital and restructure the local economy, which impinges deeply on the place-making process of contemporary China and the transformation of its factories.

Not all factories are in designated zones. Many are scattered throughout the vast semiurban and urbanizing areas. Some were township and village enterprises, vanguards in the rural industrialization period of the 1980s. With the remarkable expansion of Chinese cities, they now find themselves encircled by urban land. Meanwhile, most of them have gone through major reform, from collective ownership by the township and village to private ownership or joint-venture arrangements (N. Lin, 1995). Regardless of their location and ownership, these are overwhelmingly labor-intensive operations that employ millions of migrants, laid-off workers, and other previously unemployed or underemployed members of the urban society. This pattern applies to traditional industrial sectors as well as high-tech factories, which need to rely on the have-less workforce, especially programmable labor, to produce integrated circuits, mobile phones, laptops, and accessories. It is also the case for the new service industry firms that are essential to China's emerging information economy, for example, companies providing online and telephone booking services for travelers, telemarketing firms, and the once-popular voice information stations (*shengxuntai*). These players of the new economy will not be able to prosper without a massive supply of gray-collar labor, especially female migrant workers.[13]

Workshops engaging in the production and trading of virtual property for online gamers are another new type of informational factory, as discussed in chapter 4. This has been a rapidly emerging market known as MMORPG (massively multiplayer online role-playing games). Owners of virtual property factories hire young rural-to-urban migrants or underemployed urban youth to play online games. The job is to "strike gold (*dajin*)": to collect or produce virtual properties that can be sold for real-world currency. Working twelve hours a day, one may, for instance, collect 300 gold points in the popular game World of Warcraft. With this, the employee can earn 30 yuan ($3.80) from the employer, who can then sell the 300 points for $30 (H. He 2005). Such workshops, known as "gold farms," have spread from the coastal regions to inland cities (Chew and Fung 2007). The city of Wuhan in central China was reported to have more than two thousand gold farms in 2007. The new gold farms are in general larger in scale and serving more kinds of customers, including American, Japanese, Taiwanese, and increasingly mainland Chinese players known as renminbi players (renminbi is the official Chinese currency). Their work conditions are, however, not necessarily better: employees work in crowded spaces, a dusty environment, and with refurbished computers in rooms that are often filled with cigarette smoke. They usually sleep on the floor next to the computer they are using.

Figure 6.8 shows a typical scene of a gold farm in the northwestern city of Xi'an. Located in an urban village, this used to be one of the largest gold-farming operations in town. But it has since declined into the messy shape captured in this photograph that shows the poor work conditions most gold farmers have to put up with, usually twelve hours a day.

On October 7, 2007, an unprecedented strike of gold farmers took place in Urumqi, the capital city of Xinjiang Uyghur Autonomous Region, in China's Muslim northwest. The strikers were not migrant or laid-off workers but vocational middle school students aged sixteen to twenty. These students were supposed to study "practical computer skills," yet they were sent by their teachers into a gold farm as interns. The daily quota was to "cut 5,000 trees." While other gold farmers earned a monthly salary of

Figure 6.8
Inside an online-game gold farm in Xi'an, Shaanxi Province, October 2007. Photo courtesy Matthew Chew.

more than 700 yuan ($89.00), the interns had no income at all. But they worked the same shifts: girls on the daytime shift, boys from 11:00 p.m. to 11:00 a.m. Finally, all the male interns went on strike (*China Youth Daily* 2007). Official news media at the national level reported this case, which led to intense criticism against such shameless abuse of students as forced laborers. As the result, the Urumqi school had to stop this practice under public pressure.

Like Dafen Village and BYD in Shenzhen, the gold farms increasingly rely on ICTs for management and the economic production and delivery of services and products. This is the case with painters who reproduce e-mailed photographs as oil paintings. It is also how BYD trains its army of programmable labor in wireless phone battery production, often with the help of computer-generated graphical materials the blue- and gray-collar workers use (Zeng and Williamson 2007).

ICT applications enable Chinese factories, large and small, to tap wider regional and global markets, while also enhancing the mobility of these factories, allowing them to take advantage of sites with lower rents and higher profit margins, even if that means exploiting free child labor as in the Urumqi gold farm. While mobility increases for capital, production processes, and factory locations, this Chinese model of flexible accumulation through "cost innovation" also works to the disadvantage of employees, who are now subject to stricter labor discipline and more systematic exploitation brought about by the deployment of ICTs in their workplaces, for instance, through wireless communication, as will be discussed in the next section. Even before the spread of working-class ICTs, there had been frequent reports of poor conditions in Chinese sweatshops with workers under the surveillance of closed-circuit television. With the rise of the have-less market in China and other countries, more contracts and subcontracts are made to produce low-end ICTs at lower cost and in large quantities. This not only adds to the emergence of factories in China's urban and urbanizing areas but also furthers the tension between management and the emerging network labor, thus giving rise to new dynamics of power and place making.

The Wireless Leash

A notable recent change in factories is the adoption of personal wireless communication devices among factory workers. Newly employed workers often use their earnings for the first few months to purchase domestic-brand handsets, Little Smart, or low-end foreign-brand mobile phones. Some of these handsets were previously used and refurbished, and most of them depend on prepaid services. The second-hand market and the sales of phone cards also provide numerous jobs for underemployed members of the information have-less.

Some researchers found that workers who had acquired wireless devices were empowered by their new control over the information flow in and out of the factory. Isolating workers from the outside world used to be a regular part of labor discipline by which factory owners and managers could force workers to concentrate on their work and thereby increase the factory's productivity and profitability. However, with the spread of inexpensive handsets, the power balance tilts toward workers. This was the case, for example, for a factory in Dongguan where workers exchanged SMS in the middle of their workday about jobs in nearby plants. At the end of the day, several of them quit and went over to the factory offering better benefits (Law 2006). Frequent uses of mobile phone and SMS have also begun to shape a working-class culture among female employees in the manufacturing sector, creating a new space of expression and communication (A. Lin 2005).

These studies, however, were based on fieldwork in 2004 and 2005, which coincided with a period when there was a shortage of migrant laborers in South China. This so-called migrant dearth occurred in response to stagnant wages and rising living costs in the region, which reduced the attraction of factory work. In addition, factories in and near Shanghai in East China offered better working conditions and employment benefits (Chua 2005, S. Yang 2006). Workers became aware of these different terms of employment through their translocal networks, which increasingly involve SMS and mobile phone. They could also share this information using landline phones in long-distance phone bars, online chat services in Internet cafés, or simply face-to-face, for example, when most migrants returned to their home towns during the Spring Festival.

When I conducted my fieldwork in 2005–2006 in the Pearl River Delta, the labor shortage had become less severe. Local authorities in Shenzhen, for instance, had raised the minimum wage by 20 percent in May 2006, although there was no guarantee that all factories would observe the rule (Mitchell 2006). Moreover, factory management had become aware that workers were using mobile phones in ways that could threaten their authority. They therefore stepped up efforts to impose control over mobile phone use in the factory, for example, by banning the use of mobile phones during working hours. In some factories that produce small electronic devices such as the iPod, metal detectors originally set up to prevent workers from stealing parts and products are now used to ensure that they do not bring their mobile phones onto the assembly line (Zhang and Li 2006).

These efforts are not entirely new. Workplaces in general, not just factories, have always asserted control over workers. For examples, employees were forbidden to do online chatting or check their personal e-mail using office computers. Results from my survey groups also suggest that in 2002, 80 percent of the migrant respondents reported some restrictions on their phone use at work. The percentage rose to 100 percent in 2006.[14]

The most prevalent constraint is that employees are required to use phones owned by the employer only for work purposes. In some Taiwanese firms in Guangzhou, employees are required to specify how many personal calls they made using the workplace phone and pay for them. In other cases, like restaurants in Shenzhen, waitresses and waiters were forbidden to use the work phone at all. And in still other cases, factory workers are forbidden to make personal calls, send SMS, or even bring their mobile phone to work (Qiu 2007b).

Mobile communication also has another use: it is becoming a "wireless leash" that shop-floor management can use as a nearly complete control and surveillance system over employees. The attempt to establish total managerial domination, sometimes under the euphemism of "scientific management," was under way prior to the spread of inexpensive mobile communication (C. K. Lee 2002b). But the new mobile-based mechanism is unique in several ways.

First, the wireless system can be used to impose control over more workers, as compared to Internet or Intranet networks that can only reach employees who use computers. Second, employees are often required to keep their handsets on all the time, thus lengthening the period of control beyond the normal work hours. Third, like employers tapping landline phones and filtering employee e-mail, it is not complicated to add an intrafirm surveillance system over mobile communication—both voice telephony and SMS. This task is often assigned to the IT division in medium- and large-sized factories. It does not need to maintain constant surveillance. Merely the threat of it tilts the power balance back to management (Qiu 2007b).

A typical factory-based wireless communication system is the concentrated collective network (*jiqunwang*), which has gained popularity in urban areas. Figure 6.9 shows one such network in January 2006 in a large apparel factory in Dongguan with more than ten thousand workers (figure 6.9). In 1999, the owner bought Nokia handsets from China Mobile for communication among high-rank managers. As the cost of wireless phones

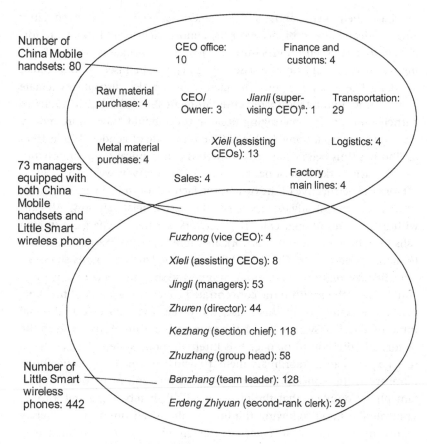

Figure 6.9
A concentrated collective network of wireless phones in an apparel factory in Dong-guan, January 2006. [a] *Jianli* (the supervising CEO) is the wife of the CEO/owner.

fell, the owner bought hundreds of new handsets, and as a result, this concentrated collective network has been expanded to include *banzhang*, the lowest rank of managers, in charge of small teams of six or seven workers.

The distribution of wireless phones reflects and reinforces the hierarchical structure of the factory. Foreign-brand handsets with China Mobile services are supplied to high-ranking managers and those who serve these top managers directly (drivers, sales, and customs affairs personnel, for example). Midlevel executives and clerks receive less expensive phones and sometimes only SIM cards without handsets, in which case they have to purchase their own handsets. Low-ranking supervisors are given Little Smarts. Meanwhile, ordinary workers, almost exclusively female, are forbidden to bring their phones into the factory. If a worker is caught checking or sending SMS on the assembly line, the handset is confiscated. Speaking like a father figure, the factory owner also discourages female workers from joining local radio entertainment shows that solicit audience participation by SMS messaging because they should "save more money for the family back home." This patriarchic mode of gendered industrialization has thus been extended to wireless communication in an attempt to influence workers' personal lives in the dormitory as well.[15]

From the perspective of the owner, the factory-controlled wireless phone system has several advantages. First, the cost is relatively low. All calls within the concentrated collective network are free of charge, although calls to or from outside the network are more expensive. Second, it is easy to manage because the China Mobile and Little Smart accounts share the same first few digits of their phone numbers so they are easier to remember and dial for others within the concentrated collective network of the same plant. The system is, in this sense, the wireless version of a traditional intrafirm landline system. Third, the owner has a team of specialists in the factory's IT division to manage this internal phone system. He also has a secretary with an extraordinary memory who can remember all the phone numbers in this concentrated collective network and many other important phone numbers that the owner needs. Remembering about a thousand numbers and following the boss at almost all times, this secretary represents an extreme instance of programmable labor—a human telephone book for the factory owner.

Most important, this wireless phone system extends control over employees, who are required to keep the phone on wherever they go so that upper-level managers can reach their subordinates immediately. The apparel factory shown in figure 6.9 has devised a penalty system for cases when the boss or other high-level administrators cannot reach those who are assigned wireless phones or phone cards. The measures go from calling the person's name over loudspeakers to the shop floor, to deducting a fine from the offender's wages, to physical punishment, and, ultimately, being fired.[16]

The emergence of the wireless system as a means of control in factories should be taken as a cautionary note on the role of not only inexpensive mobile phone but also working-class ICTs in general in the formation processes of have-less urban places. New communication technologies can liberate people from physical constraints and traditional power structures.

But they can also help strengthen managerial domination and extend the scope of influence from top down.

Dormitories, iPod City, and Uniden

Factories are not only places of production but also places where workers live. Although old-style *danwei* factories complete with their residential communities are declining, China's new factories nonetheless offer living space to their blue-collar and gray-collar employees. According to national statistics provided by MPS, 29.6 percent of registered migrants live in employer-provided dormitories. Trailing self-rented housing (31.1 percent) only by a slim margin, dorms are the second most important type of accommodation for migrant workers (Zhang, Zhao, and Tian 2003).

Although some dorms are located in urban villages and rented by employers (M. Liu 2000), dormitories inside factories remain an important mode of living, especially for the large-scale enterprises that have been playing a key role in China's export-oriented electronics industry. Although not all workers use employer-provided housing, factory dormitory is the default mode of accommodation for most low-income manufacturer employees, especially those in large-scale plants, because it is more affordable compared to rental housing in urban villages, and it is usually more conveniently located for daily commuting. From the perspective of management, centralized housing has obvious advantages, for it facilitates the enforcement of production routines by controlling the physical location of workers during and after work.

With soaring exports from China and the growth of the domestic market, overtime work is routine in many factories. Having dormitories next to production facilities is a clear advantage because it allows for longer work hours. It extends the power structure of the workplace from shop floor to places of residence, especially when the dormitories are also owned by the employer, who may impose "despotic punishment" over worker behavior by using fines and wage deductions, for example, over such offenses as littering, spitting, and physical fights between workers from different provinces (Lee 1998). Although proximity to the workplace was also a crucial factor in the old *danwei* system, these new dorms are decisively different, for most residents are migrants without local *hukou* residential status.

The spatial arrangement of the dormitory, coupled with financial penalties, can have a significant effect on labor discipline. In 2000, for example, workers died from overwork in a factory making gloves in Huizhou, Guangdong Province, because they worked regularly for more than sixteen hours a day. They earned as little as 300 yuan or $36.00 per month (Sun 2004).

In June 2006, reports were released concerning the unhealthy working and living conditions in the Foxconn plant in Shenzhen. Dubbed "iPod City" by the British press, this is a Taiwanese subcontractor firm that makes iPods. The plant accommodates more than 200,000 workers in its "regimented, spartan factory dormitories" (Webster 2006). Both Foxconn and Apple maintain that the British reports were inaccurate; however, investigative reporters from the Chinese Web site Netease found situations where about three hundred people share a single dormitory room: "In this dormitory, three beds formed one row, and the rows were very close to each other. On one side of the room, there were at least 24 rows, for a total of 72 double bunker beds. On the other side of the room, there were an equal number of beds. So about 300 people live in this dormitory. There are at least four similarly structured dormitories in the 'Peace Dormitories' courtyard, with four stories each."[17] This article also supplies photographs, available online, that show the dormitory structure with the double bunk beds. Given the extraordinary heat and humidity of the tropical climate in Shenzhen, it is easy to conceive of the terrible living condition in these dormitories.

Besides the hierarchical system of plant management, a supplementary and sometimes alternative dimension of social organization is the workers' place of origin, regional identity, and subsequent social network formation. On the shop floor and in dormitories, employees tend to identify with others from the same province or county. This was what Ma and colleagues found in a toy factory in Dongguan (E. Ma 2006). As a large portion of workers were from a few places of origin, people from these origins occupied more supervisory positions. Workers who come from the same home town are usually tightly connected; some are relatives or from the same rural village.

The strength of these translocal bonds can also be testified to by the popularity of long-distance phone bars located not far from the factory dormitories. During the week-long 2007 May Day holiday, for example, migrant workers in Shenzhen's industrial zone were reported to stand in long lines to make long-distance calls to their families and relatives back home.[18]

The centrality of regional identity in network labor can be traced back to the first half of the twentieth century as a historic hallmark of the urban underclass and labor movement in China (Chesneaux 1968, Honig 1992, Perry 1993). In today's factories, regional identity often functions as quasi-ethnicity in deciding power status in the factory. For instance, in the

Shenzhen plant of Liton Electronic Ltd., owned by a Hong Kong company to produce audiovisual equipment, employees from within Guangdong Province were reported to take top management jobs and most of the midlevel supervisory positions. Employees from outside Guangdong appeared in the lower-middle ranks of the management hierarchy, although they accounted for more than 63 percent of shop floor workers (Lee 1998).

It is crucial to note in this case that all the shop floor workers were female and most managers were male. This gendered relationship was also found in a Shenzhen factory making computer parts such as motherboards and liquid crystal displays. The control over female employees was total, as Pun notes: "Once the *dagongmei* (female migrant worker) enters the factory gate ... she is immediately placed in a specific position and nailed down into a grid of power and discipline" (Pun 2005, 80–81).

Pun, however, also maintains that, despite the suffocating domination, female factory workers adopt "a minor genre of resistance" in a variety of forms at multiple sites of social action within and outside the factory. In my focus groups of migrant workers in the Pearl River Delta, participants reported instances of employees who challenged restrictions over their ICT use at work.[19] Xiao Wu, a former security guard, discussed hacking into work phones that required a password to place long-distance calls, and another member of the focus group had also heard about this. These working-class hackers click on the hang-up flap of the telephone using different rhythms. Once they click the right rhythm, the phone security is dismantled and the phone can be used for long-distance calls. Xiao Wu claimed that he had done this successfully in the past.

At the national level, based on her fieldwork in Liaoning and Guangdong, Ching Kwan Lee contends that "the passage of state socialism ... offers the potential for labor radicalization in terms of critical consciousness and mobilizational capacity" (Lee 2002a, 218). She notes that most protests and demonstrations tend to be in the northeast and inland regions, where workers "now engage in work unit activism, the predominant mode of mobilization" (192).

Since the 1990s, the general trend has been the "increasing numbers, greater intensity, and more cohesive organization" of collective labor actions in China (Hurst 2004, 95). Most of these actions are based on networking among discontented workers physically living together, especially SOE employees in adjacent urban neighborhoods. But migrant workers have also begun to use the Internet to organize themselves, express their grievances, and ask for help from the general public. A critical event is the

December 2004 strike at Uniden Electronics Ltd., in which network labor used e-mail and blogs in their struggle.

Uniden is a Japanese electronics plant in Shenzhen, producing mainly cordless phones, VoIP devices, and walkie-talkies; half of its output is sold to Wal-Mart.[20] On December 10, 2004, most Uniden employees who had e-mail access received a message detailing fifteen demands made by workers, including better employment benefits, better working conditions, and the removal of abusive managers. The e-mail announced that if the conditions were not met, industrial action would be taken that day. When the time came and the company failed to respond, about ten thousand blue-collar workers, most of them seventeen- and eighteen-year-old female employees, walked out. On the second day, gray-collar and white-collar employees in the R&D building joined the strike, which lasted a week. At its peak, sixteen thousand workers participated in the strike.[21]

Most remarkable about this strike was that the workers used blogs to broadcast the progress of their collective action. Six blog posts were uploaded to the Chinese blog portal Blogcn.com, which was almost immediately picked up by labor observers and the press, producing, for example, a *New York Times* article on the third day of the strike (French 2004). As a result, I received an update every day in Los Angeles. This was indeed a historic moment for workers in the People's Republic of China.

Since then, these original workers' blogs have been modified, replaced with content supplied by the management, or rendered inaccessible depending on the political situation in the factory (for example, in April 2005, another large-scale strike erupted). However, although the uncensored blog posts have disappeared on the Blogcn platform, they have been reposted onto hundreds of online discussion forums, despite the company's and authorities' attempts at censorship.

The actions at Foxconn and Uniden share a few patterns. The incident at Foxconn (iPod City) was essentially the empowerment of journalists, labor activists, and concerned citizens through Internet forums and press. It started with British newspapers but quickly spread through BBS and blogs within China, resulting in a major public relations crisis for both Foxconn and Apple. The Uniden strike began with internal e-mails among employees. The strike organizers chose to use blogs strategically to appeal to the public and provide up-to-date information on the protest, which mainstream Western media like the *New York Times* picked up.

The cases share at least two important similarities. First, both involve high-profile companies in the global marketplace: Apple and Wal-Mart.

Although the plants are not directly owned by these two large multinational corporations, the fact that Foxconn manufactures iPod and Uniden produces supplies for Wal-Mart is enough to trigger a worldwide response. Second, both factories are in Shenzhen, a city of migrants, which has a more supportive local policy with regard to the development of working-class ICTs like cybercafés.[22] This is not coincidental: stronger resistance tends to exist in places with strong working-class networks.

It is of course premature to predict that working-class networks will bring about a fundamental social revolution, especially considering state and corporate reactions such as the wireless leash. However, the cases of Foxconn and Uniden show the possibility of change in Chinese factories. With the spread of working-class ICTs, workers in factory dormitories are now much less separated from urban society and much less atomized. Transnational forces like the press and labor activists have entered the struggle for justice and equality in Chinese plants. Yet on the shop floor and in the dormitories, the most powerful means of connection is still probably traditional social networks, based on regional, national, and translocal identities. If a major depression were to happen in China, it will be quite likely that the communication networks now used for job seeking, social support, and personal networking will be activated to serve purposes of collective action and lead to radical movements against the highly problematic labor-capital relationship in the rapidly industrializing cities and regions of China today.

Living beyond Oneself

Chinese network society is undergoing remarkable change. The ultimate challenge, here as elsewhere, is to develop meaningful places for living and vibrant communities for masses of strangers who are increasingly mobile and detached from a single physical locale. The process is contingent on state planning and the logic of the market. However, the information have-less—their informational needs, patterns of social networking, and collective action—matter in place making, as the diffusion of working-class ICTs breathes new life into urban villages and factory dormitories.

The emerging communities of China's new working class arise from the ashes of the Maoist city, whose main mechanisms of urban control—the *hukou* household registration system and the *danwei* work unit system—have been crippled. But the impact of market reform on the Chinese informational city is multifaceted and often paradoxical. Although migrants and laid-off workers now enjoy more freedom to move from one place to another as a result of networked connectivity, they are still subject to prejudice and discrimination, originating from the specter of institutionalized inequality in urban China, now facilitated by new technologies as well.

Within this larger historical framework, the two-tier society of the urban village has materialized with the split between indigenous villagers and migrant tenants; the workplaces from computer malls in city center to industrial zones at city periphery are constructed to reproduce the traditional power hierarchy in the ongoing spatial process of working-class network society.

However, it is crucial to recognize that the spread of working-class ICTs also creates tremendous opportunities for the formation of have-less communities, both at particular locations and translocally among the evolving social networks in the cities. These are not only employment opportunities and economic benefits that are trickling down to microentrepreneurs and their customers. More important, these open up the opportunity for grassroots networking and sociocultural uplift that may ultimately shape working-class communities above and beyond the shadows of the skyscrapers, above and beyond the elitist confinement over our imagination about the future.

These openings for social change are taking place where state officials and realtors cannot penetrate, where independent unions are yet to be established. It is in these places of struggle and of hope that we see opportunities for the have-less to transcend their narrowly defined self and participate in community building and collective action through critical events like labor strikes and mundane daily interactions in the neighborhood. Internet cafés, long-distance phone bars, convenience stores selling prepaid cards, blog posts by workers, and SMS exchange among fellow migrants: the power of these communication networks as tools of place making and class making is not to be underestimated.

7 Life and Death

The making of China's new working class is a process imbued with paradoxes and contradictions. The growth of working-class ICTs breathes life into some urban places, but it also takes life from others by reviving old ghosts and exacerbating inequality and discrimination. Although the emergence of the information have-less suggests opportunities for building more equitable urban communities, the specter of social exclusion is not easy to dispel. At times, it may even take unanticipated forms that cause fatal consequences.

The information have-less suffer because technology itself is no panacea for sick cities. While some upper-class Chinese fight for democracy and justice using new means of communication,[1] the majority of the information have-less are concerned about solving basic problems of life necessities for themselves and their families in their immediate environment. Many are obsessed with entertainment and consumption and poorly informed about public issues. Tension, misery, and resentment characterize their lives. When these burst, they can cause disruption and destroy lives. The death of victims in such situations is the ultimate expression of systemic exploitation, suppression, and despair. At the same time, some of these cases become critical media events that arouse public sentiments from all of society, in both nongovernmental and official domains. In this way, death can become the most powerful form of struggle for equality, dignity, freedom, and the true essence of human life in network society.

This chapter examines the city of the information have-less in a broader scope by first briefly introducing the city underneath: the informal economy, the places and processes of underground networks, and their relationship with working-class ICTs. Although empirical data on these subjects are rare, the matter is too important to ignore. We can nonetheless piece together a sketchy picture based on journalistic sources and my fieldwork and focus group findings, which can serve as an initial point of reference.

The chapter then provides a comparative case study of three new media events: events of major impact that are developed in an enlarged media ecology centered on the ICTs, especially low-end Internet and wireless applications in these cases. These are events with life-and-death consequences that have become indispensable to the shaping of working-class network society: the Lanjisu cybercafé fire in 2002; the murder of a migrant, Sun Zhigang, in 2003; and the Ma Jiajue murder case in 2004. These are among the most debated tragedies in urban China in the beginning years of the twenty-first century, which was characterized by the pivotal emergence of working-class network society.

The City Underneath

When Castells and Portes wrote about the informal economy, they referred to it as "the world underneath" (1989). Several of their arguments, though made in a global context with no direct reference to mainland China, are highly relevant to our discussion. Let us first encapsulate these basic characteristics of informal economy before attaching them to the Chinese context to capture a picture of working-class network society.

First, the informal economy, "unregulated by the institutions of society" (Castells and Portes, 1989, 12), is common in both advanced and less developed countries. Its wide spread is among the most notable global trends of our age. Second, this economy can represent innovative solutions from the bottom up. Third, despite its seemingly marginal or even illegal status, the informal economy is often an integral part of the urban economy. Fourth, the rise of informal economy is based on the expansion of downgraded labor, or "generic, expendable labor," as Castells (1998, 364) called it. Fifth, much of the informal sector developed under the auspices of government tolerance: "Informalization is not a social process always developing outside of the purview of the state; it is instead the expression of a new form of control characterized by the disenfranchisement of a large sector of the working class, often with the acquiescence of the state. For the latter, the loss of formal control over these activities is compensated by the short-term potential for legitimation and renewed economic growth that they offer" (Castells and Portes 1989, 27).

Although the informal economy was identified in the 1980s, these characteristics of it and its relationship to the working class and the state are strikingly pertinent to the reality of the Chinese informational city. China, of course, has a rich tradition of underground and semiunderground economies, ranging from Qing dynasty secret societies (Chesneaux 1971) to working-class street life in the post-Mao period (Dutton 1998). These encompass a variety of forms of the informal economy with a close affinity to informal working-class politics and informal working-class culture, all essential to the city underneath.

Here I map out the have-less city by looking at and categorizing its dynamics. This exploration identifies the thematic issues and common problems that run through the informal economies and unregulated urban processes.

As low-end objects of economic exchange, working-class ICTs are usually traded through cash. While China's upper classes have started to use credit cards, the information have-less use cash only. Some may have paid for content and services through SMS-based transactions, for example, by using value stored in prepaid cards.[2] But for activities in the informal economy, the primary means of exchange is still cash because there is no commercial credit system for the majority of have-less people. In addition, vendors often are not registered with the authorities and therefore, evade government taxes and other regulatory measures, for example, in the prepaid card business and Internet access services in black Net bars.

As for low-end ICT hardware, huge black and gray markets exist for used devices and parts. An example is the sales of revamped mobile phones, or black *shouji*, as discussed in chapter 3. These include used handsets sold or pawned by the original owners, such as penniless migrants selling their mobile phone for food, shelter, or a ticket to go home.[3] They also include phones that are stolen from the owners through petty theft or by organized crime. Another source is the large quantity of surplus production commodities, for instance, domestic-brand handsets that are attached with famous international brand names like Nokia. These black-market activities provide bottom-level jobs in the Chinese informational city, although they do require some basic IT knowledge in the refurbishing and sales of wireless phones.

The photo in figure 7.1 was taken in the street behind the Seibu shopping mall of Shenzhen. These were five of the eleven vendors sitting on the pavement selling their phones that evening. The adolescent had only two handsets for sale, while others had more. Male vendors in general displayed fewer phones, but they were of higher value with more recent and relatively high-end models that also looked newer. Female vendors tended to have more handsets of lower value, including Little Smarts, all resting on their laps and protected by their arms. These are moonlighters trying to make ends meet in the city underneath. But they also chatted

Figure 7.1
Moonlighting vendors selling wireless phones in Shenzhen, September 2005. Author photo.

with each other, smiling and enjoying their conversations as if the pavement were their common room.

Besides wireless handsets, the informal economy exists in the market of used computers and accessories, as discussed in the context of Guangzhou's Shipai Village in chapter 6. In July 2005, I lived in Beijing's Jianguomen area for a month. Every morning, when I walked through an underpass to cross the capital city's main strip, Chang'an Avenue, there was a middle-aged man sitting on the stairs. Beside him, a handwritten cardboard sign read, "Buying used printer cartridges." He would refill the cartridges and sell them for a fraction of the price of the original products. Scenes like this are common in certain neighborhoods of the city if the area has a considerable number of people who own printers.

The cartridge recycling business blends well with other informal economy activities. In that underpass tunnel, there were Tibetan vendors selling ethnic decorations as well as buskers playing the guitar for change from passers-by, although the man buying cartridges was there most often, almost a permanent part of that underpass. The only occasion that he disappeared, together with other hawkers, was when a high-level foreign delegation came to visit a building nearby and the police cleared out the underpass, but that was the only morning in the month that he was absent.

While hardware is recycled through the second-hand market, content and software are circulated through pirated discs and online. The informal economy of content provision dates back to the underground trading of cassette tapes in the 1980s and of *dakou* CDs in the 1990s. These were mostly popular music products smuggled into China. They were called *dakou* ("dented") because they were confiscated by customs and cut on the margin, thus bearing a physical scar (a dent) showing their illegal status. But these illicit copies nonetheless found their way on to the black market and eventually created what de Kloet (2005) terms "the *dakou* generation"—a youth subculture centered on rock music.

These *dakou* youth are going online now to use peer-to-peer (P2P) services like Bit Torrent, a popular file-sharing service among Chinese netizens. Many of them are from upper-class families, although a growing number of have-less youth are also accessing online content using P2P. On the other hand, the people selling illicit copies in the streets are members of the have-less who provide about half of all DVDs that Chinese movie audiences watch (Huang 2008). This is a high market share considering heightened official crackdowns since China entered the WTO in 2001. A main reason is that the networks of pirated DVD vendors comprise "highly sophisticated and flexible spatial organization" (Wang and Zhu, 2003, 110). A typical pattern is that copyrighted content is first illegally reproduced within China, then shipped overseas, and then smuggled back to the domestic underground economy. This pattern emerges due to China's antipiracy measures in response to pressures from foreign governments and companies, especially the United States (Wang and Zhu, 2003).

The piracy market is also closely connected to China's video disc player industry, which produces most of the world's DVD players. This "hardware-software dynamics" (Wang and Zhu, 2003, 107) demonstrates the multiple ties between the informal economy and the state-regulated formal economy. For one thing, there is simply not enough legal content to meet the massive demand for movies and other audiovisual products created by the fast-expanding disc player industry. With cutthroat competition in the disc player market, the hardware is becoming cheaper and cheaper, so that it has become a common item owned by working-class households today, yet the price of legal copies is not dropping at the same speed. The market for pirated copies therefore remains, and even enlarges. Meanwhile, the capacity of machines to play low-quality pirated discs has also become a unique selling point of domestically manufactured disc players, a peculiar change in the formal industrial system that reflects the power of the informal economy.

Besides connections with formal industrial establishments, the informal economy has multiple ties to the local state, which is among the reasons that the central government has not been able to eradicate piracy and other forms of the black market economy. As discussed in chapter 2, the practice of local state agencies is uneven across space and over time. They may play a suppressive role and clean up underground operations, but usually only once in a while. At other times, they are predators, extracting fines and confiscations, for example, from black Net bars. On certain occasions, they abuse their power to such an extent that it leads to major confrontations, as in the case of Lishui cybercafé strike.[4]

Nevertheless, local states may also be highly tolerant of informal and illegal ICT-based activities. One example is the garbage computer industry in South China. In Nanhai, Guangdong Province, for instance, long-term residents set up underground plants to refurbish used computers, which had been smuggled into China, into inexpensive computers. The migrants who revamped and polished these garbage computers worked in poor conditions, often with health hazards (Qiu forthcoming).

According to China Central Television, the underground factories had been in operation for a decade, in part due to the tolerance of local authorities. Although it violates multiple tax, environmental, and labor protection laws, this industry provides jobs and generates profits for the local economy. In Nanhai, this underground industry has ended. But elsewhere in coastal South China, it persists with the tacit protection of the state. This is a typical phenomenon of "the globalization of garbage" because the operation relied on the Internet, which allowed factory owners to place orders for tons of discarded foreign computers from the United States or Japan after browsing the photographs of the electronic garbage on the Web (Qiu forthcoming).

The globalized computer refurbishing business points to a much more encompassing aspect of the connection between working-class ICTs and the city underneath: new means of communication often serve as a critical informational and organizational basis for underground and semiunderground activities among have-less members. Without low-end ICTs, it would be much more difficult for the new working class to form grassroots networks. These include the online forums of cybercafé operators, blogs put up by migrant workers, e-commerce Web sites for working-class traders like Taobao.com, and translocal networks maintained through SMS. These are not merely commercial operations but grassroots cultural formations consisting of cross-linked interpersonal interactions that accumulate on the collective scale. But not all of them are benevolent and constructive: gangsters and organized criminals are also appropriating working-class ICTs.

As a result of criminal activities targeting personal property, security was a main concern of all focus groups that I conducted among migrants in 2002 and 2006.[5] Their mobile phones were often targeted by thieves, robbers, and tricksters. Cybercafés, and especially unlicensed cybercafés, are seen as dangerous places because of property theft, which partially explains why females tend to avoid them. Another complaint was the theft of prepaid value while using automated public pay phones:

Researcher: Anything worth noting about public phone?

Member A: Public phone . . . the main issue is stealing money.

Member B (immediately after):   Password theft . . .

Researcher: Password theft? What is it?

Member C: For example, as soon as you use a 200 card [a type of prepaid card], someone beside you looks at your password and changes it. Then he gets the value of that card.

Researcher: Oh, you mean someone can look over your shoulder and steal your PIN number? . . . Does this only happen to 200 cards? What about IP [VoIP] cards?

Member B: It happens to IP cards too.

Member C (simultaneously):   Of course! It happened to me! Once I got a new card and used it at a pay phone. I did not know [someone was looking]! The second time I used it from home, it said the password was wrong. I then knew it was stolen.

Researcher: Really? This is the first time I heard of this.

Member C (while members A and B are laughing):   Too many times this has happened!

Although such theft is common, police and local security guards seldom intervene, leaving migrant users victimized. Even if migrants saw such crime happening, they seldom dared to confront the thieves because the latter often are gangsters and work in groups. The collective response of have-less migrants was to shift from using automated pay phones to either their own mobile phones or long-distance phone bars, which provide better privacy protection.

Organized crime also targets working-class ICT providers and entrepreneurs as well. They may steal computers from cybercafés or force long-distance phone bars to pay protection fees, a practice with roots in ancient China. There are also new lines of attack and new tactics developed, for instance, those aimed at the prepaid phone card business. In July 2007, ten robbers armed with clubs and hammers attacked a car owned by a regional prepaid card wholesaler on the side of a major highway in Dongguan, stealing 2.6 million yuan ($329,000) in cash and 870,000 yuan ($110,000) worth of prepaid cards. The robbers were led by a fifty-three-year-old migrant entrepreneur who had a failed business selling prepaid cards. They knew the daily routine of the wholesaler company, which trades prepaid cards for cash with local entrepreneurs and coordinated the attack by mobile phone (Q. Sun and Xu 2007).

At the more extreme end, we see the concentration of deadly events resulting from organized crime facilitated by ICTs. The rise of online gambling, for example, during the 2006 soccer World Cup, stimulated underground gang activities relying heavily on the Internet and SMS. Although online gambling is strictly outlawed, it has spread in cities and the countryside through cybercafés (Jiu 2005). The same is happening with Internet pornography and commercial sex, when pimps can control unemployed girls and attract customers using inexpensive wireless phones. Equipped with these new devices, gangs also clash with each other in bloody confrontations and apply their enlarged, more flexible networks to engage in serious crimes such as armed robbery, drug trafficking, and murder.

A typical business based on working-class connectivity is the so-called blood black market (*maixue heishi*), which has been reported in Shanghai and Beijing. In Shanghai, blood buyers, known as blood heads (*xuetou*), advertised in online forums to recruit the poorest members of the have-less to sell their blood: laid-off workers, underemployed migrants, and students, most of whom access the Internet through cybercafés (L. Hu 2005). The blood is bought for 100 to 250 yuan ($13–32) per 100 cubic centimeters and sold for 550 yuan ($70). In Beijing, the so-called professional blood donors (i.e., those who sell their blood regularly) have challenged the safety of China's blood bank system (L. Hu 2005). Press coverage often emphasizes the subsequent health threats to the general public, for example, AIDS infection.

The most extreme form of ICT-based black market operation is probably the sale of assault weapons and the provision of gangster services such as coercion, physical injury, kidnapping, and murder. In the southern city of Zhuhai, residents receive SMS advertisements for affordable guns and grenades that are sold to anyone who can pay.[6] In another city, a Xinhua reporter received this message: "For long time our gang provides guns and ammunitions, drugs, spy ware, smuggled cars, fake currency from Taiwan, as well as private detective, professional killer, and fake ID services. Contact Ah Qiang [mobile phone number]" (XinhuaNet 2006). Although police authorities view such SMS as spam—itself an important part of the informal economy—it remains unclear how many of these messages are hoaxes, how many are real, and why this particular type of spam is reported consistently in different parts of the country.

Finally, ICT access itself gives rise to new ways of challenging the established social order, for instance, through hacking bank computer systems and official Web sites. Although many hacker attacks in China are launched by the upper-class geeks against foreign targets, a number of prominent cases have targeted domestic Chinese government sites. Some of these hackers are former computer majors, who either dropped out of college or were unemployed after graduation (Qiu 2002b). For them, hacking is a demonstration of their disobedience and disdain, which is in fact a shared element in Western hacker culture (Thomas 2003).

The Fatal Cases

We now turn to three fatal cases that victimized members of the have-less. All of them concern youth, in part because young people adopt working-class ICTs earlier than their elders. Consequently, ICTs play a more central role in the lives of young people.

These cases in which young people lost their lives triggered powerful public responses. The cases carry a special gravity in public debate because young people are the future of China, and yet they are so vulnerable in an environment that is violent and lacks equality. In this sense, although the key figures in these cases are young people, their extreme acts and experiences epitomize societal contradictions and suffering that not only these have-less youth but also their families and communities and the entire city underneath face.

Lanjisu: The Fury of the Abandoned

The Lanjisu cybercafé fire occurred in Beijing in June 2002, killing twenty-five and injuring thirteen.[7] This notorious incident was a watershed event in the evolution of China's Internet café business. This was also the most deadly fire in Beijing since the founding of the People's Republic in 1949 (*Survey of Haidian District* 2004).

There is more than one version of the story about what happened and why. Most press reports used the frame of the black Net bar, blaming the cybercafé owners for their greed and heartlessness (they allowed young customers to stay in the shop all night long) while expressing sympathy for the lives lost in this fire. Yet, as noted in chapter 2, state policies related to the cybercafé business should bear at least part of the blame. The teenage arsonists and the shop operators share responsibility, which nevertheless has to be understood in the context of severe official crackdown.

So what can we learn from this tragedy? To make full sense of the case and use it as an entry point to the city underneath, we need to examine the shop owners and operators, the customers, and the perpetrators.

Who owned and operated the shop? Why did they ignore fire code, setting up the cybercafé in an old three-story building with only one exit, plenty of flammable materials in the building, and iron bars sealing the windows? The shop owner was Zheng Wenjing, a thirty-six-year-old Beijing resident. He operated the business with his girlfriend, Zhang Minmin, "an unemployed personnel from Gaomi City, Shangdong Province" (Li and Ma 2003).[8]

Although information is limited about the lives of Zhang and Zheng—how they grew up, their educational background, and what they did besides operating the cybercafé—we can piece together how they made their business decisions under the regulatory constraints at the time. These constraints certainly were not new, and they have not disappeared since the Lanjisu fire. In October 2004, more than two years after the tragedy, the MPS still estimated that nationwide, there were twice as many black Net bars as registered legal cybercafés (Feng 2004). Zheng and Zhang's decision making with regard to their cybercafé in many ways reveals the common challenges facing microentrepreneurs who are providing ICT services in the working-class network society.

Zheng Wenjing opened his first café in Beijing's Haidian District in 1998. The timing and location suggest he was among the first generation of private Internet entrepreneurs in China, perhaps with relatively high education attainment, certainly committed to the "new economy." Zhang Minmin, his girlfriend from Shandong, did not have Beijing *hukou* residential status. But she probably had a decent education and could appreciate Zheng's ambition in order for the two to run the Net bar together. This type of ownership based on family or partner relationship is a common mode of economic organization for have-less providers, as in the case of long-distance phone bars in urban villages.

Like other microentrepreneurs, Zheng and Zhang probably had no access to bank loans. Instead, they would have had to rely on personal and family savings, as well as funds borrowed from friends and relatives. But they were unfortunate in operating the café. Before the fire, they had been caught in crackdowns and subject to fines six times. Their original shop was forced to close during the clampdown in late 2001 and early 2002. But they believed there was a huge market potential and probably thought the campaign against Net bars would end soon. Thus, when Lanjisu opened at the new site, it boasted high-configuration computers and a fast network connection (Li and Ma 2003), which means they must have invested heavily in the hardware to boost their competitiveness in the mass-service Net bars.

Zheng and Zhang must have been under serious financial constraints: they had been fined six times, were forced to relocate, and upgraded their equipment. When they opened the new café in May 2002, they hadn't completed the required paperwork. This was a financial decision for them and also common practice for cybercafé operation. The delay in paperwork was typically caused by bureaucratic inefficiency. Therefore, the regulatory authorities should also bear responsibility for the fatal consequence.

It was in this context that Zheng and Zhang chose to locate their cyber-café at this site: an old building in an ordinary low-profile residential community of Beijing. The three-story structure used to be a state-owned food and grocery store serving employees of the same work unit. After state players left the retail market, the building was rented by other business owners, one of whom put up iron bars on all windows to prevent theft. Later Zheng and Zhang were condemned for not removing these bars, which prevented their customers from escaping from the fire. They were also criticized for using cheap, flammable carpet. But given their precarious financial situation, they must not have thought they could afford fireproof materials or risk the theft of expensive equipment. Could they trust that the local police, after fining them six times, would provide enough security for their business property? Had they applied for a loan to remodel the building to meet the fire code, would any bank have considered their application?

The victims of the fire chose Lanjisu because the cybercafé offered competitive prices for Internet access, good machines, and fast connections. The Net bar operators sometimes provided free food and drink to some customers, perhaps attempting to attract them to become regular customers. But the main attraction was undoubtedly fast Internet access at an affordable price, the single most important factor in drawing large numbers of customers to mass-service cybercafés.

Lanjisu and its predecessor, Duke, were both located in the Haidian District of Beijing, an area with the largest concentration of universities in China. Moreover, it opened relatively early in the take-off period for China's Internet, and the highly educated accounted for a large percentage of users. College students are particularly early adopters.

Cybercafés are attractive precisely because schools are not. Computer labs are strictly managed and close early in the evenings. And although some students have their own computers, electricity in the dormitories is often cut off by midnight because of the university administration's belief that students should go to bed then. In 2007, three elite universities—Zhejiang University, Nanjing University, and Shanghai Jiaotong University—forbid their freshmen to have personal computers for fear of "excessive gaming" among them (Beijing News 2007). The incident triggered a public debate about the role of universities in offering Internet connections in order to compete with cybercafé access.

The attractiveness of cybercafés is thus partially a result of the failure of universities to understand the multidimensional informational needs of their students. Cybercafés are the only places that offer Internet access at affordable prices around the clock. Thus, when Lanjisu opened business in May 2002, college students flocked to it. When it was torched, twenty-one of the twenty-five victims were from the nearby University of Science and Technology Beijing; nine had been classmates in the Computer Science Department (Bai 2002).

When places of connection materialize in working-class neighborhoods, they tend to attract large numbers of have-less customers who share a similar demographic profile. The ICT services are merely part of the operation; the social functions of such places are at least equally important to students or members of other have-less groups who hang out with their friends in this shared physical space. In this way, they also become vulnerable to the unscrupulous, who now know exactly where to prey. When a tragedy happens, it affects many lives.

Lanjisu was set on fire by two young arsonists, Song Chun and Zhang Fan, aged fourteen and thirteen, respectively. There have been contradictory accounts of the immediate cause of the incident. In the online forums of cybercafé operators, one version goes that Song and Zhang were refused entry into Lanjisu because they did not meet the age requirement set by official regulation.[9] This means that the Lanjisu operators were actually law binding and were victims too.

Media and academic publications reveal that there was an argument between the cybercafé operator and the teenagers, with the operator ridiculing the young men for being penniless: "Without money, you dare to come here again?" (X. P. Liu 2002). Angered, Song and Zhang got some gasoline, poured it on the only entrance of the building, and set it afire. According to this account, the fire was a reaction to an insult. The cybercafé operators could have avoided the catastrophe had they treated the young people with respect.

The truth of what happened is probably somewhere in between these versions. The operators did not admit the boys in part because they were too young (although they were illegally offering twenty-four-hour service) and in part because they knew these two teenagers were poor. Perhaps it was wise from a financial standpoint for the owners to admit only college students or those who were older. But in the process, they were also discriminating against Song and Zhang, who had suffered prejudice and mistreatment for most of their young lives.

Song and Zhang, like many other children of the urban underclass, grew up in broken families. After the divorce of his parents, Zhang Fan was supposed to be brought up by his mother because his father was in prison for committing a violent crime. But his mother provided little care, giving him some money, a rented room, and little else. She seldom dropped by to see him (C. Wu 2002).

The main culprit of the fire, Song Cun, was brought up in an even worse environment. His parents divorced when he was just over a year old. His father won custody but was a poor parent. He was out of work, having been fired for negligence and committing a misdemeanor. He had fights with others and was sent to a detention center. Shortly after, he became a drug addict. He did not remarry but had three relationships. Two of the girlfriends frequently beat up Song Cun; one even hit the boy's head with her high heel, knocking him into coma when he was nine-and-a-half. His father was indifferent. He continued to use drugs with this girlfriend, abandoning his son to starvation and loneliness (C. Wu 2002; Shang 2003).

In February 2002, three and a half months before the Lanjisu catastrophe, Song's father was sentenced to another term in jail for repeated drug offenses. A couple of days later, Song stopped going to school for he felt he was looked down on and ridiculed by teachers and classmates (C. Wu 2002). This was a young man full of anger and hatred who did not want to be abandoned again.

Song's grandfather recalls that he was in fact a smart child, able to recognize all pieces in Chinese chess when he was only four years old. According to a teacher, when he was thirteen, he became a diligent student briefly. The reason was that he heard that his birth mother, a high-level manager of a computer company, would support him to study in America (C. Wu 2002). Although that hope soon vanished as his family life deteriorated, this short period shows that Song Chun might have been a normal member of society had he received more care and support.

Song and Zhang had bad reputations among their classmates. When their families did not give them enough money, which happened often, they bullied other students, robbed them, and treated them violently. Zhang Fan even broke the arm of one of his classmates (C. Wu 2002). Both boys were caught in a vicious circle in which their financial difficulty and lack of family support were translated into social isolation and rejection by their peers. It escalated to such an extent that they were almost completely detached from the community they lived in. The Lanjisu cybercafé was among the very few places where they could be reconnected, online and offline, with fellow human beings.

In August 2006, two months after the fire, Song received a life sentence, and Zhang was sent to juvenile reeducation center because he was under fourteen years old. Meanwhile, Zheng Wenjing, the owner of Lanjisu, was sentenced to jail for three years plus a fine of 300,000 *yuan* ($36,000), while Zhang Minmin was punished with eighteen months in prison and a fine of 200,000 *yuan* ($24,000) (Li and Ma 2003).

Urban institutions and communities too often fail to provide effective social services to troubled families. Family violence, drug abuse, and juvenile delinquency, these results of social exclusion tend to blend with and perpetuate each other at the very bottom of the have-less stratum. People in these circumstances can explode and cause catastrophic destruction.

The structural problems behind the fire remain largely unchanged, and we continue to see similar tragic events throughout the nation. In August 2003, a café operator in Ling'an City, Zhejiang Province, was beheaded by a group of furious young students because they refused to show their IDs as required by cybercafé regulation (*Eastday News* 2003). There have also been less severe attacks on operators, not to mention the many assaults, murders, frauds, and robberies of cybercafé customers.[10] Without effective intervention to reintegrate the city underneath as an essential part of the enlarged network society, tragedies like the Lanjisu fire will be repeated, taking more lives and tearing more families apart.

Sun Zhigang: Perishing in Jail

Sun Zhigang is probably the most famous migrant worker in China, but he would not have known this when he was killed at the age of twenty-seven. At the time, he was a gray-collar employee living in an urban village in Guangzhou. On his way to a cybercafé on March 17, 2003, he was detained by the police for not having a temporary residential card (*zanzhuzheng*), the official permit for migrants to reside in urban areas.[11] He was sent to a special holding center for unregistered migrants in Guangzhou Psychiatric Hospital, where he was beaten to death within sixty hours of his arrest (F. Chen 2003, W. Lin 2003, Fong 2003, Zhao 2008).

Sun grew up in a rural village in Huanggang, Hubei Province. He did well at school and managed to go to college. After graduating from the Art Department of Wuhan Institute of Science and Technology in 2001, he worked in Shenzhen until February 2003, when he joined the Daqi Clothing Company in Guangzhou as a graphic designer. When he was arrested, he had been in the city for less than a month and his temporary residential card had not yet arrived. He was therefore arrested on false ground as a "jobless vagrant" from the very beginning.

There has been widespread discrimination against migrants in Chinese cities, where illegal detainment and physical abuse are not uncommon. Sun Zhigang was not the first migrant killed in detention and will not be the last. But in a sense, despite his deadly misfortune, justice was finally done for him and his family. Due to the unprecedented public uproar in the mass media as well as online forums, Guangzhou police admitted their wrongdoing and the murderers received heavy sentences. Most important, the Beijing Central Government abolished the Regulation for Detention and Deportation of Urban Vagrants and Beggars and replaced it with a more lenient system aimed at providing help to needy migrants (*Sina News* 2004). For this historic change, Sun Zhigang will be remembered as the victim whose death had a positive impact on the lot of have-less migrants nationwide.

This tragic case had an exceptional impact on public opinion and government policy because, first, Sun Zhigang was not an average migrant. He was college educated, which led to overwhelming sympathy in mainstream society. Second, the incident occurred shortly after China's new generation of leaders, Hu Jingtao and Wen Jiabao, assumed power. This took place in the midst of the SARS epidemic, and the new government had to prioritize protecting the lives of its people more than anything else.

When Sun's death was exposed, the authorities were beginning to control the SARS outbreak, but the pandemic was still spreading. The timing was crucial because the government had to demonstrate its sincerity in carrying out its new mandate. Political control over media coverage was relaxed with respect to life-and-death cases for this brief period. Meanwhile, because SARS was not yet over, Chinese urbanites tended to spend more time online to get the latest information about disease control and because they were staying home rather than going to public places. Thus, for several weeks, the death of Sun Zhigang was discussed extensively online in mainstream Internet portals such as Sina and Sohu, with the number of click-throughs on this case trailing only SARS reports (*Sina News* 2004).

The location of the tragedy was also crucial to the national and international prominence this case achieved. Guangzhou, the capital of Guangdong Province, is a hub for have-less migrants in South China. It plays a key part in directing newcomers from the inland regions to urban villages and industrial zones. Guangzhou is also known for the plight of migrants who are uprooted, discriminated against, and victimized in urban society. The case of Sun Zhigang therefore quickly elevated from the mishap of one individual to the collective suffering of all have-less migrants.

Moreover, journalists in Guangzhou have a proud tradition of covering social ills and being empathetic with the vulnerable. The Sun Zhigang story was first reported by Chen Feng, a journalist at *Southern Metropolitan Daily*. His groundbreaking article, "The Death of Sun Zhigang, the Detainee," provided the initial and most critical ammunition for the public uproar (Zhao 2008). In fact, a year after the Sun Zhigang case, several senior personnel at *Southern Metropolitan Daily*, including the general manager and editor-in-chief, were penalized for covering this and several other cases, including the cover-up of SARS in Guangdong during the early stage of the epidemic (Watts 2005). But Guangzhou journalists have kept their high professional standards, without which the death of Sun Zhigang would probably have been merely a footnote in history.

Finally, the Sun Zhigang case has been often celebrated as a showcase for the growing power of online public opinion in China or even the invincibility of the Internet in restoring freedom and justice in authoritarian countries (Watts 2005, Q. Xiao 2004). The optimistic view has to be taken with a grain of salt given the timing and location of the case and the special status of Sun with his college education. Yet the Internet and mobile phone were essential to the dramatic outcome of the case. Chen Feng, who broke the story, learned about Sun Zhigang in an Internet forum for journalists in Guangzhou, where a college student posted the petition letter from Sun's family asking for help from journalists, legal professionals and the general public to seek justice in this case.[12] Chen followed this up and obtained the mobile phone number of Sun's high school classmate, who happened to live in the city and was trying to find out the truth about Sun's death. At the time, Sun's father and brother were in Guangzhou, where the authorities were stonewalling them. But their message was transmitted through ICT-based interpersonal networks to reach Chen and one of his colleagues at *Southern Metropolitan Daily*, where information about the case was finally released to the general public.

Had this single newspaper article provided the only information about what had happened, the case of Sun Zhigang would not have evolved into a major issue of public concern. According to my interview with Chen Feng, the tipping point was when Sina and Sohu, the two largest Internet portals in the country, put the story on their news section, which immediately generated a deluge of posts by netizens denouncing the brutality and demanding a thorough investigation. On the second day after the story hit the Web, the Guangzhou police, who had refused to cooperate for more than a month after the publication of Chen Feng's newspaper article, quickly responded by visiting the Suns to offer their condolences and seek compromise with the family so that the damage caused by this case to the image of the city could be put under control. China's new leaders also intervened quickly, bringing the murderers to justice and abolishing the discriminatory measures of 1982, all of which would have been impossible without the strong online public response.

Although the effect of online public opinion has received much attention, two important aspects in the death of Sun Zhigang remain to be addressed. One is that have-less migrants were adopting working-class ICTs for self-help by extending and strengthening their translocal networks at the grassroots level. Some of these networks are age-old, while others are new. Whichever the case, they empower less fortunate have-less people with their own system of information exchange, resource sharing, and social support.

The most crucial translocal network in this case involved the friends and former classmates of Sun Zhigang, most of them from Hubei Province. In Guangzhou, Sun was living with his friend Cheng, whom he called for help from the detention center. Cheng was among the first to learn about Sun Zhigang's death. From there, the bad news quickly spread through working-class ICTs to reach Sun's family in Hubei. When Sun's father and brother came to Guangzhou, this network of friends and classmates provided vital help in finding accommodations for them and providing financial and social support. It was through members of this network that the information was transmitted to journalists at the newspaper, through the Internet forum to Chen Feng, himself an alumnus of Wuhan University in Hubei.

Also important is to note that Sun's father and brother initially had difficulty finding legal representatives until they came across a hometown fellow (*laoxiang*) from Huanggang in Guangzhou, who happened to work for a law firm owned by another Hubei person. After hearing the details of the case, the firm agreed to provide its services at a very low fee. It was this Hubei lawyer in Guangzhou who wrote the petition letter that was later circulated in the online forum that Chen Feng was part of (*Beijing Youth Daily* 2003).

There is an important historical dimension of the Wuhan-Guangzhou connection that needs to be stressed. Since the 1980s, many college graduates from Wuhan, Hubei Province, have settled in Guangzhou and other cities in Guangdong. Besides the higher wages in Guangdong, the migration pattern is built on a legacy of the Maoist system of regional management. In this old system, Hubei and Guangdong belong to the south-central region of college administration. Thus, in the Maoist era, many Cantonese intellectuals moved to Wuhan, and in the 1980s and 1990s, they helped students find jobs in Guangzhou and other nearby cities. The historical ties become strengthened with the growth of alumni networks in Guangdong. It was hence unsurprising that Sun Zhigang, who graduated from a university in Wuhan, went to work first in Shenzhen and then in Guangzhou, where he had more access to the resources based on his college connection. ICT-based networks are built on the base of translocal ties that have accumulated over time.

The case of Sun Zhigang also shows the internal differentiation of haveless population, which sparks tension and conflict within the urban underclass along lines of migrant strata, power position, and regional identity. Under such circumstances, the use of working-class ICTs and efforts to control such use tend to reproduce and magnify existing social inequalities in the Chinese informational city.

Sun was detained in the Huang Village in Guangzhou. The young graphic designer had relatively long hair, and in the poorly lit neighborhood, he could look like a homeless person. Police stopped him and checked his temporary residential card. Upset at yet another incident of discrimination, Sun was angry. As a college graduate with a job, Sun must have thought that he deserved more respect. Yet it was exactly this mind-set that made him stand out from the rest of the inmates, because the others, including most police, had not gone to college for either academic reasons or their low family income. They probably did not think education should matter at all when someone was in custody.

While they detained Sun Zhigang, the police took away his mobile phone, thus stopping the flow of information between him and the outside world. Although Sun was healthy, he was sent to the Guangzhou City Medical Treatment Station for Detainees, housed in a branch of the Guangzhou Psychiatric Hospital in the outer suburbs (Tang 2003). This institution relied on migrant labor to serve as *hugong*, the "guard worker" or "nurse worker." Wearing military uniforms and carrying batons, these were also have-less migrants; they were poorly paid but had the power to decide the fate of inmates.

The guard who ordered the beating of Sun Zhigang was a twenty-one-year-old named Qiao from rural Shanxi Province. He had only a middle school education and was known for being rough. When Sun screamed for help, shouting that he was college educated, Qiao felt he needed to teach the prisoner a lesson. After a discussion with two fellow Shanxi guards and another from Henan, Qiao put Sun in cell 206, a room known for severe prisoner abuse.

Qiao ordered Li Haiying, the "head" of cell 206, to arrange for the beating. A junior middle school graduate from Hunan Province, Li was twenty-six and had been beaten three times since arriving at the center less than a week ago. Under Li's pressure, eight prisoners in the cell, all of them migrants, hit Sun Zhigang one after another until he lost consciousness. In this group were one senior middle school graduate, four junior middle school graduates, and three elementary school graduates.[13] Thus, in a sense, Sun lost his life because he was misplaced in the migrant strata. He was too well educated to accept what was routine in the hierarchical structure of the prison environment, where the guard gave a command and inmates who had served longer terms beat up newcomers.

Regional identity mattered in this process because northerners were known for their toughness and more likely to be in command positions. The four guards involved were all from North China. In contrast, the eight detainees who beat up Sun were from Sichuan, Hunan, and four other southern provinces. Although they were complete strangers sharing the cell for only a couple of days, they had learned to follow the orders of the northerners. The social structure of the prison reinforced the power of urban institutions, with one group of migrants suppressing another, without direct intervention by *hukou*-holding long-term residents of Guangzhou.

There was another informal system that shaped the informational structure of the detention center by controlling the use of working-class ICTs to spread fear and extract bribes from the inmates and their families, friends, and employers. After Sun Zhigang's mobile phone was taken away from him, he was able to make two brief calls to his friend Cheng so that he could come to "save" him by bringing money and the necessary paperwork. The caller ID showed that Sun was not using his own mobile phone. The other friend disclosed that Sun was "stuttering rapidly, as if he was totally frightened" (Chen 2003). Most likely, he was under close surveillance while making this call.

Confessions from the inmates who killed Sun also revealed that the guard often forced newcomers in the detention center to call people to come bail them out, using a guard's mobile phone with a prepaid phone card. Li Haiying, the head of cell 206 at the time, for example, had been forced to call his friend this way. Fortunately, the friend came in time and spent more than 70 yuan ($9) treating two *hugong* to dinner. He also gave them a bribe of 150 yuan ($19) so that Li would be better treated. It was after this that Li became the head of the cell (Tang 2003).

Along with Qiao, Li received the death penalty; the other guards and inmates who were involved received prison terms from three years to life. Remarkably, although twelve police, two doctors, and a nurse were demoted or censured for incompetence and negligence, not a single long-term Guangzhou resident was criminally charged. Justice for Sun Zhigang was therefore still only partially restored. Discrimination persists in the city underneath, which explains why, since 2003, have-less migrants have continued to be abused and occasionally murdered in detention centers.

Ma Jiajue: Another Robin Hood?

Ma Jiajue was studying bioscience in Yunnan University, the best college in the province. In February 2004, after a spat in a mah-jongg game, Ma used a hammer to kill four of his dormmates. He hid the corpses in the cabinets of his dormitory and ran away using travel plans he had made earlier based on information collected on the Internet. A month later, with high-profile coverage in both mass media and online forums, Ma was found in Sanya, Hainan Province. He showed little remorse for the murders and refused legal assistance (Jiang 2004). On June 17, he was executed at about the time when he and the four victims were supposed to graduate.

This case has deeply registered in the nation's collective memory as one of the bloodiest consequences of the commercialization of higher education and the increasing social inequality on university campuses. While mass media reports tend to frame Ma as a cold-blooded murderer, the overwhelming online opinion among have-less youngsters was to portray him as a legendary bandit, someone like Robin Hood with "the immense personal prestige of celebrated outlaws" (Hobsbawm 1969, 109).

It is not much of a stretch to extend Hobsbaum's notion of "social banditry" to include Ma Jiajue. To Hobsbaum, social banditry is "a form of individual or minority rebellion within peasant societies" (1969, 13). Although urban China today does not fit the category of peasant society, the element of rebellion—not only by Ma Jiajue the individual but also his have-less sympathizers, who formed a significant online minority group— is remarkably strong. Ma Jiajue did come from a peasant background. He grew up in Ma'er Village, Binyang County, in southwestern Guangxi Province. The village land has been encroached by the expanding Bingyang City, and Ma Jiajue's family is among the remaining few who still farm the shrinking agricultural land (Shi et al. 2004). His parents earn less than 300 yuan ($38) a month by working in the field and ironing clothes for a clothing store.[14]

Ma Jiajue, who grew up in poverty, was academically gifted. He did well in elementary school and was admitted to the best middle school in Bingyang City. There, he won a first prize in the Nanning Prefecture physics contest (Shi et al. 2004), second prize in a national physics contest (Shi et al. 2004), and third prize in a national math contest (*Sichuan Morning Post* 2004). But it was also in the city that Ma Jiajue started to taste the bitterness of poverty and urban discrimination. He often did not have enough to eat, and keeping warm was a struggle. Girls called him "Old Uncle Ma" and laughed at him, which he hated silently and could complain only in his diary (Shi et al. 2004, 8).

Feeling estranged and desperate, he began breaking high school rules and was censured repetitively (XinhuaNet 2004b). This did not prevent him from scoring high enough on the college entrance examination. He chose Yunnan University in Kunming because it was relatively close to home. Ma Jiajue was so poor that he was able to afford to go home only once during his three and a half years in college and called home only once every several months. He struggled to pay for his basic necessities, including food and shoes so he would not have to go barefoot, by working as a porter. In contrast, his affluent classmates were showing off their new mobile phones and motorcycles.[15]

The period between 2000 and 2004 was characterized by intensifying commercialization of higher education in China, as discussed in chapter 5. The year of the Ma Jiajue tragedy also marked a crucial change on university campuses because 2004 was the first year that Chinese universities nationwide admitted more students from the countryside than from cities (Yang 2005). As a result, students from extremely poor families make up about 20 percent of all Chinese college students today (Yang 2007). Financial disparity among students thus increased drastically, creating more discrimination against needy students like Ma Jiajue, who now felt that he was rejected by his peers. At the same time, university administrators and professors became more obsessed with profit making from all kinds of part-time jobs such as consultancy and a variety of lucrative "research" projects such as collaboration with corporations, thus shifting attention away from students. Finally, job prospects declined dramatically with the oversupply of college graduates. Under such circumstances, it would be unsurprising that Ma Jiajue was hopeless about his future after graduation.

Among the four whom Ma Jiajue killed, three were also from relatively poor families, all in West China (XinhuaNet-Yunnan 2004), although none of them faced as much financial difficulty as Ma had. They were in fact among Ma's best friends. But they also humiliated him. One of them used to urinate on Ma's bed comforters. In the winter, one of them paid Ma 1 or 2 yuan ($0.13–0.25) to hand-wash his laundry (there was no washing machine), and Ma did it because he needed the money.[16] Interactions like these sowed seeds of resentment and hatred that led to the murders (Y. Zheng 2004).

The case of Ma Jiajue is emblematic of social problems that face have-less youngsters in the commercialized university environment and the com-modified urban society at large. It also reveals ways of ICT application within the police system, which include working-class ICTs like prepaid services, particularly among low-rank personnel like guards, who are also have-less migrants. In order to hunt down the suspect, known for his online activities, the police monitored and tracked information flows on the Internet among the general public. But without proper checks and balance, such actions quickly became the basis for yet another crackdown campaign on working-class ICTs.

The pursuit of Ma Jiajue was among the most high-profile manhunts in the history of the PRC due to the combined use of ICTs, mass media, and rewards. When the MPS issued its A-Level Most-Wanted Alert for the arrest of Ma on March 1, 2006, the order reached all regional branches of the police system within an hour and all on-duty police and security guards within twelve hours. Until the arrest of Ma on March 15, 1.7 million police were mobilized throughout the nation. In Ma's home province, Guangxi, police made 110,000 trips to investigate more than a thousand people connected to Ma Jiajue and to check 43,000 public places, including particularly cybercafés (Y. Lan 2004).

Unlike other similar alerts, the pursuit of Ma Jiajue carried a reward of 200,000 yuan ($25,316). Information about the alert, the reward, and Ma's photograph were broadcast on national TV. The police soon received 1,560 so-called effective clues for the manhunt. In some of the cities that Ma had never been to, like Shanghai, Ningbo, and Lanzhou, the police were also "mobilized on a massive scale" due to the large number of clues (Y. Lan 2004). Cybercafés became the focus of police activity. In Wuhan, Hubei Province, yet another city where Ma had never set foot, the police checked 1,120 cybercafés. Of these, 49 of them were closed down and 8 fined for noncompliance with cybercafé regulation. That Ma Jiajue liked to go to cybercafé was now an excuse for this cybercafé crackdown (C. Zhu 2004).

The high-profile nature of the pursuit had two unintended consequences. First, the police were overloaded with information about the possible whereabouts of Ma Jiajue, especially given the reward. Most of the information, however, was useless or misleading. Moreover, it generated a large number of imposters pretending to be Ma Jiajue, online and offline. These included marginalized have-less young people who were sympathetic to Ma's suffering from the beginning and now outraged by the abusive uses of police power. "Everyday, there were suspicious information and clues and imposters pretending to be Ma Jiajue." The police stance was, however, "to believe all were true" (C. Liu 2004, 15). With the escalation of actions on both sides, the pursuit evolved into a showdown between the authorities and the less powerful, who were adopting working-class ICTs to contest power.

The image of Ma Jiajue delivered by mass media could not have been more different from the one emerging in online forums. The press and broadcasting media largely demonized Ma Jiajue, using sensational headlines such as "How a College-Student 'Butcher' Grew Up" (Shi and Ma 2004). The mass media reports typically emphasized that Ma Jiajue was a frequent visitor of "illegal Web sites," that he watched violent movies and pornography on the Internet, and that he spent hours browsing online content about how to hurt or kill people, how to hide evidence, and how to attack police. He also downloaded materials about survival skills in the wilderness, while making an escape plan based on information he had collected online (*Nanguo Zaobao* 2004).

Despite attempts to demonize Ma Jiajue in mass media, public opinion on the Internet was overwhelmingly sympathetic to him. A content analysis of 448 Internet posts in the BBS hosted by Baidu (the largest domestic search engine) showed that while 6.1 percent of them had a negative opinion of Ma Jiajue and another 8.2 percent were neutral, fully 40.8 percent thought positively about him in a sympathetic light (H. Yang 2004). To the compassionate netizens, Ma Jiajue qualified as "the noble robber" (Hobsbawm 1969, 34). He never hurt anyone during the three weeks when he was on the run, trapped by poverty and desperation, surviving on food he found in garbage bins. At school, he worked as a porter to support himself, and at home, he had a high standard of filial piety, caring especially for his mother. He was intelligent and capable of outsmarting the police, and he was fearless, embracing the death sentence to send the strongest message in defense of traditional values against the fall of the society into excessive commercialization.

Online discussions like these contain elements of fiction and should be taken as a collective making of a heroic bandit rather than an objective reflection of who Ma really was. Of the posts, two of the most widely circulated ones contributed the most to public sympathy toward Ma Jiajue in China's cyberspace. One was a report on how Ma responded after he was caught and offered a change of clothing. Wearing the detainee uniform, he sighed, "This is the best thing I've ever worn." The policeman standing next to him reportedly was moved to tears.

The other was a piece of poetry allegedly written by Ma Jiajue from his prison in Kunming, also known as the Spring City. It was in Kunming that Ma lived for three and a half years before killing his dormmates. The poem had an ancient title, *Changhenge*, meaning "The Elegy of Endless Sorrows." It was, however, written in modern Chinese, starting with his thoughts behind the prison bars (author's translation):

Rain falls on the Spring City at springtime,
with a rush of chilly air.
Looking at the rusted prison bars,
I thought of my parents, how poor they are.
To support children going to school,
from dust to dawn, they farm hard,
ironing clothes under candlelight,
half *yuan* a piece.

The poem continues to tell the story of his life: how he grew up in poverty; how he suffered from discrimination; how he fell in love with a girl who tore his love letter into pieces in public; how he learned to play computer games in college in order to socialize with classmates; and how

he could not stand being humiliated over and again by his dormmates.
It runs 255 lines and ends with a dream that at last he returns home,
"strolling slowly in my lovely, simple, dear hometown."

Ma Jiajue was executed on June 17, 2004. This, however, did not end the
story; rather, it martyred him as the ultimate legend of a defiant have-less.
Chinese netizens memorialize him in myriad ways. They identify with
him, calling him "elder brother Ma (*mage*)." His pictures, especially the
one used and popularized by the most-wanted alert, were modified into
hundreds of icons and cartoon-like images showing him laughing at the
police, ridiculing the commercial world. One netizen summarized his life
using antique language mimicking the famous *Shiji* (*Records of the Historian*)
of the Han Dynasty, and the text was posted on 4,730 Web pages as of
August 2006.[17] Two independent DV (digital video) films about Ma Jiajue's
life and death were made by college students at Peking University and
Tsingtao University, respectively, again sparking public debate two years
after the execution.[18]

Among the most illuminating multimedia materials on the Internet is a
Flash MTV entitled "Ode to Ma Jiajue (*Ma Jiajue zhige*)."[19] Indeed, Flash
animation has become a powerful tool for alternative cultural expressions
among have-less netizens. This product of grassroots creativity must have
been the result of group collaboration because it involved some sophisticated production procedures and the remixing of many cultural elements
available in the Chinese informational city and abroad. The lyric of the
Flash MTV is written from the perspective of Ma Jiajue:

Wherever I go, I see police and my picture (on the most-wanted) . . .
200,000 *yuan opens* everyone's eyes, men and women, old and young . . .
Until one day, you will find out,
I'm not as ugly as that picture . . .

The animation then superimposes Ma's picture from the most-wanted
alert over the image of the Hulk, another symbol of alienation and estrange-
ment, an avenger with anger exploding through his muscles. With a powerful blow, he swipes away a few of his brothers (*gemen'er*) in a typical scene
from the Street Fighter computer game series. He was then caught up
between merciless police and greedy people seeking the reward. Jumping
up high like a kung fu master, he swirls and smashes all his pursuers. He
then goes up to the Liangshan Mountain, the most famous gathering place
for heroic bandits in Chinese history. There he receives a call from Bin
Laden, his new comrade-in-arms. Together they use rifles to fight George

W. Bush, who is heavily armed, with missiles, bombs, and helicopter. At the end, they are hit by a grenade, and Ma Jiajue is sent to prison. The Flash MTV ends with a few sentences about the moral of the story: we have to learn to respect human life and respect each other.

More fatal assaults by college students have taken place since Ma Jiajue's execution. Some of the assailants were pursuing doctoral degrees, some came from top schools like Peking University and Tsinghua University, and some from second- or third-tier colleges. In Nanchang in 2004, a senior from Jiangxi Medical School stabbed seven people in and near a cybercafé, killing two and injuring five, toward the end of his four-year college education (XAOnline 2004). Without effective efforts to increase equality on university campuses, without the restoration of a sense of community among all students, these tragedies will continue in the city underneath.

Old Problems, New Media Events

What should we learn from the tragedies of Lanjisu, Sun Zhigang, and Ma Jiajue? The three events, occurring in 2002, 2003, and 2004, respectively, may appear to be quite different at first glance. But together they demonstrate the disastrous consequences of inequality, discrimination, and injustice. When urban institutions fail to address structural problems, tension and hatred accumulate, and there may be a deadly result. Yet the aftermath of the tragic events also shows that working-class ICTs have begun to bridge social gaps among different groups of information have-less and between them and other social groups. They have provided new means for cultural expression at the grassroots as well as opportunities for change, conciliation, and the reintegration of network society due to the momentum created by what can be called new media events.

In their influential book, Dayan and Katz (1992) developed the concept of "media event" to account for the extraordinary manifestation of media power exemplified by live-broadcast TV ceremonies that command massive audiences. These are usually grand events that are supposed to mark unique historic moments, like the Olympic Games and the funeral of John F. Kennedy, which are planned by professional event organizers, high-level state agencies, or major corporations. These media events impinge deeply on the collective memory of a society, thus creating a strong cohesive force in the media system and the social system.

The three cases discussed in this chapter qualify as media events. There were huge audiences who followed the events as they unfolded. TV was broadcasting not only the A-level alert about Ma Jiajue but also official narratives about Lanjisu and Sun Zhigang, following a typical elitist mode of top-down communication, although with much less cohesive media effects, at least along the directions expected by the authorities.

In a recent article, Katz and Liebes broadened the original idea of media events by including "disruptive events such as disaster, terror and war" in their concept because "media events of the ceremonial kind seem to be receding in importance, maybe even in frequency" (2007, 158). The cases of Lanjisu, Sun Zhigang, and Ma Jiajue might fall into the category of disruptive disasters in this more expanded concept. But these cases still differ in a few key ways to the extent that perhaps a better term is *new media events.*

At the most obvious level, the three cases relied more on new media, including Internet and mobile phones, and less on TV. Print media were also involved, as were lower-class netizens who spoke out either as individuals representing their own interests (the cybercafé operators after the Lanjisu fire) or as groups demanding a collective voice and alternative cultural expression (those who created the Flash MTV to memorize Ma Jiajue).

These were not merely new media technologies but a new ecology of multimodal communication, allowing the participation of the information have-less as not only passive audiences but also active participants in these events. Because these new participants were from different social classes, they did not share the same version approved by a centralized power authority. Discursive inconsistency and cultural conflicts were therefore a natural part of these new media events. Such internal tension prevented the cases from becoming grand "media events" in the original sense. But it was precisely because of this tension that the audiences were seriously engaged, especially those living in the city underneath, who had probably seen enough unifying harmonious official discourse detached from the reality of their lives.

Indeed, these new media events were seen as more "real" in the sense that they were relatively less manipulated as in traditional mass media channels, and they were closer to the everyday reality familiar to members of the information have-less. With the inclusion of user-generated content from the bottom of the Chinese informational city, we could see more clearly the roots of the social problems in the development of the events and the highly contentious roles played by the media, old and new.

All three incidents started with unplanned episodes: two teenagers were refused access to a cybercafé; a migrant worker failed to carry his temporary resident card; a college student had an argument with his dormmates. Things like this happen every day. But in the context of contemporary Chinese network society, with the spread of working-class ICTs coupling rapid commercialization and continued hierarchical control over urban places, the conflicts escalated and exploded when the most alienated members of the information have-less became desperate and violent. They vented their anger on others, hurting everyone and everyone's family, themselves included, through the ultimate destruction of human life.

The roots of these disasters are age-old social ills: economic disparity, the unequal distribution of power, the exclusion of the have-less from urban culture, and the lack of care for those driven to the fringes of society. In the three cases, these problems took their own forms to reflect the failure of particular urban institutions. At one level, the Lanjisu fire was about unnecessarily heightened tension in the regulatory system of cybercafés. But more fundamentally, it had to do with the lack of effective social services for disadvantaged urban families struck by divorce, unemployment, and drug abuse and for the children of these families, facing discrimination at school and in the community.

The death of Sun Zhigang exposed the horror brought about by the abuse of police power that haunts all have-less migrants. It also showed how the internal structure of the detention center could turn a group of strangers into a killing machine and how this structure could extend itself through ICTs as well. Most essentially, the case was about urban prejudice against migrants, institutionalized in the *hukou* household registration system, whose restriction has been eroded due to the public uproar following this case.

Like the teenage arsonists in the Lanjisu fire, Ma Jiajue was socially isolated. He had few friends in Kunming, and poverty prevented him from spending time with his family, even on the phone. The real culprit was, however, the excessive commercialization of education. When one of Ma's dormmates "disappeared" for several days, his girlfriend tried to find him and sought help from the university. Yet no one responded until the corpses started to decompose.[20] If this was the average level of care a college student could receive, how about other have-less people?

Ma Jiajue, Song Chun, Zhang Fan, and the inmates of cell 206 became violent when urban institutions had done violence to them by ignoring their needs, treating them with disrespect, and leaving them to the dark powers of savage capitalism. They were not born to kill. But they killed anyway because under the shadow of power and profit, the places they happened to be in were alienating and merciless.

Even after the tragedies, unequal treatment continues. Typically once these fatal events are exposed, have-less perpetrators are singled out, quickly hunted down, and sentenced to prison or executed. In the process, because targets were set on the individuals rather than the systematic problems behind them, the incidents led to heightening control over working-class ICTs and further discrimination against the have-less. Access at cybercafés, for instance, became more expensive and cumbersome, which would trigger more underground actions to subvert the inequalities of the status quo. This would then attract further crackdowns and set in process a vicious cycle of power, setting up the stage for the next disaster.

It is important to acknowledge that the three tragedies, given the gravity of their impact on public opinion, all caused some change in policy. The death of Sun Zhigang had the most obvious influence by expediting the reform of the *hukou* system, with several cities eradicating the temporary resident card system and a few provinces abolishing the distinction between rural and urban residents altogether (China News Agency 2005). Since the case of Ma Jiajue, universities have paid more attention to have-less students, giving them more loans, although that in itself is insufficient to restore equity in the education system (Yang 2007. The Lanjisu fire put the problem of cybercafés on the public agenda. It provided the justification for crackdowns locally and nationwide, leading to desired as well as unintended consequences, including the shift of national regulatory authority from the MPS to the MoC (Qiu and Zhou 2005).

Most of these changes, however, failed to address the social roots of these problems: inequality, lack of respect to the have-less, and the exclusion of the have-less from policymaking processes. Therefore, the crackdown campaigns on cybercafés in fact generated more black Net bars, and the issues facing needy families, like the family of Song Chun, remain to be solved. The trend of commercialization has not changed; rather, it has accelerated. In the university system, tuition hikes expanded from the undergraduate to postgraduate levels in 2006 (*Beijing News* 2006). Job prospects keep declining, and staff members keep focusing on profit making, leading to new conflicts such as the one in Zhengzhou (Kahn 2006). As of 2007, the temporary resident card system was still in operation in Guangzhou, where Sun Zhigang was detained for not having the card.[21] To a large extent, the discrimination of have-less migrants has persisted as the country maintains its elitist system while age-old social ills and savage capitalism continue to rule the city underneath.

Admittedly, there is a long way to go to solve the social problems of inequality and discrimination. Nevertheless, new media events should be considered an important harbinger of change. Before effective actions can be taken to restructure the problematic reality, people, especially marginalized groups, have to be able to talk about the reality they experience. In this sense, new media events present a crucial first step toward social inclusion under the circumstances of more widely available networked connectivity, which is part of the pivotal transformation toward "mass self-communication" with the "historical shift of the public sphere from the institutional realm to the new communication space" (Castells 2007, 238).

Most important is to note that the three cases demonstrate in one way or another how spontaneous grassroots formations might connect the information have-less with each other and with other social groups. Such connections could be based on traditional translocal networks such as the Wuhan-Guangzhou link in the case of Sun Zhigang, being extended through working-class ICTs. In other cases, the new means of communication may also give rise to entirely new linkages, like the online forums for cybercafé operators emerging in the aftermath of the Lanjisu fire, or the groups of netizens sympathizing with Ma Jiajue, pretending to be him in the heat of the manhunt, and exchanging Flash MTVs to commemorate their legendary bandit. While working-class ICTs may indeed be used against the have-less under particular structural constraints, the questions remain open as to if and how they can become the backbone of new infrastructures of care and of more inclusive urban communities.

The role of working-class ICTs is notable in these cases because they differ from mass media in terms of their content and organizational principles. As can be seen clearly in the cases of Lanjisu and Ma Jiajue, newspaper and TV were heavily biased toward the official version of the stories while ignoring alternative perspectives, for instance, by considering why the cybercafé operators had to set up their business as such, endangering others' and their own lives. Because the online forums were bottom-up formations of "mass-self communication" relatively free from the political and commercial constraints shaping mass media, they could foster discussions that are less simplified and more compassionate for all have-less victims, including the young perpetrators themselves, thus contributing to a less deformed collective memory. Grassroots forums enable the users and providers of working-class ICTs to speak up, share with each other, and identify with each other. It is this unique role that distinguishes them from

Networks of have-less migrants   **Mainstream urban society**

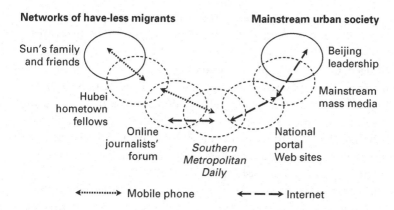

Figure 7.2

Networked communication and public opinion processes in the case of Sun Zhigang.

traditional mass media and from conventional media events, ceremonial or disruptive.

The line between old and new media, and between old and new media events, is not absolute. As figure 7.2 shows, in the case of Sun Zhigang, mass media and working-class ICTs had a close affinity with each other. Journalists at *Southern Metropolitan Daily* relied on the Web and mobile phones in an essentially translocal interpersonal network of have-less migrants from Hubei in this case to piece together the first news report. The article was then relayed to major Internet portals to create a huge impact in public opinion through more attention drawn to the event on other mainstream mass media platforms and finally the Beijing leadership of Hu Jingtao and Wen Jiabao.

This cross-media, cross-class communication pattern following the death of Sun Zhigang was more of an exceptional case due to the timing of the incident in the middle of the SARS epidemic and when the new CCP leadership had just come to power and was searching for a new basis of legitimacy. But to a lesser degree, it also happened in the case of Ma Jiajue, which highlighted the urgency for elite decision makers to increase financial aid on university campuses. However, the ending of the Ma Jiajue case was much less conciliatory with the creation of an alternative subculture celebrating and memorizing Ma as a rebel hero.

If put in perspective with the Lanjisu tragedy, we can see a progression of new media events: public discussion was dominated by traditional mass media in 2002, when cybercafé operators could share opinions only in their enclave of online forums, almost completely ignored by mainstream urban society. In 2003, grassroots networks and mass media were successfully bridged through the process visualized in figure 7.2, creating the conciliatory (albeit still discriminatory) outcome of the Sun Zhigang case. In 2004, the convergence of ICTs and traditional media happened again for the authorities such as police as well as members of the underclass, especially have-less youth sympathizing with Ma Jiajue, whose grassroots networks became more autonomous with alternative user-generated content such as poetry and Flash MTV.

It is clear that working-class ICTs can develop a close affinity with traditional mass media, at least China's new metropolitan newspapers like *Southern Metropolitan Daily* that identify more closely with the new working class. When political control loosens, the synergy between new and old communication channels, including not only formal media organizations but also interpersonal networks, can become a strong force for public opinion in an enlarged new media ecology, now realigned with the mass self-communication of the information have-less.

Such a synergy is of utmost importance because what it represents is not only intermedia relationships but also ties between the have-less and other social groups, including members of the urban elite. Indeed we can see this pattern in all three cases discussed here, albeit in different ways, when issues troubling the city underneath finally leaped from the small circles of have-less victims to mainstream public discussion.

The three fatal disasters discussed here are, in a sense, only the tip of iceberg for the vast city underneath, where the have-less live and die, where their agonies constitute the substructure of the emerging working-class network society. Gangster activities, police brutality, factory suppression of labor activists, starvation, and domestic violence within the families of the unemployed: the suffering and carnage go on. Yet most of these instances are not reported, and therefore become "uneventful," because those killed are not college educated; because female deaths are not deemed as consequential; because even the have-less themselves have grown apathetic to the silent perishing of human lives.

Nevertheless, an interim conclusion can still be reached: when it comes to the gravest tragedies, when have-less youth cannot be protected from life-threatening danger even after getting a higher education, the key channel of upward social mobility for have-less individuals, chances are that the urban society at large will be informed and engaged through the combination of new and old communication channels in an effort to protect the future of China. This collective effort is not completely immune to manipulation. But it is nonetheless a solid basis to start from in order for solutions of age-old social problems to be addressed, debated, and implemented.

As the saying goes in *The Art of War*, "Drive them into a fatal position and they will come out alive; place them in a hopeless spot and they will survive." Death in the Chinese informational city has been and will continue to be the strongest weapon of power contestation by providing the most compelling rallying call for equality and dignity in the enlarged network society.

8 Reflections

This book brings class in as a cornerstone, rather than a secondary factor, of the evolving network society in a large, industrializing country. Unlike previous China ICT studies devoted solely to the role of the state or corporate players, this book foregrounds the basic structure of informational stratification and the making of the new working class as keystones for understanding communication technology and social change.

In so doing, we have begun to synthesize and analyze two emergent processes. Technologically, Internet and wireless communication have diffused beyond the initial core of the elite, spreading into the lower strata of urban China. The consequence is the rapid materialization of working-class ICTs on a massive scale. Socially, with the integration of digital media into the everyday work and life of ordinary workers, working families, and low-income communities, we have witnessed the rise of the information have-less, which provides a crucial seedbed for the making of a new working class. The two processes interweave in the general technosocial trend toward working-class network society, whose main characteristics can be summarized:

1. Working-class ICTs have become essential to the basic human existence among the information have-less in urban China. This diffusion of communication technology enlarges network society in general and prepares a fertile technosocial foundation for the emergence of a working-class network society.
2. As a major global ICT producer, China is shaping communication technology in unanticipated ways to meet the demand of domestic and international markets, especially low-end market segments. A critical component of Chinese informationalism is the rise of network labor centered on programmable labor, which collaborates with self-programmable and generic labor, in the making of a new working class.

3. Working-class network society is emerging at the institutional and grass-roots levels. It reacts to macrotransformations of urbanization, industrialization, and globalization as well as problems in the mass media system, especially inadequate services to the lower class. Local and translocal social innovations are abundant in the appropriation of working-class ICTs among diverse social groups, including migrants and laid-off workers, young and old, providing them with solutions for existential issues caused by social transformations.

4. The information have-less include not only end users but also ICT manufacturers and providers. The involvement of have-less people in producing, distributing, and consuming working-class ICTs has led to new developments in user-generated content, suggesting that low-end technologies can respond to grassroots informational needs in unprecedented ways. This has led to important instances of working-class cultural expression and political empowerment using such tools as blogs, poetry, and mobile phones, which serve as the substance of new class dynamics in the twenty-first century.

5. Working-class network society is taking shape through processes of social differentiation and networked connectivity that crystallize the issues and questions about communication technology and social inequality in urban China. The bottom-up processes have produced distinct urban places, cultural practices, and critical events, creating working-class communities that seek to coexist with the global space of flows. They have also begun to exert a broad impact on the Chinese informational city and the global network society at large.

The technosocial emergence of working-class network society has generated a plethora of practices and structures, places and events, opportunities and controversies, policies and paradoxes. The entirety of these phenomena—their characteristics, interconnections, and transformations—may appear to be overwhelmingly complicated. This book therefore offers an inclusive framework, presented in figure 8.1, that serves as a synthesis of this book's content as well as a basis for future research.

Digital Sublime in Question

Does information technology always cause convergence, providing seamless communication and creating a unified society? Had we believed in the popular myth of the digital sublime about the miraculous power of ICTs in eradicating poverty and inequality (Mosco 2004), we would have said

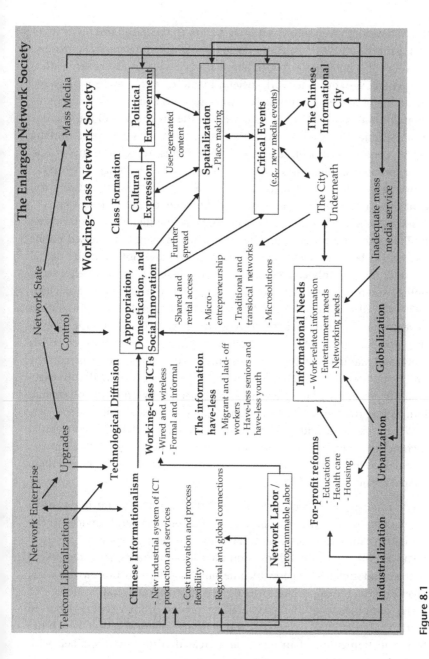

Figure 8.1
Working-class network society in urban China: A conceptual synthesis.

yes. We would have limited our imagination to the flashy images of high-end gadgets and a classless cyberspace, detached from social reality. However, this book has provided abundant evidence for divergence within the general system of network society, including a rich and multilayered clustering of low-end technologies, working-class connectivity, and grass-roots cultural and political development in the lower strata of the Chinese informational city. Confronting this divergence is a first step to rethinking digital communication technologies: their forms, roles, and impact and their problems, dilemmas, and the intellectual challenge they pose. Working-class ICTs and the information have-less have been, are, and will continue to be essential components of an enlarged network society.

Since the late 1990s, the mythical power of the digital media has been problematized by research on the digital divide, which has raised public awareness about the lack of access among the have-nots. But the digital divide is not the only conceptual tool in discussing communication technology and inequality. The knowledge gap (Tichenor, Donohue, and Olien 1970; Donohue, Tichenor, and Olien 1975) is another helpful notion developed in the mass media environment of the 1970s. In the 1980s, with the growing power of information technology, Herbert Schiller (1981, 1984) and Manuel Castells (1989) also provided systematic criticism on the problematic ways in which information is unevenly distributed, thus exacerbating power asymmetry among social classes, between labor and capital, long before the digital divide became a popular research topic.

What this book adds to this line of inquiry is that the conceptual dichotomy between the haves and have-nots no longer fully captures recent developments under the new urban circumstances given these characteristics:

• The wide spread of working-class ICTs like cybercafés and inexpensive wireless phones, including a broad range of products and services in the formal and informal economies that fill in the technology gap
• The ascendance of the information have-less—migrants, laid-off workers, retirees, and students from low-income families—who constitute a new social layer between the upper and lower tiers of informational stratification
• The prominence of the class-making process from network labor to working-class cultural expression and collective political action, which has begun to transform urban places and created critical events, albeit with limited impact at this early stage of development

Construed as such, the rise of working-class network society does not mean that the digital divide has been bridged. The logic of exclusion and inclusion still plays a role in the lives of the information have-less. The main difference now is that when it comes to working-class network society, exclusion and inclusion work not just on a single dimension of technology access, which echoes Chargravartty's argument (2004) in the Indian context about the critical importance of social, political, and cultural issues other than the issue of access itself. Although have-less people have gained access to digital technology, they may still be excluded as outsiders or, more commonly, as passive consumers excluded from policy-making processes.

The notion of the information have-less is in this sense not really about lower cost, less trendy gadgets, or lower-quality service because even working-class ICTs can be shaped into something expensive (e.g., migrants being charged for content they never subscribed to) or something with relatively high quality (e.g., Little Smart in the small city of Zhoushan). Rather, the core of the concept is the inferior market positions and the general lack of social power that prevent have-less people from obtaining more choices and using working-class ICTs to better their life chances in a wider scope of technosocial and politicocultural possibilities. This conception differs from well-received digital divide studies in the Chinese context, such as the optimistic view of China as "a success story" (Harwit 2004, 1010) or the pessimistic view about deteriorating inequality in the country "compounded by the access-to-technology gap" (Giese 2003, 52). Rather, the reality is not so clear-cut. It is full of potential for social change as well as pitfalls for what Tilly (1998) calls "durable inequality."

The key issue is not just about what happened. It is also about how we think about technosocial reality: Can we transcend the prevailing linear model of historical progression defined solely in terms of technological artifacts (Marvin 1988)? Can we interrogate the latent value issues in ICT deployment that perpetuate elite domination and hamper grassroots participation (Samarajiva and Shields 1990)? Evidence presented in this book rejects linear thinking and its obsession with "modernization," "frog leaping," or technology "upgrading" because these notions tend to ignore actual informational needs and tend to produce inadequate solutions and policies that can have serious unintended consequences.

The essence of working-class network society is about understanding the logic of the vast middle ground between the haves and have-nots, between high-end services and the absence of access, where the technosocial process often takes unexpected turns, including this turn to the new class politics of the twenty-first century.

In this often neglected gray zone, low-end ICTs have been growing on a massive scale in multifarious ways, each adapting to the needs of the information have-less in diverse places and communities. It is on this basis that the main features of working-class technologies are developed, from low price to compromise in service quality, from migrant labor to micro entrepreneurialism. These are not necessarily permanent characteristics as the technologies evolve, and they may be upgraded to high-end services. In other cases, they may involve large-scale enterprises, for instance, SMS services delivered through national telecom infrastructures belonging to SOEs like China Mobile. However, although ownership and state policy are essential to the shaping of networked connectivity, what matters more for the burgeoning working-class network society is the actual functions of the informational services, how they motivate different players, and how they facilitate social networking among the less wealthy and less powerful at the grassroots of the Chinese informational city.

Network Labor and Chinese Informationalism

"China is constructing a different model of network society" (Castells 2008, 6). What then are the main features of the Chinese model? This book maintains that a crucial answer lies in *network labor*, which plays a definitive role in China's enlarged network society.

The rise of network labor results from industrialization in early twenty-first-century Chinese cities, an ongoing process characterized by a combination of traditional-style manufacturing with ICT production and service provision and increased flexibility of work and accumulation operating on a global scale. The materialization of working-class ICTs is in this sense tantamount to the creation of an entire industrial and informational system that produces not only new technology but also new ways to organize work and the economy in urban China and beyond.

From the assembly line to call centers, from "SMS authors" to gray-collar software testers, network labor is crucial to the ascent of Chinese informationalism. Responding to demands in the highly volatile global ICT market for a huge variety of products that need to be upgraded constantly and economically (e.g., wireless phone batteries), Chinese network enterprises like BYD have created a full range of programmable labor: workers who collaborate with self-programmable and generic labor to become the foundation of China's new working class.

The key to this Chinese model is not cost advantage based on cheap labor. Rather, it is labor advantage based on the provision of an extraordinarily wide variety of blue-collar, gray-collar, and low-rank white-collar employees. These workers take up millions of jobs that are programmed and simplified; skilled, semiskilled, or unskilled; in a highly stratified structure of working conditions that is indispensable to the Chinese model. This labor advantage explains the rapid rise of China as a global IT power, exporting not only computers, mobile phones, iPods, and accessories but also content and services, from the oil painting stores in Dafen Village to online game gold farms.

Besides exports, this competitive advantage centered on network labor is also crucial to domestically oriented ICT businesses such as China's domestic brand mobile manufacturers like Bird, which deployed an army of network labor (in this case, marketers and postsale service personnel) in second- and third-tier cities to outcompete global brand names like Nokia, at least for a few years. This labor advantage in the domestic sphere of market competition has given rise to an ecology of Chinese working-class ICTs consisting of modified Little Smart base stations, waterproof cybercafé computer keyboards, SMS filtering and censorship devices, and online games specifically designed to target have-less players. The more recent policy of providing state subsidies for rural Chinese families to purchase home appliances and electronics (Subler 2008) represents another major initiative that will add to the nourishing of network labor and the subsequent evolution of Chinese-style working-class technology design.

Of course, most creative personnel in China's IT industry are still in university labs, research institutes, and corporate R&D centers. Of course, the stock market and state decisions remain essential to the future of China's new economy. But it is the network labor that provides the most distinctive feature of Chinese informationalism as compared to models in other postindustrial economies. Many of these laborers are placed in dangerous work conditions with health hazards but little protection. Most of them are poorly paid and they receive few benefits, which is why captains of Chinese informationalism could accumulate so much wealth so quickly.

This Chinese model has obvious problems. One persisting challenge is excessive labor discipline under new conditions of "process flexibility" (Zeng and Williamson 2007) controlled by management using such tools as the concentrated collective network of wireless phones (Qiu 2007b). Another is the pressure of financial markets, which distracts corporate effort away from working-class ICTs, as exemplified by the demise of pager service since 2000. In just five years, the world's largest pager market of nearly 50 million subscriptions vanished, casting off the primarily young female laborers.

In this new industrial and informational system, working-class ICTs and network labor are used as the main instruments of accumulation, whose output is transferred to feed high-end projects and traditional power structures. Structured as such, Chinese informationalism is as much about faster accumulation and more flexibility as it is about the disposal of certain "outdated" technologies and certain "older" members of the exploited network labor. This instability is a reality in Chinese informationalism despite initial signs that the authorities were trying to provide more stability and more equal standing of workers in relation to employers, especially through the new Labor Contract Law (Tsang 2008).

Globally and historically, organized labor is facing an increasing encroachment of capital. And China's political status quo poses special constraints, for example, with its control over formal organization among workers and in working-class communities. The CCP and local state authorities have also morphed into a structure of the network state, including the "network of censors" (Qiu 2004, 109): its industry connections through such projects as cybercafé surveillance software and the more recent, flexible ways of hiring people to post progovernment messages onto public Internet forums, thus creating a subtype of state-sponsored network labor.

The relationship between network labor and network state is a subject that needs more systematic research. But the general argument is clear: Although the rise of network labor is a major breakthrough in China's enlarged network society, it is not yet a self-organized, independently mobilized social force. It is instead dominated by transnational and domestic Chinese network enterprise on the one hand and the network state controlled by the CCP on the other. Network labor is a manifestation of "labor in limbo" (Solinger 2002, 31) under the specific conditions of Chinese informationalism. It is still too early to conclude that network labor constitutes a new informational proletariat comparable to the industrial proletariat of the past, as Hardt and Negri contend with their notion of "immaterial labor" being shaped in postindustrial economies (2000, 288).

Informational Needs, Existential Issues, and Microsolutions Using ICTs

Working-class ICTs constitute a new frontier for market expansion, allowing millions to be lifted from the have-not category. But why do these people—migrants and long-term city-dwellers, male and female, young and old—want to adopt new communication technology? One explanation is China's overall economic growth, some of which has trickled down to the information have-less, thus giving them more disposable income for spending on ICT. Another reason is the increasing amount and sophistication of advertising campaigns, especially targeting have-less youth. The most fundamental explanation, as we have seen in this book, is the bottom-up informational needs of these people to deal with the existential issues created by the transformations of the city, exacerbated by existing structural inequalities.

Industrialization, urbanization, and globalization are the macro agents of change for Chinese network society. They spawn not only network labor in the realm of production but also a series of upheavals in the world of the new working class, which create a chain effect. Stable employment is gone. Traditional *danwei* work units are dismantled together with the welfare systems and working-class residential communities of the old socialist city. The pillars of urban China, from education to health care to housing, are becoming commercialized at the expense of the poor into the new "three mountains" (Gu 2007, D. Yang 2007).

For upper-class Chinese urbanites today, human suffering is historical, philosophical, or artistic. It is not part of their life. But for people in the lower strata of the Chinese informational city, the pain of survival is an indispensable part of their daily struggle. Under surging population mobility and life instability, the information have-less are using cybercafés and inexpensive wireless phones to learn about what is going on around them, where to get affordable child care and medicine, how to avoid scams, and what is happening to their families and friends, even in places far away. The information function, often intertwined with grassroots networking and social support, is of utmost importance for the have-less people given the general lack of mass media and social institutional resources devoted to meeting their informational needs.

Working-class connectivity also helps have-less urbanites in seeking education and better job opportunities and, in so doing, improving their life chances overall. Although my hairdresser in Shenzhen did not know what a search engine is, he used the Internet and moved on to a new job in another city. Such applications have been insufficiently supported, not because these are low-end technologies but because commercial and state agencies are not fully committed.

In contrast, entertainment services are far more developed, especially for have-less youngsters, who spend a large chunk of their income on gaming and online chatting, including males in cybercafés and females with QQ-enabled mobile phone. Some are addicted to these games, which triggers criticism in mass media and leads to crackdowns. The subsequent moral panic is ultimately condescending and destructive, for it recycles old stereotypes while denying the right of the have-less to foster working-class connectivity in their distinct ways, beyond the usual expectations of the upper class; for it renders digital media access into a new source of vulnerability, subjugation, and disempowerment.

This is indeed a profound paradox of working-class network society. Despite the rapid expansion of the low-end market, issues of social equality have been largely shelved. Although members of the have-less have become included in the market system as consumers, laborers, and microentrepreneurs, the prevalence of discrimination and power domination—over and through the uses of working-class ICTs—proves to be an essential source of alienation.

Cognizant of these larger structural factors, it is essential that we see through the discourse of top-down social power in order to better understand what the information have-less really need, more than just ICTs. What they need, as human beings in the full sense, is not just the gadgets and commercial services offered to them so that they can be "upgraded" by upper-class standards. More important, they need respect from service providers and policymakers. They need equal treatment, sustainable solutions, and infrastructures of care.

On the contrary, when problems emerge in the realm of working-class ICTs, whose social roots are often far deeper than the technologies themselves, government and corporate intervention tend to strengthen regulatory and surveillance measures. Often only the upper classes benefit from new ways of ICT management because new regulations tend to be designed from their perspectives, whereas to the information have-less, the same would mean new upheaval. Even if some of them can continue using certain working-class ICTs, the discriminatory relationship persists and equality remains a distant dream.

The rise of working-class network society is, in this sense, a grounded transformation consisting of daily struggles by members of the have-less people to use working-class ICTs as micro solutions to meet their informational needs at the grassroots. These are bottom-up, micro answers to systemic structural change at the macro level in the rapidly changing Chinese informational city. The confrontation and negotiation between the Net and the self, materialized as such in the context of urban China, are central to the evolution of working-class network society.

From Social Innovation to Cultural and Political Empowerment?

The centrality of working-class ICTs and the information have-less is a distinct feature of the Chinese network society when compared to existing models in Western or Japanese postindustrial societies. But it is not unique when our discussion is situated in the context of the global South, including other developing regions like India. The ascendance of China as a global power in this sense carries broader geopolitical significance in that it offers an alternative model of informationalism based on creativity from the bottom up, by people of the lower class who every day face existential issues in the city underneath.

The essence of this model lies in numerous social innovations, many of them nontechnical or requiring only nonspecialized technology training. Social innovation is carried out in working-class communities in the shadow of the IT complexes, including not only random tinkering and improvisation by average end users but also systematic attempts to provide, improve, and sustain low-end services under regulatory conditions that are often less than favorable. The agent of change is usually found among members of the information have-less, especially among microentrepreneurs aided by translocal networks. The tenacity of social innovation—among the most creative members of the information have-less engaging in what Singhal and Greiner call "positive deviance" (2007) at the grassroots level—cannot be underestimated, as we have learned from the defiant upsurge of cybercafés nationwide and the prosperity of long-distance phone bars in the alleys of migrant enclaves.

A general trend in social innovation is the opening up of communication technologies originally designed for private ownership, and transforming them into shared modes of collective access, usually through rental services. Besides cybercafé and long-distance phone bars, this mode of shared access can also be observed in ADSL cooperatives, which offer informal arrangements for broadband Internet connection in high-density working-class communities.

Another key to working-class connectivity is the recycling, repackaging, and remixing of second-hand ICT products and contents that are sold in the gray and black markets, for example, used computers imported from the United States or refurbished Chinese domestic-brand mobile phones now being exported to Africa (Mooallen 2008). While some of these are transnational businesses, others are small, local, and translocal operations within urban districts, such as the transaction of used printer cartridges and accessories.

Regardless of the scale, have-less ICT providers tend to rely on horizontal grassroots networks as the most essential strategy of survival to maintain sustainability in the long run. This pattern has been recognized in other social groups as well, for instance, among farmers struggling for their rights through what they call *Lianwang*, literally "linking up with the network" (Yu 2003; Y. Zhao 2007, 107). For have-less ICT providers, these translocal social networks can be either extended from traditional relationships or created in new conditions of urban life, online and offline, as shown by networked communication processes in the Sun Zhigang case.

Hence, members of the information have-less are not always passive. The joint force of network state and network enterprise may exert control through macro and micro management, but they cannot fully preempt cultural and political empowerment at the lower strata of network society. The fact that more lower-class people have been connected through working-class ICTs indeed provides a precondition of communication and networking for the momentum of change to accumulate from the bottom up.

The availability of working-class connectivity has led to a plethora of cultural expressions among members of diverse have-less groups. These include migrant workers as exemplified by Han Ying's blog about her life and work in Chengdu as well as the New Labor Art Troupe in Beijing, which has adopted Creative Commons. The online poetry about the iron workers' strike in Hong Kong and the Flash video memorializing Ma Jiajue also belong to this category of working-class cultural expression. These are still largely communications among people who share relatively high levels of affinity with each other. Nevertheless, they need to be recognized as important harbingers of mass self-communication (Castells 2007) in working-class network society whose future impact cannot be underestimated.

Meanwhile, we have seen over and again that the majority of have-less people remain culturally dependent and politically vulnerable. Due to insufficient class consciousness among average members of the city under-neath, the information have-less should still be seen as a loosely connected assembly of people in the lower strata of China's urban society. The in-group contact and subgroup culture have significantly improved thanks to the spread of working-class ICTs. But between groups, communication is still rare, and coidentification is usually weak. Gender, age, education, ethnicity, places of origin: these lines of demarcation divide have-less people into numerous clusters, which seriously hinders the fostering of a common collective identity.

Recognizing this difficulty is not to ignore the initial signs of political empowerment, but to have a more accurate assessment of social reality. Given the newly available working-class connectivity, network labor has been mobilized in unprecedented ways, as in the Uniden strikes when workers put up blogs during their collective action against the multinational corporation or the protests of cybercafé operators in Lishui against unreasonable regulatory measures imposed by the state. But in order for such collective action to alter the structures of inequality, it is inadequate to have information flows only among the information have-less. In other words, working-class ICTs by themselves do not constitute a sufficient condition for cultural and political empowerment. Given the early formative stage of the technosocial emergence, it still has to involve larger segments of the urban society, including elite members, mass media, and institutionalized forces, especially the state.

Communication and networking through low-end communication technology remain necessary conditions in order for the concerns of the have-less to reach across social divisions and have a general impact on society. This was how news about the Sun Zhigang tragedy spread through online forums and mobile phones to influence mass media reports and then the system of urban control itself. This was how the Ma Jiajue tragedy had a broad social impact, resulting in some improvement in the financial aid system of Chinese universities. Despite the uniqueness of these cases, they nevertheless demonstrate the potentials of working-class ICTs for empowerment among the information have-less. Although there is insufficient guarantee for such instances to take place on regular basis, the ongoing struggle for empowerment deserves constant research attention.

Place, Events, and the Making of a New Working Class

Modern China has been troubled by class politics since its birth in the early twentieth century. Enormous social inequality, both between classes and within the working class, has been the key momentum for labor movements, including the communist revolution itself (Cheneaux 1968). The definition of the working class is of course not static. From previous chapters we have seen that the formation of China's new informational working class has decisively transcended the conventional category of unpropertied, male, manual laborers whose core leaders are members of a working-class political party. While the manufacturing and transportation of electronic products remain the essential occupational foundation for network labor, the rise of gray-collar workers and programmable labor has blurred the traditional boundary by filling assembly lines and call centers with female workers who perform simple skilled tasks. The decreasing cost of ICTs allows laid-off workers to become microentrepreneurs selling prepaid cards or ring tone download services. The collapse of the welfare system forces presumably nonworking populations to become network labor as well, including have-less youth working as online-game gold farmers and have-less seniors working as shopkeepers selling low-end gadgets. These groups have joined the ongoing class formation process in the enlarged network society of urban China.

This new informational working class has a broader social scope than the old blue-collar industrial working class. It is, however, of fundamental importance that we refrain from presuming the nature and social consequences of this expansion. Does it mean the working class is more empowered? More assimilated into the modern ways of urban life? With its most talented members enjoying more upward social mobility than others? These questions cannot be answered in abstract terms. Rather, we have seen that the reality is often not clear-cut: there are different kinds of labor, the propertied and the unpropertied, traditional and new social networks, and the fledgling informational working class. While some seemingly trivial developments may produce large results, other opportunities may appear to be promising in the beginning but turn out to reproduce the status quo.

Despite its fluidity and unpredictability, the class-making process has shifted from formal party politics to informal ways of contestation and negotiation. The new class politics is centered on processes of place making in its spatial patterns, while being punctuated temporally by new media events. This place- and event-centered class politics is triggered by the principal rules of the global network society—space of flows and timeless time (Castells 1996)—yet they also find innovative ways to supplement and challenge the abstract time-space of global capitalism, defying the ahistorical myths of perpetual prosperity and weightless economy.

Generally the move away from the twentieth-century model of party politics is a global trend. But in the Chinese context, the development of ICT-based informal politics is amplified by restrictions on formal organization imposed by the CCP. In other words, the prominence of informal, project-based class politics in the Chinese informational city results from the fact that no one needs formal membership to be part of the spatial and temporal construction of working-class network society.

Informational class politics take root in concrete urban places where members of the have-less population, connected through ICTs, are concentrated. Through translocal networking, different types of have-less people come together in different places with distinctive spatial dynamics. The heterogeneous urban villages like Shipai differ significantly from homogeneous migrant enclaves and from the rust belts of laid-off workers. Factory assembly line, university campus, online-game gold farm, police detention center: these are very different local power structures. Although the spread of ICTs allows higher mobility in a larger spatial scope, the actual patterns of communication, community building, and life-and-death struggles nevertheless remain place based, as in the cases of Sun Zhigang, Ma Jiajue, and Lanjisu. Urban politics is still local politics. This trend has been accentuated by the emergence of working-class network society.

What is achieved through communication technology in this class formation process is therefore not the annihilation of the local but the opportunity to allow critical local incidents to transcend social boundaries and reach other have-less groups under similar conditions of inequality and discrimination. It is through such processes of local struggle that members of other social strata, including the haves as well as have-nots, may join the cause of the have-less to safeguard the welfare of all citizens, including the right to communicate using working-class ICTs. It is also from these locally based cases of conflict and contestation that actors at multiple scales of operation become involved in the shaping of network society, locally, nationally, and transnationally.

It is unlikely that the traditional proletariat class relationship and class consciousness will be reproduced under the political reality of China today. However, issues of power persist, and they have diffused from the relatively closed realm of formal party politics. They have been played out in real-world events, now maintained and magnified through working-class ICTs and the translocal networks they sustain. In this process, internal divisions and external factors can limit the full formation of working-class network society, creating unintended consequences, sometimes with catastrophic gravity. Yet the unsatisfactory status quo calls for the creation of new social networks and the extension and reinforcement of existing ones. Despite their limited capacity now, these new and old networks are important sources of power, from the bottom up. The rise of network labor, and of working-class network society at large, provides rare openings for equality, justice, and democracy—for the information have-less, all of Chinese society, and the rest of the world.

Toward Information Technology with a Human Face

The diffusion of information technology into the everyday life of working-class Chinese urbanites has many important implications. Confirming past studies on the spread of the telephone in North America (Martin 1991, Fischer 1994), this book demonstrates how the transformation of new media services may go beyond the initial intent of technology design. The cybercafé, originally an elite business for those who were foreign-minded to seek information and higher education opportunity, has become primarily a site of entertainment for have-less youth. Little Smart, introduced to China as an economical way to provide telephone universal service in remote mountainous regions, has become a major for-profit operation in large cities as well. Few could envisage the rise of working-class ICTs on such a massive scale, in so many different forms, and so rapidly. This technosocial emergence should be seen as a strong case for social shaping, through which the unmet informational needs of the information have-less bring about new modes of networked connectivity that profoundly transform communication technology itself.

However, most observers still tend to see working-class ICTs in China from the sole perspective of the telecom industry, which has benefited greatly from this emergent market of hardware, software, service, and content. It is true that new business opportunities help attract investment and drive up stock prices. However, this narrow conception does not do justice to the fascinating and nuanced social reality at the lower strata of the enlarged network society. As Castells maintains, "Most analyses are related to China as the savior of global capitalism, forgetting that ultimately the dynamics of society, including the socio-political dynamics, is what determines the process of development" (2008, 6).

As we have seen, the commercial logic may become harmful to the sustainability of low-end technologies, for the process of upgrading can be easily turned into processes of exclusion, as happened to the pager industry and its primarily female workforce. It is, however, important to note that telecom liberalization played a role in opening up the new development trend. Without the partial destruction of telecom monopoly, without the state-owned telcos being listed on stock markets, the drive to foster working-class ICTs would have been much weaker on the structural level.

In important ways, these new services reinforce existing tendencies among the have-less people toward translocal networking, information exchange and social support at the grassroots, and entertainment, particularly for young people. In so doing, low-end services like the cyber-café, SMS, prepaid cards, and Little Smart have all developed their distinctive features, indicating the latest trend in the social shaping of technology, no longer solely dominated by the elite as was the case in China until recently. Rather, this process is driven by social forces from the bottom up, by hope and suffering at the grassroots, and by formerly excluded groups like migrants and laid-off workers. For the first time, the complexity and volatility of the city underneath in China are reflected and incorporated in the development of digital media. This is indeed a change of epic proportions.

The specter of inequality and discrimination is still part of urban China. But the emergence of working-class network society opens up alternative ways of seeing and thinking, based on which we can see a genuine opportunity to foster "information technology with a human face" (Castells 1999, 25). To seize this opportunity, public and private actors need to work with the information have-less and their grassroots communities in facing key challenges such as sustainability and profound dilemmas such as commercial alienation. This book provides a realistic picture for the hopes and hindrances here.

What we need now are not just new ways to see ICTs from the perspectives of the have-less and, in so doing, drawing the issues and problems closer to home. Only highlighting the serious consequences that affect real human lives is not enough. More important, we need to seize this opportunity afforded by the emergence of working-class network society as a fresh point of entry to the transformation of communication technology and the class politics it has given rise to.

Precious as it is, the window of opportunity does not warrant sustainable growth. Without systematic ways of support through long-term policy and stable institutions, what happened to the pager industry may recur with other low-end services; this is already underway with Little Smart. Indeed, even pager service in China was not the first time when upgrading had a devastating impact on working-class communities. The area of Lower Manhattan where the World Trade Center was located had been known as "Radio Row" and "Electrical District" because of the large number of electronics shops concentrated in this area of blue-collar New Yorkers. But the entire community was dismantled to make room for the twin towers (Mosco 2004). From a longer historical point of view, the cost of neglecting working-class technologies and the jobs, families, and communities they produce is too high and too painful for any society.

Once we are able to envision the information have-less previously rendered invisible by elite discourse, we open ourselves up to new questions, new solutions, and new practices in the areas of policymaking, technology design, and cultural development. The totality of these possibilities constitutes a new technosocial imagination about the most fundamental components and the restructuring of network society. To this end, the new working class will face challenges, paradoxes, and fallibilities; these are inevitable in any historic process of this proportion. For too long, the new working class has been the silent cogwheel of China's new economy. Now their destiny depends on the future of networked connectivity among the information have-less: if and how the modes of connection today will be sustained, transformed, and used to build civic bonds among members of the new working class and between them and other citizens of the Chinese informational city with its global reach.

Afterword

China's industrialization in the contemporary era of globalizing capitalism is rewriting the history of rapid development. By comparison to the experiences of countries whose industrialization spanned the turn of the nineteenth century, China's entry into the world economy over the past thirty years has met intensified conditions of globalization. As connections between places, globalization and its range of new international institutions, economic practices, and technological possibilities have transformed space-time relations and the possibilities of relations between local, regional, and national scales and their global reach. As a consequence, conceptualizing China's contemporary transformation compels consideration of domestic, transnational, and geopolitical complexities, ties, and transactions as never before.

This project's origins—in the realities of people's diverse informational experiences across the landscape of uneven societal development in contemporary China—have yielded a rich empirical context for original perspectives on the information have-less and working-class ICTs, at once transcending the conceptual problems of the digital divide and training our focus on people's pursuit of information and information technologies as daily life strategies. Through these discerning interpretations, we learn how people in diverse places and with limited means, many in the process of migrant journeys from rural to urban lives, bring into reach hitherto unattainable means of communication through which they choose to manage and enhance the present and begin to change the future.

This informational society in the making also demonstrates intensification of significant transhistorical and transnational connections at work in China's contemporary transformation. Through the use of ICTs, domestic translocal home town networks and international diasporic networks are now enabled anew in realities of daily communication, from mountainous interiors to coastal factory towns and from Guangzhou apartments to

Hong Kong high-rises. The South China at the center of this project structures around dense social and economic networks that transcend borders,
boundaries, and histories—a region of networks before the emergence of
the contemporary network society—the region of the South China coast
that is at the heart of the historic Chinese diaspora. At the suprastate scale,
contemporary China is integrating into an Asian region already characterized by the highest rates of ICT adoption in the world, from Japan and
South Korea to Hong Kong and Singapore. Foreign direct investment from
these countries and outsourcing of information industry labor to China,
and the transformational space economies they produce, together neces-
sitate relations of communication that lead to the adoption of ICTs across
the socioeconomic spectrum.

The phenomenon of working-class ICTs and rapid change-over in ICT
adoption and use is also a parallel concept for social mobility—for those
workers whose luck, information management capacity, sheer will, good
connections, training and education, and hard work open up avenues
to new plateaus. The sheer scope of the market for mobile devices and
the incomparable array of consumer product choices in handsets and
related items, in addition to the market for used products, generate a
wider stream of possibilities for new users and lower-income and thrifty
users—as well as for those seeking the next hot item. The near ubiquity
of the mobile phone in some cities and regions, and early adoption in
the cities and economic zones that were "one step ahead under reform,"
where local innovations in ICT use have especially emerged, lead to
a redefinition of the empirical contexts of the network society idea.
China's centers of capital concentration are increasingly wired, and
working-class ICTs are filling in the wide gaps of uneven informational
development.

Locating the informational city in the Chinese city is an especially significant exercise. The restructuring of the city in China under reform has
witnessed nothing less than the wholesale decanting of urban residential
neighborhoods for commercial real estate development and high-end com-
modity housing. In the process, the producer city of the Maoist vision and
the *danwei,* or work unit compound, has nearly totally succumbed, compelling long-time residents to relocate to distant suburban ring roads, often
without adequate compensation or transportation. The realities of such
new urban lives in China depend on distance-transcending technologies
for essential community maintenance like never before. The massive
restructuring of the Chinese city under reform is an exercise in the production of *disan chanye,* or third sector industries, the services industry economies of world cities that lie at the foundation of China's urban economic

restructuring and planned urban futures. Anyone harboring doubt about the role of state vision in the transformation of the contemporary Chinese city need only visit the Shanghai Urban Planning Exhibition Center in People's Square, where the exhibit on the top floor presents the primary goals of the current and future five-year plans: building information industry infrastructure and transforming Shanghai into one of the leading information and telecommunications hubs of the Asia-Pacific region.

Among this book's many astute observations about the information have-less is the condition that those among this arena are, on balance, more likely to lack social power than market position. This reality of the contemporary information society in China—the importance of certain kinds of information for negotiating contemporary society and its quickly morphing conditions and opportunities—also maps on to the transhistoric practice of *guanxi* and *guanxi* networks as contexts of effective operation in a society characterized by constraints on resource access and agency-based decision making through bonds of affinity and familiarity. Certainly such traditional networks have been breaking down here and there in favor of contemporary meritocratic and social and professional ties, while they are also maintained among diverse classes, including officials and ranking bureaucracies, whose hold over information control shores up their power.

Evolving state-society relationships in contemporary China make governance and governmentality—governing power deployed in the widespread general interest of social order, discipline, and control—more important than government in many arenas, especially from perspectives of the grassroots and its capacity to share and transmit information across space, social classes, and other territorial and social divisions. It is well known that expressions of citizen concern have grown in recent years at the local level in China, while media about local demonstrations, strikes, and other forms of organized civil action are highly limited in circulation. Some media controls have also loosened up, yet the state continues to exercise particular interest in the content of information flow. So from perspectives of both the idea of public space for citizen expression in the Chinese city and the public sphere of civil society and its dependence on a critical media, the evolving information society in China will continue to depend on the use of ICTs and their informational potential. This is one of the outstanding conditions of the contemporary global era, and one of the central challenges to the future of state-society relations in China.

Carolyn Cartier
Hong Kong,
June 2008

Methodological Appendix

The research that supports this book is based on empirical evidence collected since 2002. Some data were gathered through conventional social science methods such as fieldwork, interviews, focus groups, and secondary data and news archive analysis. Other data collection methods include some new elements to suit the technosocial reality of urban China today, for example, the examination of user-generated content, the survey group design, and sociospatial mapping of commercial informational services in a working-class community. Because the survey group and mapping exercises require a lengthier explanation, I first introduce the other methods.

Fieldwork was a main data collection method of this study, which was conducted in more than twenty cities in eleven provincial-level administrative units located in China's southern, eastern, northern, western, and central regions. During the fieldwork, I submerged myself in many working-class communities, using many low-end information and communication technologies (ICT) businesses, and visiting a range of labor activists, nongovernmental organizations, and state regulatory agencies.

Semistructured interviews were conducted with small-scale working-class ICT providers (especially cybercafé and long-distance phone bar operators), larger-scale ISPs and ICPs (including regional telcos, prepaid phone card companies, and UTStarcom managers), and local officials in charge of IT and telecommunications projects in the city or province.

In these interviews, I asked questions about the local or regional histories of ICT development, the unique characteristics of interviewees' private or public enterprise, their strategies and competitors, the problems they face, and future development prospects. The length of the interviews varied from thirty minutes to two to three hours. I interviewed some cybercafé and phone bar operators multiple times to gain more in-depth knowledge. Most interviews were carried out in the interviewee's workplace. Some were over meals or in local teahouses. The interviews were transcribed and then analyzed.

To understand ways of technology appropriation from the perspective of users, I lived with migrant workers in South China and interviewed them in their dormitories and working-class communities. I also carried out interviews with ordinary urbanites, especially workers, retirees, and students. The length of these user interviews was shorter, usually from twenty minutes to one hour, and explored basic behavioral and cognitive aspects of how the interviewees use and perceive ICTs, what their goals are, and what problems they face. These interview data served as a basis for the construction of a questionnaire used in the survey groups.

After initial affinity was established with interviewees, thirteen focus groups of low-end ICT users were organized in Guangdong and Shanghai, in 2002, 2004, 2005, 2006, and 2007. Six of them were with migrant workers as part of the survey group design; the other seven were with long-term residents and students, with their *hukou* residential status being officially registered in the city. Each focus group had four to seven participants and lasted about two hours. The setting was usually in a quiet room in a local restaurant, although two were in university classrooms in Shenzhen and Shanghai, respectively, because the participants were college students.

While most focus groups were conducted in Mandarin, the official Chinese language, two were administered in the Cantonese dialect by native Cantonese speakers hired and trained in order to better involve long-term-resident participants, particularly elderly males and females who could speak only Cantonese. These focus groups were audiorecorded and then transcribed for data analysis.

Another important source of data is online content, especially Internet forums, BBS, blogs, and Web sites that provide crucial platforms for networking and cultural expression among the more articulate members of the information have-less. These include key forums for cybercafé operation (e.g., World Net Alliance, http://www.txwm.com/), migrant worker poetry (e.g., Dagong Poets, http://sh.netsh.com/bbs/8832/), migrants' blog (e.g., by Han Ying, http://hybh3399.blog.163.com/), and the New Labor Troupe http://www.dashengchang.org.cn/.

Texts, images, and audiovisual materials from these sources well reflect the ways by which working-class network society takes shape in cyberspace and in the offline world, not only on the basis of everyday interactions but also during critical events. This user-generated content is, however, not stable online because of fast content updates, limited server space, and sometimes censorship, for example, in the aftermath of the Uniden factory strike in Shenzhen and the Shengda College uprising in Zhengzhou, when participants' blogs were removed or whitewashed. These online discussions, blogs, poems, and animations were therefore saved as soon as they were retrieved and deemed valuable for archiving, in either hard copy or electronically, as the events unfolded.

This project also relied on secondary data compiled by state and corporate research institutes, including the MII, CNNIC, CASS, CCIDNet (*Saidi*), and annual reports of China's four national telcos: China Mobile, China Telecom, China Netcom, and China Unicom. At the subnational level, I collected official regulations and news releases by provincial, municipal, and district-level state agencies in Guangdong, Shanghai, Jiangsu, and Zhejiang. Using the databases of LexisNexis and WiseNews, I traced relevant news coverage in both English- and Chinese-language publications.

Survey Groups of Young Migrant Workers

A survey group is a data collection method that combines quantitative and qualitative techniques with action research and empowerment. It mixes a face-to-face survey with focus groups, both involving have-less migrants as grassroots opinion leaders above and beyond the role of survey administrators and focus group participants. The design is built on the assumption that migrant workers are capable of observing, articulating, and deliberating key issues regarding working-class ICTs and related social issues so long as they are organized in equitable peer groups, because from a communication perspective "empowerment process fundamentally consists of dialogic communication . . . especially in small groups" (Rogers and Singhal 2004, 82).

Figure A.1 shows the design of survey groups as they were conducted in three major cities in South China: Guangzhou, Shenzhen, and Zhuhai. Guangzhou is the provincial capital of Guangdong Province. Shenzhen and Zhuhai are China's most prominent special economic zones. The three cities were selected because they are among the top migration destinations in South China with a wide variety of service and manufacturing jobs being filled by millions of migrants from all over the country.

The survey group design allowed me to work closely with three to five migrant workers at a time for a period of four days. Altogether six survey groups were carried out, involving twenty-two migrants and two student helpers. In phase I of the study, I organized three survey groups between May and August 2002. In phase II, from January to March 2006, I repeated

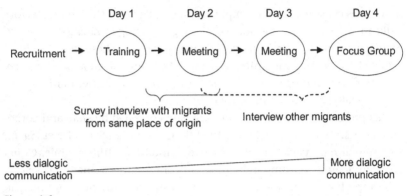

Figure A.1
Survey group design.

the procedure with additional help from two graduate students on the Shenzhen campus of Peking University, who had been interprovincial migrants themselves working and studying in the region for a few years. Over the four-day period, the survey group met daily. At the end of the period, a focus group was held when a high degree of rapport had already been built among members of the survey group, who had also been oriented to have more communication with each other on subjects related to working-class ICT services. Such a design based on intensive, interactive, collegial teamwork with empowered migrant workers ensures relatively high data quality.

Given the difficulty of constructing an all-inclusive sampling frame for the migrant population, purposive sampling procedures were employed to identify respondents from diverse groups of migrants. A basic factor was the migrant's place of origin due to the networked, translocal pattern of migration. First, we (including myself in phase I and myself and the two student helpers in phase II) went to the largest labor markets of the three cities on the first morning of the study period and identified four to five migrants in each labor market who came from different regions of China. Most identified migrants who agreed to join the project were young (their average age was twenty-four) and female, except two males. Seven of them had no income at the time, being either students or unemployed. Others had an average monthly income of 1,400 yuan (about $170) by working as clerks, factory workers, and waitresses. The average education attainment of all survey group participants was high school.

After recruitment, a training session of about two hours was held among the migrant participants and survey administrators, who were briefed about the project. They conducted their first face-to-face interviews with each other. These first interview results were checked and discussed on site to make sure all questions were answered and clearly recorded. After this, the survey administrators were instructed to interview fellow migrants from their places of origin, preferably using their local dialects. As a result, while 71 percent of survey interviews were conducted in Mandarin, 259 survey interviews were conducted in seventeen dialects as the preferred means of communication by respondents.

The migrant survey administrators signed a contract that protected their rights and specified their duties. They received 6 yuan ($0.73) for each finished questionnaire. All expenses incurred by the research project such as public transportation were reimbursed. The participants were entitled to receive a per diem allowance of 30 yuan ($3.63) for food and drink. This meant that each of them earned about 350 yuan ($42.30) in four days, almost doubling their average daily income.

Each administrator was asked to complete forty questionnaires, half with young migrants and the other half with senior citizens. A quota system was used to include equal numbers of men and women through purposive sampling, which involved roughly the same number of respondents identified in labor markets (job seekers), factories (manufacturing workers), and service industry settings (service sector workers). Survey administrators were also sent to different districts of the city to collect data. Altogether 899 questionnaires were completed, of which 478 were from young migrant workers. After the data were cleaned up, deleting, for example, those who reported they were older than forty-five or had too high an income (5,000 yuan or above), 390 were retained for the analysis about have-less migrants; the results are presented in chapters 4 and 7. The other half of the quantitative data concerning have-less seniors is still being analyzed, although the qualitative findings, for instance, about the practice of "beeping" among the elderly, have been incorporated in chapter 5 of this book.

A meeting of the survey group was held daily during the data collection period when we cross-checked and confirmed the number of completed questionnaires. The administrators received payment for their finished questionnaires plus their daily allowance and reimbursement for project-related expenses. In the day 2 meeting and to a lesser extent the day 3 meeting as well, some questionnaires were returned because they were incomplete. Since in this early stage, most survey respondents were acquaintances in the personal social networks of the administrator, he or she could interview the respondents again, face-to-face or over the telephone, to complete the unfinished parts of the questionnaires.

Through daily meetings, the survey group participants interacted with each other in a natural work setting, comparing their experiences and observations, raising questions and discussing them with me and the graduate student helpers. They were reminded to take notes of the additional, more qualitative findings that could not be recorded in the survey, which would be shared later in focus groups.

The final focus group at the end of the four-day period included discussion topics concerning the behavioral, perceptual, and socioorganizational issues involved in the diffusion, uses, and appropriation of working-class ICTs. In particular, migrant participants were asked to identify the main benefits and key problems brought about by informational services. They were also asked to identify what caused the problems and how they could be overcome. Held in a quiet room, the focus groups lasted on average for two hours and were audiorecorded and transcribed for analysis.

Sociospatial Mapping of Commercial Informational Services in a Working-Class Community

While the survey groups were focused on the experiences of low-end ICT users, the sociospatial mapping was designed to unveil deployment patterns of working-class ICTs from the perspective of service provision at the grassroots. Due to the absence of systematic research on this subject, I attempted to use the mapping exercise as a first step to establish benchmark databases for more in-depth examination in the future. The goals were threefold: to conduct an exhaustive census of existing low-end informational services and locate them spatially in a working-class community; to develop a coding system for different kinds of working-class ICT services; and to shed light on the general patterns of spatial distribution for commercial ICT businesses in a particular community. The mapping instrument was tested in Shipai Village, Guangzhou, in 2007 and is being replicated in Shixia Village, Shenzhen.

Shipai Village was selected because it is the most researched heterogeneous migrant enclave, but its media and communication system has not been examined much. The decision to map all commercial informational services reflects two judgments based on my initial fieldwork between April and September 2007: on the one hand, services that meet the informational needs of have-less people in this community are almost exclusively for profit, which confirms the dominance of the commercial logic; on the other hand, there are traditional informational services not based on digital media such as bookstores, although many of the businesses are also related to mobile phones, computers, and the Internet.

During the first phase of research from April to September 2007, I visited Shipai Village numerous times with Kitty Chen, who had lived next to Shipai Village for several years and was the main research assistant for this mapping project. With help from other students at Jinan University and after studying sociological, anthropolitical, and planning documents about Shipai, we developed the first research plan and pretested the coding system for informational services, which at this point contained thirty-one types of services (twenty-five formal businesses and six informal ones). A detailed map of the community was obtained, digitized, and cleaned up as the basis of the mapping exercise.

In October 2007, we identified and trained four students from Sun Yat-Sen University in Guangzhou to implement the census and mapping of commercial informational services. A half-day training session was held when the student research assistants were briefed about the design and objectives and then trained on site in Shipai Village. The four assistants worked in two groups, each including one male and one female student, who were assigned to cover half of the working-class community by walking shop to shop, street to street.

Because the purpose of this exercise was to establish a baseline data set for sampling and further exploration in the next phase, the assistants were asked not to conduct any interviews. Instead, they were to record only what they could observe from the streets or inside the shops: shop or business identification number; time of recording or observation; name or signage of the shop; the type of business, using the coding system to specify the main business type as well as secondary business type, if any, while also recording new types of services not yet included in the system; and spatial location of the business, including street address (or nearby landmark for those without address), vertical location (street level, upstairs, or basement level), and grid location (both according to the grid on the digitized map, e.g., A5 or D2, and marking on a hard copy of the map using a fine-tipped pen). For the most widespread service, long-distance phone bars, student assistants were also asked to record the pricing information, usually prominently displayed on signs put up by shop owners.

Group members needed to cross-check and discuss the coding result for each informational business site, paying special attention to the diversity of services offered. They also recorded other outstanding observations during the data collection process, which were then reported in group discussion at the end of the day. Besides the first day of training, the mapping exercise was conducted over three weekends in October 2007, and the student assistants each received a stipend of 2,000 yuan ($250).

Through the mapping exercise, 481 individual business sites were identified. Because some of them could not be grouped into the thirty-one items of the original coding system, the system of commercial informational services was expanded to forty-six types: thirty-seven types of formal or legal businesses and nine types of informal economy businesses. (The full list is in chapter 6.)

These data were entered into a database containing the main variables being recorded: identification number, shop name/sign, address/landmark, grid position, main business type, secondary business types, and time of observation. They were also color-coded and entered onto the digital map whose selected results are presented in figures 6.2, 6.3, and 6.4 in chapter 6. The database and the map have allowed an overall assessment of the sociospatial patterns with respect to low-end informational services in this working-class community. They have facilitated sampling for a deeper examination of a particular street or a particular kind of informational service in Shipai Village, while offering a baseline for future exploration in other urban communities of the information have-less.

Internet Resources

There is a wealth of online resources about the evolving working-class network society in China. The list below includes a sample of the most prominent ones that have been active and accessible until spring 2008. Most of these Internet resources are only presented in Chinese, while some English content is available in certain e-commerce platforms, nongovernmental organization Web sites, and documentary Web sites. The great majority of the content consists of texts, accumulated in large quantity, in online forums, blogs, and Web sites. There are also multimedia content such as animations, music, and visual art resources created or archived by members of the information have-less.

Online Forums
World Net Alliance: http://www.txwm.com/
Net-bar Guide: http://www.netbarguide.com/
17173 Online Game Portal: http://www.17173.com/
Guangdong Migrant Worker Forum: http://bbs.gddgw.com/
China Laoxiang Club: http://www.cnlxh.com/
China Gray-Collar Network: http://www.huikecn.cn/
China Labor Dispute Network: http://www.btophr.com/

Literature and Blogs
United Web of Dagong Literature: http://www.dgwxlw.com/
Migrant worker poetry: http://sh.netsh.com/bbs/8832/
Rural Women blog: http://blog.sina.com.cn/njn
Han Ying's blog: http://hybh3399.blog.163.com/
Old Kids blog: http://blog.oldkids.cn/
Xie Lihua's blog: http://blog.sina.com.cn/xielihua
Yu Dianrong's blog: http://yudianrongxs.blog.163.com/
Laid-off worker in Daqing: http://blog.newstarnet.com/?author=1504

Documentaries and Animation
Ode to Ma Jiajue: http://www.flash8.net/flash/15776.shtml
Chinese Gold Farmers: http://www.chinesegoldfarmers.com/

E-Commerce Platforms
China Used Computer Network: http://www.2it.com.cn/
China Used Handset Network: http://www.2sjsj.com/
Flea Channel: http://flea.zol.com.cn/
Taobao Net: http://www.taobao.com/
Huanla Barter Net: http://www.huanla.com/
Wuhan Barter Net: http://www.e1515.com/
Dafen Village Oil Paintings: http://www.dafencun.com.cn/
Shipai Village Information: http://www.shipaicun.com/

Nongovernmental and Nonprofit Organizations
New Labor Art Troupe: http://www.dashengchang.org.cn/
Net for Migrant Youth Labor Force: http://www.dgqn.net/
Old Kids Network: http://www.oldkids.cn/
Education Network for Liushou Kids: http://www.liushouedu.com/
Migrant Workers' Network: http://www.mingong123.com/
China Labor Forum: http://www.labourforum.com/
Family of Floating Population: http://www.ldrkzj.com/

Notes

Chapter 1

1. See chapters 4 and 5 for more systematic discussion on the demographic estimates.

2. The survey was conducted by the Informatization Office of Beijing Municipality in 2005 among long-term residents and migrants in Beijing's eight urban and four suburban districts. It measured respondents' technosocial positioning along four dimensions: (1) ownership and access to ICTs, (2) ICT knowledge and skills, (3) behavioral patterns related to ICTs, and (4) attitudes toward and benefits gained from ICTs. Detailed explanation on methods and implementation procedures is available in the Informatization Office of Beijing Municipality (2005, 2–12).

3. *Informationalism* refers to the contemporary mode of production that relies on the processing of information technology and ICT-based innovation for the generation of wealth. See Castells (1996).

4. By "self-programmable labor" and "generic labor," Castells (1998) understands the better-paid and skilled employees who enjoy more work autonomy but need to constantly update their skills and knowledge by themselves due to increasing competition in the labor market (i.e., "self-programmable labor") and those who are unskilled, or whose skills are regarded as valueless and disposable in the new economy and can only sell their physical labor with minimum knowledge/expertise input for very low wages (i.e., "generic labor"). I propose to add "programmable labor" as a specific layer of workers that emerges between self-programmable and generic labor in the context of China's new ICT industry. See detailed discussions in chapters 4 and 6.

Chapter 2

1. See Whyte (1955) for his classic work on street corner societies. Chapters 6 and 7 in this book more systematically examine China's street corner societies and working-class ICTs in the urban context.

2. See the collection of articles on the fall of Info Highway Co. at http://tech.sina .com.cn/focus/ihw.shtml (accessed on January 11, 2007).

3. Interview, Guangzhou, June 2002.

4. Interview, Hong Kong, April 2006.

5. See http://www.feiyu.com.cn/jianjie/feiyu.htm (accessed on April 8, 2006).

6. Author's translation from http://www.feiyu.com.cn/jianjie/HTML/hhtsj.htm (accessed on April 9, 2006).

7. Personal interview, Beijing, July 2002.

8. Calculation based on interview with Wang Yuesheng, cited in Dong (2003).

9. For an overview of collective hacker activities in China, see Qiu (2002b).

10. Interviews with provincial-level, city-level, and district-levels officials in South China's Pearl River delta (summer 2002–spring 2005) and East China's Yangtze River delta (December 2003–January 2004).

11. See Lishui City Government Web page, http://www.lishui.gov.cn/xsls/ (accessed on April 22, 2006).

12. See http://www.zetronic.com.cn/aboutus.asp (accessed on January 15, 2007).

13. See http://www.pconline.com.cn/customer/2002/haoyi/ (accessed on April 21, 2006).

14. Interview with cybercafé manager, Sichuan, May 2002.

15. Interview with cybercafé manager, Shanghai, January 2004.

16. The highest tax rate of 40 percent was reported in Jiaxing, Zhejiang Province, during my interviews with cybercafé owners in the city in December 2003.

17. Fieldwork in Guangzhou, July–August 2002.

18. Interview with Ringo Lam in Hong Kong, November 2005.

19. Interviews with cybercafé operators in Shanghai, December 2003.

20. See www.txwm.com/about.htm (accessed on February 17, 2008).

21. See http://www.snda.com/en/about/overview.htm (accessed on February 17, 2006).

22. Author's translation. See the full poem at http://tech.blogchina.com/152/ 2005-03-31/361461.html (accessed on April 20, 2006).

23. It takes dozens or hundreds of hours of playing these games to accrue valuable items, which make it easier for players to fulfill the goals of the game. So if a player wants a more powerful character but doesn't want to spend all that time playing,

he or she can buy the necessary virtual items from a gold farmer. For example, in World of Warcraft, players' characters advance through seventy levels of "skill" by killing virtual bad guys. Some people consider reaching level 70 to be when the game really gets interesting. Killing those bad guys goes much faster with a higher-level weapon. Hence, buying such a weapon to get to the end game state might make sense. See the introductory text and trailers at http://www.chinesegoldfarmers .com/Index.html (accessed on February 17, 2008).

24. Interview with cybercafé manager, Guangzhou, July 2002.

Chapter 3

1. Field observations in Sichuan (May–June 2002), Zhejiang (December 2004) and Guangdong (March 2005).

2. See the company profile at http://www.chinamobileltd.com/about.php (accessed on January 17, 2007).

3. Interview with female migrant worker, Shenzhen, February 2006.

4. Starting in 1999, the State Council issued a series of preferential policies aiming at fostering domestic handset producers. The MII has also invested about 1.4 billion yuan (nearly $170 million) in domestic manufacturers. See Le, Qiao, and Sun (2006).

5. See http://www.chinabird.com/bird2004/about/about1.htm (accessed May 8, 2006).

6. Interviews in Shanghai, Hangzhou, Ningbo, Wuhan, and Zhaoqing (2002–2007); focus groups in Shanghai and Zhaoqing (2003–2004).

7. See the analysis on India in Castells, Fernandez-Ardevol, Qiu, and Sey (2006).

8. Interviews in Guangzhou (August 2002) and Suzhou (January 2004).

9. Interview with UTStarcom manager, Hangzhou (December 2003).

10. Focus group findings from Shanghai (January 2004), Zhaoqing (April 2005), and Guangzhou (August 2005).

11. Personal interview, Ningbo, December 2003.

12. Word association function was originally developed for computers. Based on commonly used Chinese phrases, it allows the automatic listing of a number of characters that are most frequently associated with the character that the user enters. Thus, after entering the first character, the user only needs to press one button to select the next character. The function also exists for entering English words (not phrases), although the Chinese word association function can work more efficiently in the construction of phrases and sentences.

13. Fieldwork in Guangdong (June–August 2002), Shanghai (December 2003–January 2004), and Beijing (July 2005).

14. See Katz and Aakhus (2002) and Fortunati, Katz, and Riccini (2003) for discussions on this phenomenon in contexts other than China.

15. See the company Web site at http://www.venusense.com/ (accessed on February 20, 2008).

16. Focus groups conducted in Shanghai (January 2004) and Guangdong (January–March 2006).

17. See the discussions in chapter 2.

18. Focus groups in Guangzhou, Shenzhen, and Zhuhai, July–August 2002 and January–March 2006.

Chapter 4

1. General Office of the State Council, "Announcement on Improving Employment Management and Services for Rural-to-Urban Peasant Workers," January 15, 2003.

2. *China Population Statistics Yearbook* (2005, 315).

3. See chapter 6 for more discussion on urban villages.

4. Notably, total urban employment was 264.76 million in 2004. Thus, there are still other employees besides the 164.5 million shown in table 4.2.

5. Calculated in current prices by *Annual Economic Report of China* (1981). Comparatively, the increase of industrial output was about thirty-five times during the twenty-five years from 1979 to 2004, as calculated in current prices based on *China Economic Yearbook* (2005).

6. Hence scholars like Hui Wang (2004) argue that the persistent influence of the Cold War in the Asian Pacific is an integral part of the region's economic achievements in recent decades.

7. In table 4.5, the 1985 and 1995 data were from the former Ministry of Electronic Industry (MEI), whereas the 2004 data were from the Ministry of Information Industry (MII). There is inconsistency in how they define the electronics industry. It is therefore more important to look at the structural composition under different ownership systems rather than the aggregated totals.

8. *Research Report on China's Exports of Electronic and Information Products* (2004). Beijing: China Economic Publishing House, p. 55.

9. Interviews with cybercafé operators in Sichuan (May 2002), Zhejiang (December 2003), and Guangdong (summer 2002, spring–summer 2005).

10. Interview with Li Dongming, director of China Social Survey Research Institute.

11. Focus groups in Shenzhen (August 2002, February 2006), Zhuhai (July 2002, April 2006), and Guangzhou (August 2002, March 2006).

12. Personal interview with MMORPG virtual property trader (Guangzhou, March 2006); see also Chew and Fung (2007).

13. Focus group with students in Shanghai (January 2004) and Shenzhen (December 2005) and with migrant workers in Guangzhou (February 2006) and Shenzhen (January 2006).

14. Some of these top-level Internet policymakers in Beijing basically laughed at me when I raised the problem of female Internet dropouts to them in a meeting in 2005. See chapter 5 for a full discussion on the curricula design of ICT classes in high schools that did a poor job of treating gender issues.

15. C. K. Lee (1998) and Pun (2005) offer detailed accounts of the work conditions in electronics factories in Shenzhen.

16. See the detailed descriptions on the role of mistress (*xiaojie*) in linking businessmen with local officials in X. Liu (2002). See also T. Zheng (2004).

17. Focus group findings from Zhuhai, March 2006.

18. Personal interview with Deng Qiyao, Guangzhou (January 2007). Deng conducts regular fieldwork in the ethnic regions of southwest China.

19. Personal interviews, Sichuan Province (May 2002).

20. *China Demographic Science*, 1998(5); cited in Yu and Ding (2004).

21. Calculation based on MII monthly reports for the telecom industry. Note that the landline figures include Little Smart using MII's regulatory definition.

22. Personal interview, Shenzhen, July 2002.

23. Creative Commons is a nonprofit organization that helps digital content producers to distribute and share their products legally outside the control of large media corporations. Creative Commons-Mainland China is the chapter of Creative Commons in mainland China. For more information, see http://creativecommons.org/international/cn/.

24. See http://sh.netsh.com/bbs/8832/ (accessed on February 25, 2008).

Chapter 5

1. The "three mountains" is a metaphor used in the Chinese Communist revolution to refer to the domination of imperialism, feudalism, and bureaucratic capitalism.

In the context of contemporary urban China, the new three mountains stand for the heavy burden imposed by for-profit reform in housing, health care, and education.

2. MoE, "Guidelines on Accelerating the Construction of Information Technology Curricula in Middle Schools and Primary Schools (in Chinese)." http://www.edu .cn/20030210/3077057.shtml (accessed on July 3, 2006).

3. Fieldwork in Wuhan, Shanghai, and Beijing (summer 2002 and winter 2004). Survey in Guangzhou, Shenzhen, and Zhuhai (summer 2002 and spring 2006).

4. China Market and Research (2004), quoted in *China New Telecom Network* (2006).

5. Seniors aged fifty-five to sixty-five represent 9.88 percent of China's total urban population, *Almanac of China's Population* (2005).

6. Focus group with college students in Shenzhen, January 7, 2006.

7. See Qiu (forthcoming) for discussions on the global flows of used computers into China.

8. See chapter 5 and the methodological appendix for detailed explanations for this project and the survey group design.

9. If the sample is split into younger migrants (age twenty-five or under) and older migrants (twenty-five or older), then the relationship of stronger ICT connectivity and less control over ICT budget, is much more prominent among younger migrants (coefficient = .45, $p < .001$) than older ones (coefficient = .21, $p < .05$).

10. Focus group in Nanhai (July 2002).

11. See http://blog.chinesenewsnet.com/?p=12467 (accessed on July 8, 2006).

12. Search conducted on July 8, 2006.

13. National Survey on Hygiene Services (1993, 1998, 2003), cited in Gu, Gao, and Yao (2006).

14. China Market and Research (2004), quoted in *China New Telecom Network* (2006).

15. See chapter 5 and the methodological appendix for detailed explanations for this project and the survey group design.

16. The survey was carried out by a group of medical researchers from the University of Southern California in 2002. Personal interview with Ping Sun, a member of the research group (May 2003, Los Angeles).

17. See http://oldkids.com.cn/ (accessed on July 11, 2006).

18. See the brief introduction of the Web site at www.oldkis.com.cn/main/about/ jianjie.htm (accessed on July 11, 2006).

19. Telephone interview with administrative staff at Old Kids, July 11, 2006.

20. See the Web site for left-behind children at http://www.liushouedu.com/English .aspx (accessed on March 2, 2008).

21. See the workshop's Web site at http://www.sintef.no/content/page1_9425.aspx (accessed on July 14, 2006).

Chapter 6

1. See the discussion in chapter 4 about Chinese online-game "gold farmers" and their "guilds."

2. Interview with a taxi driver in Guangzhou (January 2007).

3. For a focused discussion on the reproduction of the *danwei* system in Beijing's high-tech sector, see Francis (1996).

4. See the Dafen Village oil painting selling Web site at http://www.dafencun.com .cn/index_en.asp (accessed on March 4, 2008).

5. Interview with urban village residents in Guangzhou (April–October 2007) and Shenzhen (December 2007).

6. *China Demographic Science*, 1998(5), cited in Yu and Ding (2004, 34).

7. Focus group discussion with residents of Shipai Village (September 2007).

8. Ibid.

9. Interview with a manager in the Pacific Computer City (October 2007).

10. See http://2it.com.cn for the company Web site (accessed on March 5, 2008).

11. Author's translation. Quoted from Zheng (2006, 161).

12. See Walcott (2003) for the development of Chinese high-tech parks. See chapter 4 for the rise of electronics as a main category of China's exports to the world.

13. See the discussion in chapter 4.

14. See the methodological appendix and the discussion in chapter 4 about the survey groups.

15. Interview with a former member of the factory managerial staff (Shenzhen, January 2006).

16. See the fuller discussion in Qiu (2007b).

17. Zhang and Li (2006). The original Chinese article is no longer available online. The story was translated into English by Roland Soong and, with photographs, posted at http://www.zonaeuropa.com/20060623_1.htm (accessed on August 10, 2006).

18. Personal communication with graduate students at the Shenzhen campus of Peking University, which is located next to a community of migrant workers (June 2007).

19. See the methodological appendix and the discussion in chapter 4 about the survey groups.

20. *Investigation Report* (*diaocha baogao*) compiled by labor organizers in Shenzhen in April 2005, provided by Pun Ngai.

21. See http://www.blogcn.com/user24/unidenppl/blogs (accessed on December 21, 2004). A few weeks after the strike, most of the contentious information about Uniden on this blog was removed. In summer 2006, it was closed down.

22. See the related discussions in chapters 2 and 4.

Chapter 7

1. A good example is the effort of a lawyer in Beijing, Pu Cunxin, who used SMS and a blog to commemorate the 1989 Tiananmen tragedy on June 3, 2006. See Pu (2006).

2. See chapter 3 for discussions on SMS-based charging schemes and their problems—for example, migrant workers being charged for content they never ordered.

3. Findings from the migrants' focus group conducted in Shenzhen in spring 2006. In summer 2002, I also came across a migrant next to the Guangzhou East Railway Station who tried to sell his pager after his wallet was stolen.

4. See the discussion in chapter 2.

5. See chapter 4 and the methodological appendix for the survey group design.

6. Personal communication with a student who has family in Zhuhai (April 2006, Hong Kong).

7. See also the discussion in chapter 2.

8. This quotation from the news report is probably from the legal verdict. But Zhang is in fact a cybercafé operator, which contradicts her "unemployment" status.

9. See http://news.sina.com.cn/z/wangba/index.shtml for a comprehensive collection of reports on this incident (accessed on March 7, 2008).

10. See a comprehensive listing of the unfortunate incidents at China Education Online BBS: http://bbs.eduol.cn/printpage.asp?BoardID=14&ID=65147 (accessed on August 18, 2006).

11. See the related discussion on *hukou* and *zanzhuzheng* in chapter 6.

12. Interviews with Chen Feng by telephone and e-mail, November 2004.

13. Each cell is called a *cang*. Since it is routine for every newcomer to receive at least one beating, the physical abuse of new arrivals is called *guocanggui*, or "passing the routine of the cell."

14. Defense statement by Ma Jiajue's lawyer.

15. Ibid.

16. Ibid.

17. Search conducted on Baidu.com on August 26, 2006. See http:// wang123654789wang.blogchina.com/ for full text (accessed on August 26, 2006).

18. For an introduction and screenshots of the DV films, see http://bn.sina .com.cn/dv/2006-01-23/152813924.html and http://cnsn.com.cn/edunewsview .asp?id=10088 (accessed on August 15, 2006).

19. See http://www.flash8.net/flash/15776.shtml (accessed on August 15, 2006).

20. Defense statement of Ma Jiajue's lawyer.

21. Interview with taxi driver in Guangzhou (January 2007).

References

Aldrich, B. C., and Sandhu, R. S. (eds.). (1995). *Housing the Urban Poor: Policy and Practice in Developing Countries*. New Delhi: Vistaar Publications.

Almanac of China's Economy. (1981–2005). Beijing: Economic Management Publications.

Almanac of China's Population. (1985–2005). Beijing: China Social Sciences Publications.

Associated Press. (2002, December 27). China closes 3,300 cybercafés.

Baark, E. (1997). *Lightning Wires: The Telegraph and China's Technological Modernization, 1860–1890*. Westport, Conn.: Greenwood Press.

Bai, X. (2002, June 17). Most Internet users were students. *XinhuaNet*. http://www
.cctv.com/news/china/20020617/371.html (accessed April 9, 2006).

Bao, D. (2004). How far can Little Smart go down the road? *Information Networks* [*Xinxi wangluo*], *11*: 22–31.

Bao, X. (2001). *Holding Up More Than Half the Sky: Chinese Women Garment Workers in New York City, 1948–92*. Urbana: University of Illinois Press.

Barboza, D. (2008a, January 7). In many Chinese factories, loss of fingers and low pay. *International Herald Tribune*, p. 1.

Barboza, D. (2008b, March 29). In life and death, Tibet victims belie official account. *International Herald Tribune*, pp. 1, 6.

Barendregt, B. (2005). The ghost in the phone and other tales of Indonesian modernity. In *Proceedings of the International Conference in Mobile Communication and Asian Modernities*, Hong Kong, pp. 47–70.

Barmé, G. R., and Ye, S. (1997). The great firewall of China. *Wired, 5.06*: 138–150, 174–178.

Beijing News. (2007, October 11). Don't blame the computer if you fail to take good care of college students, p. A13.

Beijing Statistics Information Network. (2005, October 14). Most support real-name registration system for mobile phone. http://www.bjstats.gov.cn/zwxx/tpbd/200510140022.htm (accessed February 8, 2006).

Beijing wanbao. (2005, October 11). Police announces SMS scam cases today (Jingfang jingongbu duanxin zhapian'an), p. 16.

Beijing Youth Daily. (2003, April 28). Interview with Sun Zhigang's families, p. A12.

Bell, D., and Jayne, M. (eds.). (2004). *City of Quarters: Urban Villages in the Contemporary City*. Aldershot, U.K.: Ashgate.

Blogchina. (2005, March 20). China Net-bar Sunny Plan formally launched. http://tech.blogchina.com/7/2005-03-20/36184.html (accessed April 20, 2006).

Bolt, D., and Crawford, R. (2000). *Digital Divide: Computers and Our Children's Future*. New York: TV Books.

Booth, M. (2000). *The Dragon Syndicates: The Global Phenomenon of the Triads*. London: Bantam Books.

Borja, J., and Castells, M. (1997). *Local and Global: Management of Cities in the Information Age*. London: United Nations Centre for Human Settlements.

Bray, D. (2005). *Social Space and Governance in Urban China: The Danwei System from Origins to Reform*. Stanford, Calif.: Stanford University Press.

Bu, W. (2007). ICT, gender, and communication activism. Paper presented at the Information Technology and Social Responsibility conference, Hong Kong, December 17–18, 2007.

Bu, W. (2008). *Analytical Report on Rural Left-Behind Children and Models of Supportive Action*. Beijing: Chinese Academy of Social Sciences.

Bu, W., and Guo, L. (2000). *Research Report on the Uses and Influences of Internet among Youth*. Beijing: Chinese Academy of Social Sciences.

Bu, W., and Liu, X. (2003). *Research Report on the Adoption, Uses and Influences of Internet among Youth*. Beijing: Chinese Academy of Social Sciences.

Bu, W., and Liu, X. (2004). *Research Report on Media Advocacy Strategies for Reproductive Health among Migrant Youth in Henan and Shaanxi*. Beijing: Chinese Academy of Social Sciences.

Bu, W., and Qiu, J. L. (2002a). *Report on Informational Education and Communication Strategies against the Trafficking of Women in Sichuan Province*. Beijing: UNICEF China.

Bu, W., and Qiu, J. L. (2002b). *Report on Media Usage among Vulnerable Groups in Southwest China: Qualitative Survey Interpretation for the TB IEC Mission*. Beijing: World

Bank and U.K. Department for International Development China Tuberculosis Control Project.

Business Weekly. (2002, August 14). State prudent on reviving cyber cafés. http://www.china.org.cn/english/BAT/39371.htm (accessed April 7, 2006).

Cao, Y., and Liu, H. (2006). How do urban peasant workers perceive their self-image in mass media: The case of Nanjing. In G. Zhang, K. Zhao, and Y. Zhang (eds.), *Mediated Society: Current State and Trends,* 83–91. Shanghai: Fudan University Press.

Cartier, C. (2001). *Globalizing South China.* Oxford: Blackwell.

Cartier, C., Castells, M., and Qiu, J. L. (2005). The information have-less: Inequality, mobility and translocal networks in Chinese cities. *Studies in Comparative International Development, 40*(2): 9–34.

Castells, M. (1977). *The Urban Question: A Marxist Approach.* Trans A. Sheridan. London: E. Arnold.

Castells, M. (1989). *The Informational City: Information Technology, Economic Restructuring, and the Urban-Regional Process.* Oxford: Blackwell.

Castells, M. (1996). *The Rise of the Network Society.* Oxford: Blackwell.

Castells, M. (1997). *The Power of Identity.* Oxford: Blackwell.

Castells, M. (1998). *The End of Millennium.* Oxford: Blackwell.

Castells, M. (1999). The informational city is a dual city: Can it be reversed? In D. A. Schön, B. Sanyaland, and W. J. Mitchell (eds.), *High Technology and Low-Income Communities: Prospects for the Positive Use of Advanced Information Technology,* 25–41. Cambridge, Mass.: MIT Press.

Castells, M. (2007). Communication, power, and counter-power in the network society. *International Journal of Communication, 1*: 238–266.

Castells, M. (2008). Interview with Manuel Castells. *Chinese Journal of Communication, 1*(1): 3–6.

Castells, M., Fernandez-Ardevol, M., Qiu, J. L., and Sey, A. (2006). *Mobile Communication and Society: A Global Perspective.* Cambridge, Mass.: MIT Press.

Castells, M., and Portes, A. (1989). World underneath: The origins, dynamics, and effects of the informational economy. In A. Portes, M. Castells, and L. Benton (eds.), *The Informal Economy: Studies in Advanced and Less Developed Countries,* 11–37. Baltimore, Md.: John Hopkins University Press.

CCID Net. (2004, November 1). Protecting network environment, 1600 illegal Net-bars lost licenses in rectification. http://news.ccidnet.com/art/1032/20041102/171879_1.html (accessed January 11, 2007).

Chan, K. W., and Zhang, L. (1999). The *hukou* system and rural-urban migration in China: Processes and changes. *China Quarterly, 160*: 818–855.

Chakravartty, P. (2004). Telecom, national development and the Indian state: A postcolonial critique. *Media, Culture and Society, 26*(2): 227–249.

Chen, F. (2003, April 25). The death of Sun Zhiguang, the detainee. *Southern Metropolitan Daily*, p. A2.

Chen, Q. (2001, December 26). How college students perceive pre-marital sex. *China Youth Daily*, p. 5.

Cheng, T., and Selden, M. (1994). The origins and social consequences of China's *hukou* system. *China Quarterly, 139*: 644–668.

Chesneaux, J. (1968). *The Chinese Labor Movement, 1919–1927*. Stanford, Calif.: Stanford University Press.

Chesneaux, J. (1971). *Secret Societies in China in the 19th and 20th Centuries*. Hong Kong: Heineman.

Cheung, A. (2003). The business of governance: China's legislation on content regulation in cyberspace. Paper presented at the China and the Internet: Technology, Economy, and Society in Transition conference, Los Angeles, May 30–31.

Chew, M., and Fung, A. (2007). Virtual property problems in China. Paper presented at the Information Technology and Social Responsibility conference, Hong Kong, December 17–18.

China Economic Yearbook. (2005). Beijing: China Economic Yearbook Publications.

China Electronics Daily. (2005, December 2). MII launched heavy rectification campaign against "black shouji," p. 3.

China Hygiene Statistical Yearbook. (2005). Beijing: Ministry of Hygiene.

China Labor Watch. (2007). *The Long March: Survey and Cases of Work Injuries in the Pearl River Delta Region*. http://www.chinalaborwatch.org/2007FinalWorkInjury Report.pdf (accessed February 24, 2008).

China Netizens Daily. (2006, January 23). Little Smart shopping recommendations for Spring Festival. http://wy.cnii.com.cn/20041105/ca333573.html (accessed July 5, 2006).

China News Agency. (2005, October 27). Eleven Chinese provinces and municipalities began to use single *hukou* for urban and rural residents.

China News Agency. (2006, April 18). MII repeats storm against "black shouji."

China New Telecom Network. (2006). Old companion handsets accessing old companion market. http://www.telenews.com.cn/Article/911-1.htm (accessed July 5, 2006).

China Population Statistics Yearbook. (1996, 2006). Beijing: China Statistics Publications.

China Statistics Yearbook. (2005–2007). Beijing: China Statistics Publications.

China Telecom World. (2004, August 2). How far can dual-mode Little Smart go? http://tech.sina.com.cn/it/t/2004-08-02/0949396319.shtml (accessed January 17, 2007).

China Trade and External Economic Statistical Yearbook. (2007). Beijing: China Statistics Publications.

China Youth Daily. (1997, January 15). How far are Chinese people away from Information Superhighway? p. 6.

China Youth Daily. (2007, October 10). Interns "cutting trees" all day in online game: Xinjiang school questioned for using students as online-game substitutes, p. 6.

China Youth Network. (2004, August). *Survey Report on Nationwide Net-Bar Survival Condition.* Beijing.

Chua, C. H. (2005, May 19). Labor woes spread to west China: Region now suffering shortage of migrant workers that has hit southern and coastal areas. *Strait Times.* Retrieved from LexisNexis Academic.

Cline, R. J. W., and Haynes, K. M. (2001). Consumer health information seeking on the Internet: The state of the art. *Health Education Research, 16*(6): 671–692.

CNNIC (China Internet Network Information Center). (October 1997–January 2008). *Semi-Annual Survey Report on the Development of Internet in China.* http://www.cnnic.net.cn/ (accessed February 25, 2008).

Collection of Data from the Third Census of the Electronics Industry. (1996). Beijing: Ministry of Electronics Industry.

Cui, C. (2004a). The flow of rural labor. In H. Deng and B. Lu (eds.), *Changing Binary Structure,* 190–199. Beijing: China Development Press.

Dayan, D., and Katz, E. (1992). *Media Events: The Live Broadcasting of History.* Cambridge, Mass.: Harvard University Press.

De Kloet, J. (2005). Popular music and youth in urban China: The *dakou* generation. *China Quarterly, 183*: 609–626.

Dong, J. (2003, September 28). Feiyu Net-bar boss Wang Yuesheng. *China Management Daily.* http://telecom.chinabyte.com/336/1732836.shtml (accessed April 8, 2006).

Dong, X. (2006, May 25). Little Smart location services provide peace of mind for the elderly to go outdoors. *News Network.* http://xlt.qd.sd.cn/buynews/qingdao/2006-05-25/164833.stm (accessed July 5, 2006).

Donner, J. (2004). Microentrepreneurs and mobiles: An exploration of the uses of mobile phones by small business owners in Rwanda. *Information Technology and International Development*, 2(1): 1–21.

Donner, J. (2006). The use of mobile phones by microentrepreneurs in Kigali, Rwanda: Changes to social and business networks. *Information Technology and International Development*, 3(2): 3–19.

Donohue, G. A., Tichenor, P. J. and Olien, C. N. (1975). Mass media and the knowledge gap. *Communication Research*, 2: 3–23.

Drakakis-Smith, D. W. (1987). *The Third World City*. London: Methuen.

Du, Q., Chen, L., and Chang, Q. (2005).Exploring the reform of urban villages. *China Economic Weekly*, 27: 34.

Dutton, M. (ed.). (1998). *Streetlife China*. Cambridge: Cambridge University Press.

Eastday News. (2003, August 28). Students in Ling'an, Zhejiang Province killed Net-bar operator in the streets. http://tech.tom.com/1121/1861/2003828-57191.html (accessed August 28, 2006).

Education Statistics Yearbook of China. (2000, 2004). Beijing: People's Education Press.

Einhorn, B. (2006, March 29). Tech's faster boat to China. *Business Week.* http://www.businessweek.com/globalbiz/content/mar2006/gb20060329_117943.htm (accessed April 21, 2006).

England, R. S. (2005). *Aging China: The Demographic Challenge to China's Economic Prospects*. Westport, Conn.: Praeger.

Epstein, D. G. (1973). *Brasilia, Plan and Reality: A Study of Planned and Spontaneous Urban Development*. Berkeley: University of California Press.

Euromonitor. (2003, July). *Cellular and Wireless Communications Systems in the USA*. Global Market Information Database.

Evans, P. (2002). Introduction: Looking for agents of urban livability in a globalized political economy. In P. Evans (ed.), *Livable Cities? Urban Struggles for Livelihood and Sustainability*, 1–30. Berkeley: University of California Press.

Fan, C. (1999). Migration in a socialist transitional economy: Heterogeneity, socio-economic and spatial characteristics of migrants in China and Guangdong Province. *International Migration Review*, 33(4): 954–987.

Fan, C. (2004). Out to the city and back to the village: The experience and contribu-tions of rural women migrating from Sichuan and Anhui. In A. M. Gaetano and T. Jacka (eds.), *On the Move: Women in Rural-to-Urban Migration in Contemporary China*, 177–206. New York: Columbia University Press.

Fan, H. (2004, August 13). Nine billion yuan appeared overnight, Chen Tianqiao becomes China's richest man. *Beijing Youth Daily*, p. A15.

Feigenbaum, E. (2003). *China's Techno-Warriors: National Security and Strategic Competition from the Nuclear to the Information Age.* Stanford, Calif.: Stanford University Press.

Feng, D. (2004). MPS claims black Net-bars are at least twice the number of legal Net-bars. *YeskyNet.* http://news.chinabyte.com/315/1870315.shtml (accessed April 24, 2006).

Feng, Z. (2005). Guangzhou Tianhe Constructs No.1 IT Street in South China. *Southern Network.* http://gd.southcn.com/zwdt/xxjd/200511280038.htm (accessed July 25, 2006).

Fischer, C. (1994). *America Calling: A Social History of the Telephone to 1940.* Berkeley: University of California Press.

Fishman, T. C. (2005). *China Inc.: How the Rise of the Next Superpower Challenges America and the World.* New York: Scribner.

Fong, T.-H. (2003, May 2). Seeking answers to a death in detention. *South China Morning Post*, p. 8.

Fong, V. L. (2002). China's one-child policy and the empowerment of urban daughters. *American Anthropologist, 104*(4): 1098–1109.

Fortunati, L., Katz, J., and Riccini, R. (eds.). (2003). *Mediating the Human Body: Technology, Communication and Fashion.* Mahwah, N.J.: Erlbaum.

Francis, C. B. (1996). Reproduction of *danwei* institutional features in the context of China's market economy: The case of Haidian District's high-tech sector. *China Quarterly, 147*: 839–859.

Franklin, J. (2006, June 7). Protests paralyze Chile's education system. *Guardian.* International Section, p. 14.

Frazier, M. W. (2002). *The Making of Chinese Industrial Workplace: State, Revolution, and Labor Management.* Cambridge: Cambridge University Press.

French, F. W. (2004, December 16). Workers demand union and Wal-Mart supplier in China. *New York Times*, p. A3.

Frost and Sullivan. (2003, February). *The "PAS" Phenomenon: Revolutionizing Local Wireless Telephony.* Frost and Sullivan White Papers.

Gaetano, A. M., and Jacka, T. (2004). *On the Move: Women in Rural-to-Urban Migration in Contemporary China.* New York: Columbia University Press.

Galperin, H., and Bar, F. (2007). The microtelco opportunity: Evidence from Latin America. *Information Technologies and International Development, 3*(2): 73–86.

Galperin, H., and Mariscal, J. (eds.). (2005). *Digital Poverty: Perspectives from Latin America and the Caribbeans*. Ottawa, Canada: IDRC.

Gandy, O. (1993). *The Panoptic Sort: A Political Economy of Personal Information*. Boulder, Colo.: Westview Press.

Giese, K. (2003). Internet growth and the digital divide: Implications for spatial development. In C. Hughes and G. Wacker (eds.), *China and the Internet: Politics of the Digital Leap Forward*, 30–57. London: RoutledgeCurzon.

Graham, S. (1999). Global grids of glass: On global cities, telecommunications and planetary urban networks. *Urban Studies, 36*(5–6): 929–949.

Gu, X. (2007). To cure the "Chinese disease": Struggling between two roads of healthcare system reform. *The Twenty-First Century [ershiyi shiji]*, (December): 4–13.

Gu, X., Gao, M., and Yao, Y. (2006). *China's Healthcare Reforms: A Pathological Analysis*. Beijing: Social Sciences Academic Press.

Guangming Daily. (2006, July 8). MoC releases survey report on Internet café industry, p. 2.

Guo, L. (ed.). (2004). *Approaching the Internet in Chinese Small Cities*. Beijing: Research Center for Social Development, Chinese Academy of Social Sciences.

Guo, L. (2005). *Research Report on the Uses and Influences of Internet*. Beijing: Research Center for Social Development, Chinese Academy of Social Sciences.

Guo, L., and Bu, W. (2000). *Research Report on the Uses and Influences of Internet among Adults*. Beijing: Chinese Academy of Social Sciences.

Haddon, L. (2003). Domestication and mobile telephony. In J. Katz (ed.), *Machines That Become Us*, 43–56. New Brunswick, N.J.: Transaction Publishers.

Han, L., and Yang, Q. (2007, July 13). More than 2000 "black gaming workshops" exist in Wuhan. *Changjiang Commercial Daily*. http://game.people.com.cn/GB/48644/49662/5983548.html (accessed March 12, 2008).

Hanna, N. (1996). *The East Asian Miracle and Information Technology: Strategic Management of Technological Learning*. Washington, D.C.: World Bank.

Hardt, M., and Negri, A. (2000). *Empire*. Cambridge, Mass.: Harvard University Press.

Harwit, E. (2004). Spreading telecommunications to developing areas in China: Telephones, the Internet and the digital divide. *China Quarterly, 180*: 1010–1030.

Harwit, E., and Clark, D. (2001). Shaping the Internet in China: Evolution of political control over network infrastructure and content. *Asian Survey, 41*(3): 377–408.

Harvey, D. (2005). *A Brief History of Neoliberalism*. New York: Oxford University Press.

He, H. (2005, October 22). Chinese "farmers" strike cyber gold. *South China Morning Post*, p. A8.

He, L. (2005, June 20). Marketization is not the direction for reform. *China Youth Daily*, p. A7.

He, Z. (1997). A history of telecommunications in China: Development and policy implications. In P. Lee (ed.), *Telecommunications and Development in China*, 55–87. Cresskill, NJ: Hampton Press.

Hobsbawm, E. (1969). *Bandits*. London: Weidenfeld & Nicolson.

Honig, E. (1992). *Creating Chinese Ethnicity: Subei People in Shanghai, 1850–1980*. New Haven, Conn.: Yale University Press.

Hsing, Y.-T. (1997). *Making Capitalism in China: The Taiwanese Connection*. New York: Oxford University Press.

Hu, A. (2001). *Regions and Development: New Strategies for Western-Region Development*. Beijing: China Planning Publications.

Hu, A. (2005). Health: The greatest safety challenge for Chinese. *Zhongguancun, 23*: 63–65.

Hu, L. (2005, January 31). The urban black market of blood. *China Newsweek* [*Zhongguo xinwen zhoukan*], pp. 23–24.

Huang, M. (2008). Report on the measurement and evaluation of Chinese movie audiences. *Media Digest* [*Chuanmei toushi*], *2*: 8–11.

Huang, J., and Cheng, G. (2005). Market, society, state and education for the children of migrants. *Youth Studies* [*Qingnian yanjiu*], *8*: 1–10.

Huang, P., and Domenach-Chich, G. (eds.). (2006). *Urban Poverty Reduction among Migrants: Problems and Policy Orientation in China*. Beijing: Social Science Academic Press.

Huang R. (2005). Household conditions of Chinese empty-nest seniors. *Population and Economics* [*Renkou yu jingji*], *2*: 57–62.

Huang, Y. (2001). Gender, *hukou*, and occupational attainment of female migrants in China (1985–1990). *Environment and planning A, 33*: 257–279.

Hummert, M. L., and Nussbaum, J. F. (eds.). (2001). *Aging, Communication, and Health: Linking Research and Practice for Successful Aging*. Mahwah, N.J.: Erlbaum.

Hurst, W. (2004). Understanding contentious collective action by Chinese laid-off workers: The importance of regional political economy. *Studies in Comparative International Development, 39*(2): 94–120.

IDG and WCGCP (Working Committee on Gaming of China Publishers Association). (2006). *2006–2010 Market Analyses and Predictions for the Gaming Industry in China*. Beijing: March 2006.

ILO (International Labor Organization). (2002). *Current Dynamics of International Labor Migration: Globalization and Regional Integration*. http://www.ilo.org/public/english/protection/migrant/about/index.htm (assessed May 27, 2006).

Informatization Office of Beijing Municipality. (2005). *Research Report on Digital Divide in Beijing Municipality*. Beijing: China Development Publications.

Iredale, R., Bilik, N., and Su, W. (eds.). (2001). *Contemporary Minority Migration, Education, and Ethnicity in China*. Cheltenham, U.K.: Edward Elgar.

Iredale, R., Bilik, N., and Guo, F. (eds.). (2003). *China's Minorities on the Move: Selected Case Studies*. Armonk, N.Y: M. E. Sharpe.

Jensen, R. (2007). The digital provide: Information (technology), market performance, and welfare in the South Indian fisheries sector. *Quarterly Journal of Economics, 122*(3): 879–924.

Jiang, Y. (2003, June 18). *How Lethal Is PHS? Little Smart the "Shooting Star."* Beijing: China IT Market Information Center.

Jiang, Y. (2004, June 19). Conversation with Ma Jiajue's lawyer. *Southern Metropolitan Daily*. http://news.sina.com.cn/c/2004-06-19/09243460046.shtml (accessed March 23, 2006).

Jin, L. (2005, December 20). Domestic handset producers to be slashed by half next year? *New Express Daily* [*Xinkuaibao*], p. 1.

Jiu, T. (2005, October 2). Underground lottery. *Nanfang Daily*, p. 7.

Johnson, K. A. (1983). *Women, the Family, and Peasant Revolution in China*. Chicago: University of Chicago Press.

Johnson, B. (2008, March 14). China: US overtaken in global Internet league. *Guardian*, p. 26.

Jung, J.-Y., Qiu, J. L., and Kim, Y. C. (2001). Internet connectedness and inequality: Beyond the digital divide. *Communication Research, 28*(2): 507–535.

Kahn, J. (2006, June 22). Rioting in China over label on college diplomas. *New York Times*, p. A1.

Katz, A., and Liebes, T. (2007). "No more peace!" How disaster, terror and war have upstaged media events. *International Journal of Communication, 1*: 157–166.

Katz, J., and Aakhus, M. (eds.). (2002). *Perceptual Contact: Mobile Communication, Private Talk, Public Performance*. Cambridge: Cambridge University Press.

Koh, E. K. (2005). *Bridging Digital Divide: Satellite Solution.* Tokyo: Asian Development Bank.

Kuo, K. (2004, March 11). Little Smart "cell" phone very, very smart in China. *Asia Times.* http://www.atimes.com/atimes/China/FC11Ad02.html (accessed January 17, 2007).

Labi, A. (2006). Greek students protest proposals to reform universities. *Chronicle of Higher Education, 52*(42): 45.

Lan, A. (2005, February 6). Boom in SMS greetings over the Spring Festival, Shenzhen provider earned 800 million per day. *Shenzhen Special Economic Zone Daily,* p. B5.

Lan, Y. (2004, April 1). Revelations from the conclusion of the chain murder case. *Nanfengchuan,* pp. 36–38.

Lan, Y., and Zhang, R. (2005). Analysis of the reasons for the formation of urban villages. *China Rural Economy [Zhongguo nongcun jingji],* 11: 68–74.

Lanfranco, E. (2005, September 27). China's tech commissars target SMS porn. UPI.

Larmer, B. (2006, September). The Manchurian mandate. *National Geographic,* pp. 42–73.

Law, P. (2006). The use of mobile phones among migrant workers in southern China. In P. Law, L. Fortunati, and S. Yang (eds.), *New Technologies in Global Societies,* 245–258. Singapore: World Scientific Publishing.

Le, N., Qiao, N., and Sun, H. (2006, April 10). Secret stories of wireless communication in China. *Communications World Weekly [Tongxin shijie],* 13: 32–39.

Lee, C. C. (ed.). (2000). *Power, Money, and Media: Communication Patterns and Bureaucratic Control in Cultural China.* Evanston, Ill.: Northwestern University Press.

Lee, C. C. (ed.). (2003). *Chinese Media, Global Contexts.* London: Routledge Curzon.

Lee, C. K. (1998). *Gender and the South China Miracle: Two Worlds of Factory Women.* Berkeley: University of California Press.

Lee, C. K. (2002a). From the specter of Mao to the spirit of the law: Labor insurgence in China. *Theory and Society, 31*: 189–228.

Lee, C. K. (2002b). Three patterns of working-class transitions in China. In F. Mengin and J.-L. Rocca (eds.), *Politics in China,* 62–92. New York: Palgrave Macmillan.

Lerner, D. (1958). *The Passing of Traditional Society.* Glencoe, IL: Free Press.

Li, J. (2004). *The Redevelopment of Urban Villages.* Beijing: Science Publications.

Li, J. (2005). *Research on the Development of China's Tertiary Sector*. Beijing: People's Press.

Li, P. (2002). Metamorphosis: The end of villages. *China Social Sciences [Zhongguo shehui kexue]*, 1: 168–179.

Li, P. (2007, September 25). Beijing accelerates the fostering of Five-mao party. *Apple Daily*, p. A27.

Li, W. (2004, May 29). Ban on wireless phone at school triggers argument with parents. *Chongqing Wanbao*, p. 12.

Li, Y. (2005). *The Structure and Evolution of Chinese Social Stratification*. Lanham, Md.: University Press of America.

Li, Y., and Ma, J. (2003, April 29). Fined six times before, Lanjisu boss still operated black Net-bar. *Beijing Youth Daily*, p. A9.

Liang, Z., and Chen, Y. P. (2004). Migration and gender in China: An origin-destination linked approach. *Economic Development and Cultural Change*, *52*(2): 423–443.

Light, I., and Bonacich, E. (1991). *Immigrant Entrepreneurs: Koreans in Los Angeles, 1965–1982*. Berkeley, Calif.: University of California Press.

Light, I., and Gold, S. (2000). *Ethnic Economies*. San Diego, Calif.: Academic Press.

Lin, A. (2005). Romance and sexual ideologies in SMS manuals. Paper presented at the International Conference on Mobile Communication and Asian Modernities, Hong Kong.

Lin, D. (2006, April 6). The "heart"less pain of domestic handsets. *Guangming Daily*, p. 10.

Lin, N. (1995). Local market socialism. *Theory and Society*, *24*(3): 301–354.

Lin, W. (2003, April 30). A company employee died in Guangzhou detention center for the lack of temporary resident card. *China Youth Daily*, p. 7.

Lin, Y. (2005). *The Legend of Little Smart [Xiaolintong chuanqi]*. Beijing: China Water Power Press.

Ling, R. (2004). *The Mobile Connection: The Cell Phone's Impact on Society* (3rd ed.). San Francisco: Morgan Kaufmann.

Liu, C. (2004, July). How police nailed down Ma Jiajue. *People's Public Security [Renmin gong'an]*, 14–15.

Liu, M. (2000). A case study of Shipai migrant community. *Market and Demographic Analysis [Shichang yu renkou fenxi]*, *6*(5): 41–46.

Liu, H. (2004, March). *Research on Market Dynamics of Little Smart in China*. Beijing: TeleInfo Institute, China Academy of Telecommunications Research of MII.

Liu, W. (2005). Three medical problems. *China Reform [Zhongguo gaige]*, 9: 46–49.

Liu, X. (2002). *The Otherness of Self: A Genealogy of Self in Contemporary China*. Ann Arbor: University of Michigan Press.

Liu, X. P. (2002). Seeing through the Net-bar incident. *Current Affairs: Version for Middle School Students [Shishi baogao: Zhongxueshengban]*, 1: 58–59.

Lu, H. (2005). *Focusing on Chinese Migrant Workers*. Beijing: China Economic Publishing House.

Lu, W. (2004, November 30) Net-bar owners attempt collective boycott against Shangda. *Youth Daily* (Shanghai). http://news.chinabyte.com/147/1882147.shtml (accessed April 24, 2006).

Lu, X., and Perry, E. J. (1997). *Danwei: The Changing Chinese Workplace in Historical and Comparative Perspective*. Armonk, N.Y.: M. E. Sharpe.

Lyon, D. (ed.). (2003). *Surveillance as Social Sorting*. London: Routledge.

Ma, E. (2002). Translocal spatiality. *International Journal of Cultural Studies*, 5(2): 131–152.

Ma, E. (2006). *Bar and Factory: Studying Urban Culture in South China*. Nanjing: Jiangsu Renmin Publications.

Ma, E., and Cheng, H. (2005). "Naked" bodies: Experimenting with intimate relations among migrant workers in South China. *International Journal of Cultural Studies*, 8(3): 307–328.

Mackenzie, P. (2002). Strangers in the city: *Hukou* and urban citizenship in China. *Journal of International Affairs*, 56(1): 305–319.

Manion, M. (1994). Survey research in the study of contemporary China: Learning from local samples. *China Quarterly*, 139, 741–765.

Mao, T. (2006, April 26). Prevalent requests for the lowering of phone charge during the golden week. China News Agency.

Martin, M. (1991). *Hello Central? Gender, Technology and Culture in the Formation of Telephone Systems*. Montreal: McGil–Queen's University Press.

Marvin, C. (1988). *When Old Technologies Were New*. Oxford: Oxford University Press.

McDonald, J. (2003, May 14). China cracks down on high-tech spread of SARS rumors. Associated Press.

McLaughlin, K. (2005, September 22). China's model for a censored Internet. *Christian Science Monitor*, p. 1.

Meiers, R. L. (1962). *A Communications Theory of Urban Growth*. Cambridge, Mass.: MIT Press.

Ministry of Education. (MoE). (2003). Guidelines on accelerating the construction of information technology curricula in middle schools and primary schools. http://www.edu.cn/20030210/3077057.shtml (accessed July 3, 2006).

Ministry of Information Industry. (1988–2007). *Annual Statistical Reports on the Telecommunications Industry*. Available: http://www.mii.gov.cn/ (accessed March 26, 2008).

Mitchell, T. (2006, May 31). China's Shenzhen to lift minimum wage by 20%. *Financial Times*. http://www.ft.com/cms/s/2348c8f6-f094-11da-9338-0000779e2340.html (accessed February 7, 2007).

Modern Life Daily. (2002, June 4). Teacher on sick leave worked as voice information mistress, p. A0.

Mooallen, J. (2008, January 13). The afterlife of cellphones. *New York Times*, p. 38.

Mosco, V. (2004). *The Digital Sublime: Myth, Power, and Cyberspace*. Cambridge, Mass.: MIT Press.

Mueller, M., and Tan, Z. (1997). *China in the Information Age: Telecommunications and the Dilemmas of Reform*. Westport, Conn.: Praeger.

Murelli, E. (2002). *Breaking the Digital Divide: Implications for Developing Countries*. Commonwealth Secretariat: SFI Publications.

Murphy, R. (2002). *How Migrant Labor Is Changing Rural China*. Cambridge: Cambridge University Press.

Murray, B. (2003, June 4). Internet café regulation in China: A policy review. *MFC Insight*. http://www.mfcinsight.com/files/030604Oped3.pdf (accessed March 8, 2004).

Nanguo zaobao. (2004, March 16). Being from very poor family, Ma Jiajue had strong sense of inferiority. http://news.sohu.com/2004/03/16/90/news219449083.html (accessed March 23, 2006).

National Comprehensive Statistics on Education Equipment in Primary and High Schools. (2004). Beijing: Ministry of Education.

National Telecommunications and Information Administration (NTIA). (1995). *Falling Through the Net: A Survey of the "Have Nots" in Rural and Urban America*. http://www.ntia.doc.gov/ntiahome/fallingthru.html (retrieved March 29, 2006).

National Telecommunications and Information Administration. (2000). *Falling through the Net: Toward Digital Inclusion.* http://search.ntia.doc.gov/pdf/fttn00.pdf (retrieved November 10, 2006).

New Weekly (2001, September 7). The eight-year pain of Peking University's south wall. http://cul.book.sina.com.cn/s/2001-09-07/3564.html (accessed January 11, 2007).

Norris, P. (2001). *Digital Divide: Civic Engagement, Information Poverty, and the Internet Worldwide.* Cambridge: Cambridge University Press.

Oakes, T., and Schein, L. (2006). *Translocal China: Linkages, Identities, and the Reimagining of Space.* London: Routledge.

Oi, J. (1992). Fiscal reform and the economic foundations of local state corporatism. *World Politics, 45*(1): 99–126.

Oreglia, E. (2007). *The Service Industry and Young Migrant Women in Beijing: A Report for Intel.* Berkeley: School of Information, University of California.

Organization for Economic Co-operation and Development (OECD) (2006). *Information Technology Outlook 2006.* Paris: OECD.

Padovani, C., and Nordenstreng, K. (2004). From NWICO to WSIS: Another world information and communication order? *Global Media and Communication, 1*(3): 264–272.

Pang, Y. (2003, February 20). Careless consumption by college students. *Life Times* [*Shenghuo shibao*]. http://www.ecjtu.net/news/list.asp?ID=870&SpecialID=0 (accessed January 29, 2007).

PC Online. (2004, November 3). Shanghai: Old items revitalized. http://www .pconline.com.cn/mobile/market/sh/0411/483680.html (accessed July 5, 2006)

Pday Research. (2006). *Research Report on Overseas Market Expansion of Handset Manufacturers, 2006.* Beijing: Tsinghua University.

Pei, Z. (2006, April 12). Suggestions of NPC Standing Committee on the twelve confirmed priority tasks for 2006. *People's Daily,* p. 1.

People's Telecommunications Daily. (2003, December 3). Analysis of the production and sales situation for domestic handsets. http://www.cnii.com.cn/20030915/ca212113.htm (accessed January 17, 2007).

Perry, E. J. (1993). *Shanghai on Strike: The Politics of Chinese Labor.* Stanford, Calif.: Stanford University Press.

Pertierra, R., Ugarte, E. F., Pingol, A., Hernandez, J., and Dacanay, N. L. (2002). *Txt-ing Selves: Cellphones and Philippine Modernity.* Manila: De La Salle University Press.

PRC 1985 Industry Census. (1988). *Materials Volume 7: Electronics Industry*. Beijing: China Statistics Publications.

Pu, C. (2006, August 10). "June Fourth" seventeen years later: How I kept a promise. *New York Review of Books*, *53*(13). http://www.nybooks.com/articles/19198 (accessed February 9, 2007).

Pun, N. (2005). *Made in China: Women Factory Workers in a Global Workplace*. Durham, N.C.: Duke University Press.

Qian, Q., and Chen, Y. (2003). Preliminary research on migrant enclaves in China's large cities. *Urban Population [Chengshi renkou]*, *27*(11): 60–64.

Qiao, X. (2006, October 9). Purchase of computer and mobile phone disqualifies people from low-income welfare. *Xinmin Evening News*, pp. A1, 12.

Qingdao Morning Post. (2006, March 24). Three-yuan Little Smart hot in Qingdao. http://it.sohu.com/20060324/n242451074.shtml (accessed July 11, 2006).

Qiu, J. L. (2002a). Coming to terms with informational stratification in the People's Republic of China. *Cardozo Arts and Entertainment Law Journal*, *20*(1): 157–180.

Qiu, J. L. (2002b). Chinese hackerism in retrospect: The legend of a new revolutionary army. *MFC Insight*.

Qiu, J. L. (2004). The Internet in China: Technologies of freedom in a statist society. In M. Castells (ed.), *Network Society: A Cross-Cultural Perspective*, 99–124. London: Edward Elgar.

Qiu, J. L. (2006). From the information have-less to the pillar of information society. *Twenty-First Century [Ershiyi shiji]*, (October): 101–110.

Qiu, J. L. (2007a). The accidental accomplishment of Little Smart: Understanding the emergence of a working-class ICT. *New Media and Society*, *9*(6): 903–924.

Qiu, J. L. (2007b). The wireless leash: Mobile messaging as means of control. *International Journal of Communication*, *1*(1): 74–91.

Qiu, J. L. (forthcoming). A city of ten years: Public/private Internet development in Nanhai City. *Positions: East Asia Culture Critique*.

Qiu, J. L., and Chan, J. M. (2003). China Internet studies: A review of the field. In M. Price and H. Nissenbaum (eds.), *The Academy and the Internet: New Directions in Information Scholarship*, 275–307. London: Peter Lang Publishing.

Qiu, J. L., and Thompson, E. (2007). Editorial: Mobile communication and Asian modernities. *New Media and Society* (Special Section on Mobile Asia), *9*(6): 895–901.

Qiu, J. L., and Zhou, L. (2005). Through the prism of the Internet café: Managing access in an ecology of games. *China Information*, *19*(2): 261–297.

Reporters without Borders. (2004, July 3). China to censor mobile text.

Rice, R. E., and Katz, J. (eds.). (2001). *The Internet and Health Communication: Experiences and Expectations*. Thousand Oaks, Calif.: Sage.

Rogers, E. (1962). *Diffusion of Innovations*. New York: Free Press.

Rogers, E., and Singhal, A. (2003).Empowerment and communication: Lessons learned from organizing for social change. *Communication Yearbook, 27*: 67–85.

Rong, D. (2000, June 19). Peking University has a networked wall. *Beijing wanbao*, p. 3.

Roudanjia, V. (2007). A case study about cell phone usage in Amdo Tibetan society. Paper presented at the conference Living the Information Society: The Impact of ICTs on People, Work and Communities in Asia. Makati, Philippines, April 23–24.

Samarajiva, R., and Shields, P. (1990). Value issues in telecommunications resource allocation in the Third World. In S. Lundstedt (ed.), *Telecommunication, Values, and the Public Interest*, 227–253. Norwood, NJ: Ablex.

Schiller, D. (2005). Poles of market growth? Open questions about China, information, and the world economy. *Global Media and Communication, 1*(1): 79–103.

Schiller, H. (1981). *Who Knows: Information in the Age of the Fortune 500*. Norwood, N.J.: Ablex.

Schiller, H. (1984). *Information and the Crisis Economy*. Norwood, N.J.: Ablex.

Servon, L. J. (2002). *Bridging the Digital Divide: Technology, Community, and Public Policy*. Malden, Mass.: Blackwell.

Shang, L. (2003). A sociological analysis of the Lanjisu Net-bar fire. *Journal of Beijing University of Chemical Technology: Social Sciences Edition, 2*: 20–24.

Shanghai Oriental TV. (2004, February 22). *Police life [Jingcha rensheng]*.

Shen, J. (2005, March 21). Separate-card Little Smart available in May. *First Financial Daily [Diyi caijing ribao]*. http://mobile.21tx.com/2005/03/21/11811.html (accessed March 12, 2008).

Shen, L. (2003, February 22). National Internet café number reduced by half. Xinhua News Agency. http://bf3.syd.com.cn/gb/sywb/2003-02/22/content_355431.htm (accessed March 4, 2005).

Shi, X., Yang, S., Mo, S., Ma, L., and Huang, W. (2004, July). The lonely trip of Ma Jiajue. *People's Public Security [Renmin gong'an]*, pp. 4–13.

Shi, Y., and Ma, H. (2004). How to inform and to guide? Reflections on the reports of Ma Jiajue. *News and Writing [Xinwen yu xiezuo], 6*: 33–35.

Short, S., Zhai, F., Xu, S., and Yang, M. (2001). China's one-child policy and the care of children: An analysis of qualitative and quantitative data. *Social Forces, 79*(3): 913–943.

Sichuan Morning Post. (2004, March 16). Ma Jiajue once won third prize in national math contest. http://www.sohu.com/2004/03/16/90/news219449054.shtml (accessed March 23, 2006).

Sina News. (2004, January 14). Sun Zhigang incident demonstrates the power of online public opinion. http://tech.sina.com.cn/other/2004-01-14/1830282409.shtml (accessed August 18, 2004).

Singhal, A., and Greiner, K. (2007). *Do What You Can, with What You Have, Where You Are.* Allentown, N.J.: Plexus Institute.

Silverstone, R., and Haddon, L. (1996). Design and the domestication of ICTs: Technical change and everyday life. In R. Silverstone and R. Mansell (eds.), *Communication by Design*, 44–74. Oxford: Oxford University Press.

Slater, D., and Tacchi, J. (2004). *Research on ICT Innovations for Poverty Reduction.* New Delhi: UNESCO. http://cirac.qut.edu.au/ictpr/downloads/research.pdf (accessed November 2, 2006).

Solinger, D. (1999). *Contesting Citizenship in Urban China.* Berkeley: University of California Press.

Southern Metropolitan Daily. (2008, March 17). Focus Media owns information about half of China's mobile phone subscribers, sending out hundreds of millions of spam SMS everyday. p. A15.

Stacey, J. (1983). *Patriarchy and Socialist Revolution in China.* Berkeley: University of California Press.

Su, Q. (2005, June 8). Clean-Net vanguard frequently disabled. XinhuaNet. http://soft.yesky.com/security/289/2012789.shtml (accessed April 20, 2006).

Subler, J. (2008, February 22). Beijing's appliance rebates are "like free food falling from the sky." *International Herald Tribune*, p. 16.

Sun, L. (2006). Breakdown: The stratification structure of Chinese society since the 1990s. In Y. Li, L. Sun, and Y. Shen (eds.), *Social Stratification in Contemporary China*, 1–35. Beijing: Social Sciences Academic Press.

Sun, Q. (2003). Rural urbanization and the clan life of urban villagers. *Contemporary Chinese History Studies* [*Dangdai zhongguoshi yanjiu*], *10*(3): 96–104.

Sun, Q., and Xu, Y. (2007, July 17). 2.6 million being robbed: Crime committed by acquaintances, mostly "old thieves." *Southern Metropolitan Daily*, pp. A05–06.

Sun, W. (2002). *Leaving China: Media, Migration, and Transnational Imagination.* Lanham, Md.: Rowman & Littlefield.

Survey of Haidian District, Beijing Municipality. (2004). Beijing: Beijing Press.

Tabulation on the 2000 Population Census of the PRC. (2001). Beijing: China Statistics Publications.

Tan, Z., Chen, S., and X. Liu (2005). Adoption of limited mobility services: Little Smart in China as a case. Paper presented at the Hong Kong Mobility Roundtable, June 2–5.

Tang, J. (2003, June 16). The truth about Sun Zhigang's death. *China News Weekly,* pp. 18–25.

Tao, J. (2005). Survey research on media access and media evaluation of migrant workers. *Chinese Communication Studies Review [Zhongguo chuanboxue pinglun],* 1: 132–139.

Taylor, R. (2006, April 9). China wrestles with online gamers. BBC News. http://news .bbc.co.uk/1/hi/programmes/click_online/4887236.stm (accessed April 10, 2006).

Thompson, E. P. (1966). *The Making of the English Working Class.* New York: Vintage Books.

Thomas, D. (2003). *Hacker Culture.* Minneapolis: University of Minnesota Press.

Tichenor, P. J., Donohue, G. A., and Olien, C. N. (1970). Mass media and differential growth in knowledge. *Public Opinion Quarterly, 34*: 158–170.

Tilly, C. (1998). *Durable Inequality.* Berkeley: University of California Press.

Toral, J. (2003). State of wireless technologies in the Philippines. In *Proceedings for Closing Gaps in the Digital Divide: Regional Conference on Digital GMS,* 173–177. Bangkok.

Tsang, D. (2008, March 17). Tensions at the top over contract law. *South China Morning Post,* p. 6.

Van Dijk, J. A. (2005). *The Deepening Divide: Inequality in the Information Society.* Thousand Oaks, Calif.: Sage.

Walcott, S. M. (2003). *Chinese Science and Technology Industrial Parks.* Burlington, Vt.: Ashgate Publishing Co.

Wang, D., and Yang, Y. (2004). Brief analysis of gray-collar labor crisis in the manufacture sector. *Population and Economics [Renkou yu jingji],* 2: 59–63.

Wang, H. (2004). *China's New Order.* Cambridge, MA: Harvard University Press.

Wang, J. (2005a). Youth culture, music, and cell phone branding in China. *Global Media and Communication, 1*(2): 185–201.

Wang, L. (2006) How the children of peasant workers in Suzhou receive basic education. *Educational Review [Jiaoy du pinglun],* 1: 82–86.

Wang, L., Xu, H., and Huang, A. (2004, January 5). Gray-collar strata. *News Weekly [Xinwen zhoukan],* pp. 56–59.

Wang, S., and Zhu, J. J. (2003). Mapping film piracy in China. *Theory, Culture and Society*, *20*(4): 97–125.

Wang, W. (2003). Analysis on the implementation of compulsory education policy among children of migrants in Beijing. *Journal of the Chinese Society of Education* [*Zhongguo jiaoyu xuekan*], *10*: 9–12.

Watts, J. (2005, July 1). Print and be damned—China's paper tigers fight on. *Guardian* (Foreign Pages), p. 17.

Webster, N. (2006, June 14). Welcome to iPod City: The "robot" workers on 15-hour days. *Mirror*, p. 24.

Whyte, W. F. (1955). *Street-Corner Society: The Social Structure of an Italian Slum*. Chicago: University of Chicago Press.

Wilson, E. J. III (2004). *The Information Revolution and Developing Countries*. Cambridge, Mass.: MIT Press.

Wu, A. (2005, September 28). *Shouji* should not be barrier for assistance to poor students. *China Women's News*, p. 64.

Wu, C. (2002, June 28). I want to kill them: Young Net-bar arsonists uttering shocking words. *Southern Weekend*. http://news.sina.com.cn/c/2002-06-28/1101619333.html (accessed August 21, 2006).

Wu, I. (2007). The triumphant consumer? VoIP, "Little Smart," and telecom service reform in China. *Information Technology and International Development*, *3*(4): 53–66.

Wu, W. (2002). Temporary migrants in Shanghai: Housing and settlement patterns. In J. R. Logan (ed.), *The New Chinese City: Globalization and Market Reform*, 212–226. Oxford: Blackwell.

Wu, W., and Shi, Y. (2001, November 11). Guangdong Province forbids pager stations to suddenly disappear. *Nanfang Daily*.

Wu, X. (2007). Network commentation is propeller for political democracy. *Xinmin Evening News*, p. B6.

XAOnline. (2004, June 22). Nanchang "Ma Jiajue" on killing spree in Net-bar. http://www.oplay.com/info/content/4709.htm (accessed August 15, 2006).

Xi, E. (2004, January 12). Care about the forgotten corners of high technology. *Telecom World Network*. http://www.cww.net.cn/Mobile/Article.asp?id=9396 (accessed July 5, 2006).

Xiao, C. (2001, April 16). Peking University plans to re-establish South Wall. *China Computer World*. http://www.ccw.com.cn/htm/news1/net/affair/01_4_16_15.asp (accessed April 9, 2006).

Xiao, Q. (2004). The rising tide of Internet opinion in China. *Nieman Reports*, (Summer): 103–104.

Xie, L. (2006, February 8). Domestic handsets to reach bottom and bounce by yearend. *China Electronics Daily [Zhongguo dianzibao]*, p. 17.

Xin, H. (2000a, November 12). His Net-bar is probably the largest chain-store Net-bar in the world. *Sina News*. http://tech.sina.com.cn/r/m/50989.shtml (accessed April 9, 2006).

Xin, H. (2000b, December 7). On-the-spot report of Feiyu, Beijing's largest Net-bar, being rectified. *YeskyNet*. http://tech.sina.com.cn/i/c/45322.shtml (accessed April 8, 2006).

Xin, M. (2004, September 24). Will chain-store management improve the image of black Net-bars? *PCOnline*. http://www.pconline.com.cn/news/hy/0409/460243.html (accessed January 15, 2007).

XinhuaNet. (2003, April 10). Little Smart using countryside to surrounding cities? http://news.xinhuanet.com/fortune/2003-04/10/content_825207.htm (accessed January 17, 2007).

XinhuaNet. (2004a, January 9). Shanghai population in negative growth for 11 years. http://www.csonline.com.cn/news/guonei/t20040109_96207.htm (accessed June 30, 2006).

XinhuaNet. (2004b, March 17). Revealing the growing-up process of the murder suspect in Yunnan University death case. http://www.yn.xinhuanet.com/topic/2004/gxfz/xlym/1_01.htm (accessed August 24, 2006).

XinhuaNet. (2005, March 31). Who did Henanese offend? http://news.xinhuanet.com/forum/2005-03/31/content_2767963.htm (accessed June 10, 2006).

XinhuaNet. (2006, April 15). Selling guns and professional killers: Crazy SMS frightens receivers. http://www.cnonline.org/2004/article/4669.html (accessed August 18, 2006).

XinhuaNet-Yunnan. (2004, March 17). No graduation diploma in heaven. http://www.yn.xinhuanet.com/topic/2004-03/17/content_1800746.htm (accessed March 23, 2006).

Xinhua News Agency. (2002, June 4). Porn-chat at voice information station corrupted children.

Xinhua News Agency. (2003a, February 21). Internet cafés still subject to strict control.

Xinhua News Agency. (2003b, October 29). Short message system, on-line gaming make Ding Lei China's richest man.

Xu, Y., and Yu, F. (2004, August 31). Little Smart location service. *China Data Communications*. http://www.chinabyte.com/telecom/157/1848657.shtml (accessed July 11, 2006).

Yang, D. (2005, January). Correct errors in the "industrialization of education." *Nanfengchuang*, pp. 52–54.

Yang, D. (2007). The problems and prospects of educational equity in China. *Twenty First Century [Ershiyi shiji]*, (December): 14–22.

Yang, D., and Zhao, Y. (2004). The current state and policies for China's empty-nest seniors. *Modern Clinical Nursing*, 3(5): 60–62.

Yang, H. (2004). An analysis of the role of Internet audience from the perspective of agenda-setting theory: A case study of the Ma Jiajue incident. *Journalism and Communication Studies [Xinwen yu chuanbo yanjiu]*, 2: 35–39.

Yang, M. (ed.). (1999). *Spaces of Their Own: Women's Public Sphere in Transnational China*. Minneapolis: University of Minnesota Press.

Yang, S. (2006) Economic reflections on the problem of migrant dearth. *Study and Exploration [Xuexi yu tansuo]*, 2: 242–244.

Yang, W. (2004, December 10). Insider report on the collective stoppage of Lishui Net-bars. *eTime Weekly*. http://www.etimeweekly.com/h/2194.asp (accessed April 22, 2006).

Yangtze River Archives. (2005). *Reservoir Migration and Area Construction, Volume 18*. Shanghai: China Encyclopedia Publications.

Yardley, J. (2005, September 4). The Chinese get the vote, if only for "Super Girl." *New York Times*, p. 3.

Yearbook of China's Cities. (1991, 2001, 2006). Beijing: Publishing House for the Yearbook of China's Cities.

Yearbook of China's Information Industry. (2007). Beijing: Electronics Industry Publications.

YeskyNet. (2004). How did domestic handset giants fail? http://news.chinabyte.com/134/1893134.shtml (accessed May 8, 2006).

YeskyNet. (2005, November 10). Pubwin EP spurs a storm in Net-bar management. http://news.chinabyte.com/118/2189618.shtml (accessed April 21, 2006).

Young, G. (2005, September 28). China's Dalian becoming Japan's call center hub. Japan Economic Newswire.

Yu, J. (2003). Farmers' organized resistance and its political risks. *Strategy and Management [Zhanlue yu guangli]*, 3: 1–16.

Yu, H., and Ding, P. (2004). *Survey on China's Peasant Workers*. Beijing: Kunlun Publishing House.

Zeng, M., and Williamson, P.J. (2007). *Dragons at Your Door: How Chinese Cost Innovation is Disrupting Global Competition*. Boston, MA: Harvard Business School Press.

Zhan, S. (2006). Peasant workers' mobility and poverty in China. In P. Huang and G. Domenach-Chich (eds.), *Urban Poverty Reduction among Migrants*, 1–32. Beijing: Social Sciences Academic Press.

Zhang, J. (2004). Analysis of the current state of China's handset market. *Communications Today [Xiandai tongxun]*, 3: 53–55.

Zhang, J., and Li, Q. (2006, June 19). Foxconn Workers. *NetEast Technology Report*. http://www.zonaeuropa.com/20060623_1.htm (accessed August 10, 2006).

Zhang, L. (2001). *Strangers in the City: Reconfigurations of Space, Power, and Social Networks within China's Floating Population*. Stanford, Calif.: Stanford University Press.

Zhang, L., Zhao, S., and Tian, J. (2003). Self-help in housing and Chengzhongcun in China's urbanization. *International Journal of Urban and Regional Research*, 27(4): 912–937.

Zhang, Y. (2005, December 26). The past and present of pharmaceutical representatives. *Caijing Magazine*, 26: 52–53.

Zhao, H. (2005). Analysis on the reasons for dropouts from primary and secondary schools. *Education Exploration [Jiaoyu tansuo]*, 2: 37–38.

Zhao, H. (2006, May 8). The secrets why Bird Handset had a huge loss. *China Computers Daily [Zhongguo jisuanji bao]*, p. A19.

Zhao, S. (2004). The conflict of order and the reform of governance. In H. Deng and B. Lu (eds.), *Changing Binary Structure [Zouchu eryuan jiegou]*, 349–372. Beijing: China Development Press.

Zhao, S. (2005, Winter). Peasant migration: Order building and policy re-thinking. *Social Sciences in China [Zhongguo shehui kexue]*, pp. 168–176.

Zhao, Y. (1998). *Media, Market, and Democracy in China: Between the Party Line and the Bottom Line*. Campaign: University of Illinois Press.

Zhao, Y. (2003). The role of migrant networks in labor migration: The case of China. *Contemporary Economic Policy*, 21(4): 500–511.

Zhao, Y. (2007). After mobile phones, what? Re-embedding the social in China's "digital revolution." *International Journal of Communication*, 1: 92–120.

Zhao, Y. (2008). *Communication in China: Political Economy, Power and Conflict.* Lanham, MD: Rowman & Littlefield.

Zheng, M. (2006). *The Urbanization of Shipai Village.* Beijing: Social Sciences Academic Press.

Zheng, T. (2004). From peasant women to bar hostesses: Gender and modernity in post-Mao China. In A. M. Gaetano and T. Jacka (eds.), *On the Move: Women in Rural-to-Urban Migration in Contemporary China,* 80–206. New York: Columbia University Press.

Zheng, Y. (2004). Analysis of Ma Jiajue's criminal psychology. *Issues in Juvenile Delinquency,* 3: 28–30, 34.

Zhong, J. (2004, September 21). Will sub-nuclear technology help domestic handsets blossom? *Business Weekly [Shangwu zhoukan].* http://news.sohu.com/20040921/n222158852.shtml (accessed January 17, 2007).

Zhong, Y. (2004, February 9). Three youngsters and their Old Kids website. *Xinmin wanbao,* p. 30.

Zhong, Z., Liu, L., Liu, P., and Mo, X. (2005). Student loans going astray. *Capital Markets [Ziben shichang],* 10: 41–52.

Zhou, Y. (2005). Paradox in development. *Social Sciences [Shehui kexue],* 8: 22–27.

Zhu, C. (2004, March 12). Forty-nine Ma Jiajue's, all are fake. *Changjiang Daily.* http://news.sohu.com/2004/03/12/51/news219405137.shtml (accessed March 19, 2008).

Zhu, D. (2006, April 7). Opening-up Net-bar registration showing change in regulatory approach. *Youth Daily* (Shanghai). http://news.sohu.com/20060407/n242685754.shtml (accessed March 19, 2008).

Zhu, S., and Zhao, L. (2000, September 24). Zhongguancun never sleeps. *New Weekly [Xinzhoukan].* http://edu.sina.com.cn/job/2000–09–24/12770.shtml (accessed April 9, 2006).

Zinn, H. (2001). *A People's History of the United States, 1492–Present.* New York: Perennial Classics.

Index

Printed in the United States
by Baker & Taylor Publisher Services